FREDRIC JAMESON

FREDRIC JAMESON

Marxism, Hermeneutics, Postmodernism

Sean Homer

Routledge
New York

Published in North America by
Routledge
29 West 35th Street
New York, NY 10001

First published in Great Britain by Polity Press
in association with Blackwell Publishers Ltd.

ISBN 0 415 92030 2
ISBN 0 415 92031 0 pbk

A catalog record has been applied for from the Library of Congress.

Typeset in 10½ on 12 pt Palatino
by Ace Filmsetting Ltd, Frome, Somerset
Printed in Great Britain

This book is printed on acid-free paper.

For Eugenie

Contents

Acknowledgements

This book is the product of many intellectual and personal encounters over the last ten years or so; unfortunately I can only acknowledge the most recent debts here. First and foremost, I am deeply indebted to Eugenie Georgaca and Nick Stevenson for the time they have taken away from their own work to read and comment on draft chapters. Their detailed criticisms have alerted me to many errors of judgement and have served as a constant reminder of the complexity and overdetermined nature of any theoretical endeavour. Their support and friendship have been invaluable. I would also like to thank Douglas Kellner for his very positive response to earlier drafts of some of this material; his enthusiasm for, and encouragement of, this project has been greatly appreciated. The account of the Marxist Literary Group was written with the assistance of members of the MLG e-mail list; I would especially like to thank Fredric Jameson, Walter Cohen, Paul Smith, Peter Fitting, John Beverley, Tom Moyland, Melani McAlister and all those who took the time to respond to my postings. I am grateful to Rebecca Harkin, Gill Motley and unknown readers at Polity Press for their help, encouragement and advice, and Ann Bone for her suggestions in editing this text. I am particularly grateful to my friends, colleagues and students at the Centre for Psychotherapeutic Studies, University of Sheffield, for providing the intellectual environment in which this project could be realized. Finally, I should like to thank my children, Ella, Alice and James, for their love and friendship as well as their unwavering faith in my ability to finish this book. Needless to say, the ultimate responsibility for the arguments herein is all my own.

x   *Acknowledgements*

The author and publishers are grateful for permission to quote from the following works by Fredric Jameson: *The Political Unconscious: Narrative as a Socially Symbolic Act*, Cornell University Press, Ithaca, N.Y., © 1981 by Cornell University Press, used by permission of the American publisher, and Methuen, London, also by permission; *Postmodernism, or, The Cultural Logic of Late Capitalism*, Duke University Press, Durham, N.C., © 1991, Duke University Press, reprinted with permission, and Verso, London, 1991; *Marxism and Form: Twentieth-Century Dialectical Theories of Literature*, © 1971 by Princeton University Press, reprinted by permission of Princeton University Press.

Abbreviations

The following abbreviations have been used in references to works by Jameson:

SOS   *Sartre: The Origins of a Style* (1961)
MF   *Marxism and Form: Twentieth-Century Dialectical Theories of Literature* (1971)
PH   *The Prison House of Language: A Critical Account of Structuralism and Russian Formalism* (1972)
FA   *Fables of Aggression: Wyndham Lewis, the Modernist as Fascist* (1979)
PU   *The Political Unconscious: Narrative as a Socially Symbolic Act* (1981)
LM   *Late Marxism: Adorno, or, The Persistence of the Dialectic* (1990)
SV   *Signatures of the Visible* (1990)
PLC   *Postmodernism, or, The Cultural Logic of Late Capitalism* (1991)
GPA   *The Geopolitical Aesthetic: Cinema and Space in the World System* (1992)
ST   *The Seeds of Time* (1994)

Introduction

Fredric Jameson has been described as 'probably the most important cultural critic writing in English today'[1] and he is widely acknowledged as the foremost proponent for that tradition of critical theory known as Western Marxism. Through his early critical surveys on the Frankfurt School and the Hegelian tradition of dialectical criticism in *Marxism and Form* (1971) to those on Russian formalism and structuralism in *The Prison House of Language* (1972), Jameson has perhaps done more than any other figure to contribute to the renaissance of Marxist criticism in the US since the early 1970s. These two early books represent key texts in the dissemination of continental theory and Western Marxism in the North American academy, where these traditions were at the time still relatively unknown. These books were also central to re-establishing Marxism and specifically Marxist cultural theory as one of the most challenging and radical currents of contemporary critical practice competing within the universities. With the publication of *The Political Unconscious* (1981) and his first sustained engagement with post-structuralism and Althusserian Marxism, Jameson emerged as a major theoretician in his own right. *The Political Unconscious* established him as one of that small group of international theorists whose work defines the parameters of contemporary theoretical debate. Jameson's reputation as one of the most significant theorists working today was further enhanced with the publication of his seminal essays on postmodernity in the early 1980s, culminating with the monumental study *Postmodernism, or, The Cultural Logic of Late Capitalism* (1991). His analysis of the spatio-temporal dynamics of postmodernity and its cultural logic has provided some of the most influential, as well as the most controversial, ideas produced on this theoretically and textually saturated subject. His work in the 1990s on globalization and geopolitical aesthetics has only served to confirm Jameson's status as a singularly unique and audacious critic as he attempts to map the cultural and political implications of capitalism's universalizing logic.

Within the United States Jameson is a central figure in contemporary theoretical and cultural debates, his work providing an essential point of reference for Marxist and non-Marxist critics alike. He has received relatively little critical attention within Europe, however; one does not find for example the sheer welter of Readers or introductory and expository texts that one does for Derrida, Baudrillard, Foucault and most other major continental theorists.[2] How can we account for this relative paucity of critical attention to Jameson, particularly in Europe? He is undoubtedly a difficult theorist to read and I have not tried to evade or gloss over these difficulties in this study, but is he really any more difficult than either Derrida or Lacan? Theory is now ubiquitous within the academy and most academics are at least familiar, if not altogether comfortable, with the presentation of complex and at times bizarre notions in difficult languages and opaque styles. And yet Jameson can still be seen as too difficult to include on many undergraduate courses, while students who profess not to understand the first chapter of *The Political Unconscious* one week can be found quoting freely from *Of Grammatology* or *Écrits* the next.

There would appear, therefore, to be a deeper logic at work here, one which involves, on the one hand, the historical specificity of Jameson's own discourse and, on the other, the political fate of Marxism itself. Jameson has consistently argued for the importance of retaining a conception of history and above all a sense of the historicity of our own political and theoretical practice. It is somewhat ironic, then, that his own work is frequently criticized for being too historically and culturally constrained. Jameson's view of Marxism and the emphasis he puts on particular philosophical dilemmas such as reification and the subject–object split, as well as his stress on the unifying characteristics of class and totality, are frequently perceived from a European perspective as specifically North American preoccupations. Thus his overriding concern with the universalization of capitalism and with thinking or representing the totality of the world economic system cannot be separated from his position as a theorist within the only country, the United States, that can at present aspire to global hegemony.

I shall return to these criticisms in relation to history and narrative, to postmodernism and spatial theory and finally in relation to the questions posed for Marxism by contemporary cultural politics. It is worth recalling at the outset, however, that – as Slavoj Žižek has also taken to reminding us – the rejection of totalizing theory in favour of concepts of heterogeneity and difference is itself a peculiarly Eurocentric ideology.[3] The post-structuralist critique of Marxism, and specifically Hegelian Marxists such as Jameson, rests on the assertion that Marxism represents an overly totalizing theory and thus reduces difference and specificity to identity and homogeneity. There is clearly justification for this criticism in relation to the more reductive and deterministic forms of Marxism. However, capitalism *is* undoubtedly a universalizing system; it increasingly structures every aspect of our subjective experience, while at the same time, and most visibly since the collapse of the Soviet Union in the late 1980s, it can be seen to be embarking on a new wave of global expansion and standardization. The rejection of Marxism's totalizing narrative from the post-structuralist perspective of difference and heterogeneity may on reflection come to be seen as somewhat precipitate.

This is not to suggest, as will be evident from the various criticisms I advance throughout this study, that Jameson's work is unproblematic in this respect; but it is to accept that the systemic and structural characteristics of capitalism remain as fundamentally important today as its nomadic, heterogeneous, schizophrenic logic. Jameson's perspective on global capitalism is, to be sure, historically and culturally specific. However, it is the very uniqueness of his historical position, as a cultural theorist within the first country to approach global political and cultural hegemony, that makes it possible for him to write against the main current of much contemporary theory. Jameson's attempt to trace the sedimented representations of an unrepresentable social totality – to dialectically think both the structural and the fragmentary, the systematic and the reifying nature of capitalism – is indeed a scandalous and inconceivable endeavour from the perspective of continental Europe or the UK today. But therein lies its significance and challenge for contemporary political, cultural and social theory.

Among certain strands of contemporary post-Marxist social theory we are now informed that any theory having recourse to economic and class determinates is *a priori* taken as essentialist, reductive and ideologically bankrupt.[4] Yet it seems somewhat perverse that, at the very moment when the political right, from the US and UK in the 1980s to Russia and Korea in the 1990s, openly acknowledges the *primacy* of the economic in social and political matters, large sections of the radical and 'cultural' left should abandon this traditional terrain of critique altogether. Contrary to some of the more inflated claims of the postmodernists concerning free-floating signifiers, new technological revolutions and notions of hyperreality, the economic would appear to be more and not less determinate of social relations today than at any time in our previous history. The lessons Jameson has to teach us, therefore, on certain fundamental questions of the relations between politics, culture and the economic may be more timely than we care to recognize.

Again this is not to suggest that the Marxist left can simply brush aside the critiques of postmodernism and post-Marxism and assert that its own analysis of history and society is axiomatically correct. Many of the criticisms of the orthodox left from the perspectives of gender, race, sexuality, ecology and other so-called 'marginal' political formations remain substantively valid. The question, however, is whether or not this rules out the Marxian critique and 'traditional' socialist politics *per se*. This study originated with the view that Jameson's work makes significant advances in formulating a viable Marxist critical practice that can at once accommodate and address many of the criticisms of orthodox Marxism and at the same time retain Marxism's key analytic categories. To put it another way, the present political imperative for a Marxist or the radical left is not to sunder the relations between culture and the economy as the post-Marxists would have us do, nor alternatively to blandly reassert the primacy of economic determination as orthodox Marxism does; rather the task is to develop a theory flexible enough to articulate the increasingly complex mediations between a global economic market and our discrete, fragmented, cultural experience. Jameson provocatively and controversially entertains the possibility that such a discourse is not only desirable but feasible.

The second aspect of the relative lack of critical attention Jameson has received in Europe is a consequence of the fate of Marxism itself. While Marxism and work within a Marxist problematic has undergone a significant revival in the US since the early 1970s, in continental Europe there has been an unremitting 'demarxification', to use Jameson's term, of political and cultural theory over the same period. Since mid-1970s, Marxism has been displaced by a series of alternative theoretical discourses: structuralism, deconstruction, psychoanalysis and postmodernism to name just a few. According to Perry Anderson this topographical shift of the predominate centres of Marxist intellectual activity from Germanic and Latin Europe to English-speaking countries cannot simply be explained away by reference to Marxism's `intellectual defeat at the hands of a superior alternative'.[5] Indeed, close scrutiny of the encounter between Marxism and continental philosophy reveals it to have been rather negligible and of insufficient depth `to present any real challenge to a historical materialism confident of itself'.[6]

The declining influence of Marxism within European radical and critical theory cannot be accounted for intrinsically, therefore, in terms of the history of ideas, but must be seen in the context of politics and society at large. Eurocommunism, Maoism and Trotskyism all in their different ways suffered political defeat in the 1970s and proved unable to meet the aspirations of a generation radicalized through the student protests of 1968 and the emerging new social movements. These defeats raised questions of concrete political strategy which European Marxism failed to address adequately. Jameson's project, therefore, is instructive in the sense that it developed in an entirely different context, one in which Marxism was not the predominant conceptual or political paradigm. Indeed, Jameson's reflections on the possibilities for a Marxist cultural politics and the need for a sympathetic dialogue with non-Marxist theory may be more appropriate for a readership in the 1990s than in the 1970s, when a more self-confident and robust cultural left still dominated the theoretical scene.

Jameson, as I shall discuss below, has consistently argued for an open, pluralistic, Marxist political and cultural discourse. Marxism, he contends, is not so much a self-consistent, internally coherent, philosophical position, but rather it functions as a corrective to other forms of thought, as the de-idealization of bourgeois philosophy and theory. Thus Jameson can appropriate and incorporate the insights of alternative and non-Marxist theory while retaining Marxism's overarching historical narrative. Jameson effectively ascribes local or contingent validity to many of the postmodern and post-structuralist critiques of Marxism while in turn foregrounding the limitations and historical constraints of their positions. In short, Jameson has rigorously and persuasively sought to produce a sophisticated, non-reductionist, non-mechanistic form of Marxism able to meet the challenge of providing an understanding and critique of contemporary society and culture, of addressing the critique of post-Marxist theory and, finally, of reasserting Marxism's traditional emancipatory narrative. I shall be considering the extent to which Jameson achieves this goal.

I have suggested that Jameson is a difficult theorist to read; this is in part a question of style and his particular adherence to a dialectical tradition of thought that remains alien to many students brought up on the playful, fragmentary and aphoristic styles of postmodern textuality. Jameson is an unashamedly systematic thinker who constantly strives to enact or encapsulate the movement of the dialectic within his own texts. Over the last thirty years he has produced a body of work that combines a formidable degree of philosophical breadth, political integrity and intellectual rigour. His great philosophical-literary models remain Sartre, Lukács and Adorno, but he is equally at home engaging with such figures as Lacan, Derrida and Baudrillard. Moreover, he presents an astonishing range of cultural analyses from 'high' literature to science fiction, from popular music, film and video to painting, sculpture and architecture. Jameson will slip from a discussion of Heidegger to pop art and Hollywood film with an ease that is at once breathtaking and unsettling. The conjuncture of radically divergent, and even antagonistic, theorists and ideas within his work provocatively challenges many of the complacent assumptions and pre-set ideas concerning the nature of Marxism and the discrediting of its sociocultural critique today. Jameson's oeuvre presents one of the most sustained and unequivocal arguments *for* Marxism's continuing relevance to the field of cultural politics today. His achievement is once again to remind us that the much heralded 'death of Marxism' is somewhat premature.

The aim of this book is threefold. First, it is to provide, as comprehensively as possible, an introduction to Jameson's work as critic and theorist. Secondly, it is to situate Jameson's theoretical and political project in relation to the philosophical traditions from which his work emerges and within which he continues to operate and develop. I work through such influential figures as Sartre, Hegel, Adorno, Lukács, Althusser, Lacan, Deleuze, Baudrillard, Mandel and Lefebvre, focusing on Jameson's specific interest in their work and how he incorporates such a diverse body of theorists into his own Hegelian-Marxist framework. At the same time I have sought to situate Jameson's own texts historically. Finally, this book seeks to advance a critique of Jameson's work. I focus on six key areas: issues of form; the representation of history; the politics of pleasure and desire; postmodernism as a cultural logic of late capitalism; globalization and the spatial theory of postmodernity; and finally his conception of the social totality. In each of these areas I identify the problematic, analyse Jameson's own intervention and then draw out some of the theoretical and political implications of his dialectical and incorporative procedure.

Jameson, correctly I believe, insists on the continuing relevance of 'traditional' Marxist concepts of history, class struggle, commodity fetishism, reification, utopianism or transformative politics and the totalizing nature of late capitalism. Marxism has not been invalidated through post-structuralist and deconstructive critiques, nor has postmodernism discredited its hist-orical and emancipatory narrative. On the other hand, the radically changed political and theoretical climate has meant that Marxism has had to rethink and reconceive many of its foundational tenets. Jameson's work has been central to this project and the force of many of my criticisms derives from his attempt to subsume and reconcile often contradictory theoretical positions within a Hegelian-Marxist framework. Jameson's work, however, remains exemplary in its integrity and commitment to formulate a radical, pluralistic and non-dogmatic Marxist cultural practice and politics appropriate to advanced capitalism in the closing years of the twentieth century.

Sartre: From Situation to History

Jameson's formative political experience was marked by two interrelated events, the aftermath of McCarthyism and the emergence of the New Left. The key figure in his early political and philosophical development was the French existentialist Jean-Paul Sartre. Jameson's first published work, *Sartre: The Origins of a Style* (1961), originated as his doctoral thesis in the late 1950s, a period when New Criticism was still hegemonic in the United States.[7] One of the principal contenders against this conservative hegemony was the phenomenologically informed criticism of George Poulet and J. Hillis Miller, while the first works of what we now call 'theory', specifically the early Roland Barthes and some of Adorno's work, were only slowly becoming known and had as yet to make a strong intellectual impact. Jameson's own existential phenomenological study, therefore, was part of a wider attempt within the academy to radically break with the dominant critical paradigm of a conservative New Criticism. The study of Sartre, though, rather than the more pure phenomenology of Husserl or Merleau-Ponty, is significant in one respect. As Frank Lentricchia has observed, the impact of Sartre on literary criticism in the US was at the time rather small; he was not an obvious choice for a phenomenologically informed literary criticism.[8] Furthermore, Sartre was by the late 1950s emerging as the most radical of the existential phenomenologists. The choice of Sartre, therefore, would suggest a more overtly political intent than an initial reading of *The Origins of a Style* might convey.

The figure of Sartre has had an enduring influence on both Jameson's theoretical and political development. The chapter on Sartre and history in *Marxism and Form* is by far the most extended analysis of any single theorist in the book, while the existential analysis of Conrad's *Lord Jim* in *The Political Unconscious* or Jameson's defence of the concept of totalization in *Postmodernism, or, The Cultural Logic of Late Capitalism* attest to Sartre's continuing influence. Moreover, Sartre's conceptual framework can be seen to inform a number of Jameson's own theoretical formulations. Philip Wood, for example, has drawn attention to the striking similarity between Jameson's conception of three concentric horizons of interpretation in *The Political Unconscious* and Sartre's 'hierarchy of significations'.[9] Jameson's insistence on history and political interpretation as 'the absolute horizon of all reading and interpretation' also has more than a mere echo of the Sartre of *Search for a Method*.[10] In addition, Jameson's continuing commitment to an analysis of lived experience and the central role he accords to consciousness in such notions as 'cognitive mapping' betray the persistence of the central themes of classical existentialism in his thinking.

There is a deeper sense, however, in which Sartrean theory can be said to be embedded in Jameson's texts and political project, that is, through the problematic he first encountered in his engagement with existentialism. As Jameson himself has described it, 'the "conversion" to "Sartreanism" was itself always rather different from more conventional modernist conversions of either the aesthetic or the philosophical type'.[11] Unlike Kantianism, Heideggerianism or even, more recently, the deconstruction of Derrida, a commitment to Sartreanism was 'more a matter of a general problematic than of agreement with Sartre's own positions'.[12] In a personal account of his own existential moment and its relationship to his later understanding of Marxism, Jameson has described Sartre as a role model of the politically engaged intellectual: 'for a whole generation of French intellectuals, but also for other Europeans, most notably the younger British left, as well as for Americans like myself, Sartre represented the model of the political intellectual, one of the few role models we had, but a sufficient one.'[13]

Sartre was, as Douglas Kellner has pointed out, Jameson's 'original choice', that is, the initial gesture or unjustifiable decision which, in existential terms, inaugurates one's 'project'. Kellner goes on to observe that in the 1950s Sartre was received in the United States as an exemplary figure of the `individualist radical intellectual' and a `rebel against convention of all sorts'.[14] In adopting Sartre as a role model, Jameson was signalling his own radical, non-conformist aspirations, while at the same time adopting a role model who, to the end of his life, remained staunchly individualistic. Sartre perhaps more than any other figure on the left came to symbolize the figure of the *intellectuel engagé*, the committed intellectual who sought to intervene politically but from outside any mass political organization or traditional party structure. Sartre's search for a viable form of Marxism, both politically and theoretically relevant to contemporary France and divorced from the dogmatism of the Communist Party and the Soviet Union, resonates strongly with Jameson's view of Marxism elucidated in *Marxism and Form*. For Jameson, Marxism is not a rigid system one applies to a given state of affairs but a situated discourse, an open and flexible body of thought that develops according to the specific historical circumstances. It is perfectly consistent, writes Jameson, `with the spirit of Marxism – with the principle that thought reflects its concrete social situation – that there should exist several different Marxisms in the world today, each answering the specific needs and problems of its own socio-economic system' (*MF*, xviii). As with Sartre, therefore, the task was to develop a viable form of Marxism appropriate to the needs of contemporary North American society and the `unique questions raised by monopoly capitalism in the West' (p. xviii).

As its title suggests, the Sartre book is concerned with the development of a particular writer's style. Even in this early work, though, Jameson's conception of style is neither individualistic nor purely aesthetic but is conceived as a historical phenomenon. Style, according to Jameson, is not simply a question of personal expression or a purely literary effect but, in its modern sense, a given style can be seen to take on a significance above and beyond the meaning of the text or the individual sentence itself. As readers, our sense of a particular unique style is cumulative, the gradual assemblage of fragments, words, phrases, sentences and books which come together to give the impression of a unique style as a coherent entity, but one which is nowhere present in its full effects. This particular attention to style is itself a modern phenomenon, where we have come to expect a radical disjuncture between new styles of writing and older forms of literature. On the other hand, there have been moments when what Jameson calls, in *Sartre: The Origins of a Style*, 'the inherited form and the style that fills it in spite of itself with more modern content' coexist in a work. Such a moment, writes Jameson, 'reflects not so much a weakness of the writer's talent but a new problematic moment in his situation, a moment of crisis in the history of the

development of writing itself' (*SOS*, vii). Sartre's literary achievement was to articulate just such a moment.

Jameson's close reading of Sartre's style has all that we have now
come to expect from a Jamesonian analysis: the attention to form as
well as content, the subtle philosophical understanding and Jameson's
own elegant prose. What is missing from the analysis and the study
as a whole is any attempt to embed the analysis of texts in their own
historical moment. Paradoxically for a philosophy grounded on the
situatedness of consciousness and action, Jameson's analysis is surprisingly ahistorical. The failure to historically account for the conditions of possibility of this crisis of narratability is not simply a
methodological failing on Jameson's part, it rather demarcates one of
the limitations of existentialism itself. Retrospectively we can now see
that individual biography was not only Sartre's preferred form but
also the ultimate limit of the Sartrean system itself,[15] and it is this limit
that defines the horizon of Jameson's own study with its pervasive
meditation on the relationship between consciousness and things.
The study never makes the next move to situate these philosophical
concerns in their social and historical context. As Jameson observes,
most of Sartre's work stops just at the point where 'the problem of the
individual life can no longer be isolated from the society in which it
is to be lived, and is suddenly subordinated to history and social
change' (*SOS*, 7). The theoretical limit Jameson first encountered in
the work of Sartre of how to begin to articulate the complex relationship, or mediations, between individual experience, history and
social change delineates the problematic of much of Jameson's subsequent work – in other words, how can we begin to theorize isolated
cultural artefacts in relation to wider historical forces and individual
agency in an increasingly globalized system.

There is more than a sense of circularity to *Origins of a Style*, as
Jameson himself acknowledges; Sartrean existentialism and phenomenology provided both the object of the study and its methodology.
The categories Jameson employs in his analysis are the self-same
categories through which Sartre elaborated his own philosophy: the
'instant', the 'act', the 'event', the 'look', the 'situation', etc. Thus
Jameson reads Sartre's plays as a formal embodiment of Sartre's
founding opposition between subject and object. Paradoxically, on
the one hand Jameson is placed in the position of vigorously defending the distinction between the philosophical and the literary and
dramatic texts, insisting that Sartre's plays can only be thought of as
'idea-plays' if we accept that 'the "ideas" of this philosopher's play[s]
are wholly different in quality from the thoughts developed in the

philosophical works' (*SOS*, 3). On the other hand, Jameson seemingly unproblematically shifts register from the fictional texts to the philosophical works in order to validate his interpretation, and with very little attention to the distinction between the quality of the ideas involved. Indeed, when this is coupled with the overall valorization of language to the detriment of other formal considerations,[16] one is left with the strong impression that Adorno's criticism of Sartre's work as merely 'thesis plays' and 'philosophical novels' is strongly founded.[17] Similarly, we find that Jameson's analysis of temporality in *Le Sursis* (*The Reprieve*) will be `familiar to readers of Sartre's philosophic works', where it can be found `unashamed and unconcealed' (*SOS*, 61). There is a remarkable self-referentiality to this study as Jameson moves between Sartre's literary production and the philosophical works but never moves beyond Sartre's corpus. Kellner interprets the lack of citations and references to other critics in Jameson's text as a manifestation of the phenomenological desire for the thing-in-itself, eschewing other methodological approaches and approaching the object of study without preconceptions.[18] The methodological double-bind presented by *The Origins of a Style* is also instructive in another sense. First, as I have suggested, it points to the limitations of existentialism itself; secondly, it can be seen to inscribe the historical determinates, or conditions of possibility, for Jameson's own text.

Distanced from their own national traditions and resources, American intellectuals looked to Western Europe for role models, and for Jameson this meant initially the figure of Jean-Paul Sartre and later the Frankfurt School. In this respect Jameson's path to Marxism was part of a generational shift, a generation 'whose members moved to the most radical alternatives within contemporary politics and theory'.[19] On the one hand, the turn to Western Europe signalled the 'isolation of the radical intelligentsia in the McCarthyist era and its aftermath which lacked a tradition at hand which could be brought to bear on its cultural concerns, or which could politically mobilize it or offer models of radical self-identification',[20] and on the other, it signified a search for new theoretical resources appropriate to the given historical moment. For Jameson, then, the path through Sartre and the New Left to Marxism was not simply a case of following the trajectory of Sartre's own political thought. On the contrary, Jameson's 'conversion' to Marxism was more a consequence of his encounter with a particular problematic at the limits of existential phenomenology, a problematic of human agency and social change, of the isolated cultural artefact and its place in history. This problematic could be

Introduction

successfully articulated and resolved only if Sartre's own discourse could be reinserted into history itself, and for this Jameson required a more fully dialectical view of history and historical agency. Reading Jameson contextually, writes Kellner, one 'encounters a young literary critic radicalized by study in Europe during the 1950s and by the political movements of the 1960s, turning to Marxism as the solution to his own theoretical and political dilemmas'.[21] In the following chapter I will examine Jameson's attempt to resolve some of these dilemmas through a systematic reading of some of the major figures of the Western Marxist tradition. I situate this work in relation to the academy and the formation of the Marxist Literary Group, and finally I delineate Jameson's initial formulation of dialectical method, that is to say, 'metacommentary'.

1

The Dialectics of Form

Throughout the late 1960s and early 1970s Jameson engaged in a series of readings of the major figures of Western Marxism, studies which were subsequently collected together as the early chapters of *Marxism and Form*.[1] This work has been described as the Ur-text for the renaissance of Marxist criticism in the US academy throughout the 1970s; it also maps some of the central concerns of Jameson's theoretical project. The present chapter, therefore, will be largely expository as I introduce the terrain of Hegelian Marxism and, at the same time, seek to clarify and define certain key Jamesonian concepts which find their first formulation in *Marxism and Form*. It is only with a clear understanding of Jameson's early conception of dialectical method that we will be able to mark the extent to which his ideas have evolved and changed over the years to confront the challenge to Marxism posed by post-structuralism and postmodernism. *Marxism and Form* is itself in large measure an expository text and there is a tension present, as Terry Eagleton has pointed out, between textual exegesis and critique.[2] Jameson's method of 'immanent critique', of the sympathetic working through of an opponent's position has frequently led to a confusion between survey and critique and an identification of Jameson with those very positions he is explicating. In Jamesonian terms, such a confusion between the critic and the object of study will itself only be overcome by more fully historical and dialectical thinking. For reasons of space I will not address this dilemma here, restricting myself, especially in the second and third sections of the chapter, to an exposition of Jameson's ideas and reserving my own critique of his work for the chapters that follow.

I examine *Marxism and Form* under three general rubrics: the logic of form, the logic of content, and metacommentary. The logic of form considers Jameson's conception of form as in-itself political and ideological. I outline Jameson's critique of the practices of empiricism and logical positivism and, at greater length, his alternative tradition of Hegelian dialectical method; finally I provide an analysis of Jameson's own style and practice of dialectical writing. The logic of content will address what Jameson considers to be a fundamental dialectical law of form, that is to say, a work's ultimate determination by its content. The determination of Jameson's own text, therefore, will involve the historicization of Jameson's own practice and a further examination of the situation of Marxist cultural discourse within the US academy. Finally, I sketch Jameson's initial formulation of dialectical method in his seminal essay 'Metacommentary'.

The Logic of Form

I suggested in the introduction that Marxism is not so much a coherent set of ideas or positions in its own right as a critical or corrective discourse. Marxism operates, according to Jameson, as the rectification of other modes of thought. We cannot, therefore, fully understand a given set of ideas or a text until 'we understand that which it is directed against, that which it is designed to correct' (*MF*, 365–6). This applies as much to Jameson's own work as to the work for which he provides an introduction and critique. In the preface to *Marxism and Form*, Jameson identifies his conceptual opponents as that amalgam of 'political liberalism, empiricism, and logical positivism which we know as Anglo-American philosophy' and suggests that it is the critique of this tradition 'which makes up the tendentious part of my book, which gives it its political and philosophical cutting edge' (p. x). *Marxism and Form*, however, undertakes no such critique in terms of its content; nowhere in this text does Jameson explicitly and systematically contest the ideas and presuppositions of empiricism or positivism. Indeed, Jameson does not even go so far as to identify any particular currents or tendencies of Anglo-American philosophy which he is against. So in what sense can a critique of empiricism and positivism be said to provide the political and philosophical cutting edge of *Marxism and Form*?

It is in the 'form' of the text that Jameson's critique operates, that is to say, in its particular style of writing and the thought processes that that style entails, or more precisely, that that particular style embodies and enacts. Style, for Jameson, is not merely a matter of adornment, the expression of an individual taste or personal preference, but rather an 'enactment': style is performative. It is in the very form of Jameson's text, in the shape of his individual sentences, through his syntax and punctuation, that he conducts his polemics against Anglo-American philosophy. For Jameson, a particular style or form is inherently ideological and what he rejects in Anglo-American philosophy is its tendency to separate out distinct spheres of social life, through its emphasis on the individual fact or object, while refusing to make connections at the level of the social totality. He writes of Anglo-American empiricism:

> The method of such thinking, in its various forms and guises, consists in separating reality into airtight compartments, carefully distinguishing the political from the economic, the legal from the political, the sociological from the historical, so that the full implications of any given problem can never come into view; and in limiting all statements to the discrete and the immediately verifiable, in order to rule out any speculative and totalizing thought which might lead to a vision of social life as a whole. (*MF*, 367–8)

In place of the anti-speculative and individuating bias Jameson identifies with Anglo-American philosophy, *Marxism and Form* adumbrates an alternative mode of thought, that of dialectical thinking. Speculative, or dialectical, thought directly challenges those isolating and inhibiting tendencies of empiricism and positivism by foregrounding the essential interrelatedness of events and phenomena. Unlike traditional Anglo-American philosophy, dialectical thought moves from the whole to the part and back to the whole again. Dialectical thought, therefore, forces its practitioner not only to reflect on its own object of study, but also on its own situation and status, and consequently, Jameson argues, to draw unavoidable conclusions on the political level.

The very density and self-consciousness of Jameson's prose eschews the quick and superficial reading and makes serious demands on its readers. In his 1982 *Diacritics* interview Jameson responded to a question on the difficulty of his style with the observation: 'Why should there be any reason to feel that these problems [of culture and aesthetics] are less complex than those of bio-chemistry?'[3] The difficulty of dialectical thought and writing is proportionate to the difficulty of the ideas with which it is dealing; 'real' thought, suggests Jameson, whether it be about bio-chemistry or literature, is difficult and an insistence on the virtues of 'clarity' does not necessarily correlate with greater insight and understanding. The difficulty that many readers encounter with dialectical prose is not so much a stylistic one but rather 'a measure of the unfamiliarity, in our society, of attempts to think the total system as a whole'.[4] This is a concept that, as we shall see throughout this study, Jameson's own work will relentlessly pursue, and perhaps more than any other the single concept that defines Jameson's corpus as a distinctive body of work in relation to contemporary theory. If his style is difficult, that difficulty is proportionate to the complexity of the problematic with which he is wrestling, that is, the position and function of culture within the now globalized system of market capitalism. In emphasizing the difficulty of dialectical prose, however, we should not overlook its pleasure, both the pleasure in reading Jameson's texts and, as I shall point out below, the very obvious pleasure Jameson takes in writing them. Before directly considering Jameson's own dialectical style I shall briefly reflect on the process of dialectical thought itself.

According to Jameson, the basic story the dialectic has to tell us is that of the dialectical reversal, 'that paradoxical turning around of a phenomenon into its opposite of which the transformation of quantity into quality is only one of the better known manifestations' (*MF*, 309). Every object can be said to carry within itself that which it is not, that is, it carries within itself its own opposite as an implicit comparison or differential perception which, even if unacknowledged, is always made. In other words, one identifies an object by differentiating it from what it is not, what is known in classical Hegelian dialectics as the 'identity of identity and non-identity'. Jameson sees this paradoxical reversal and transformation as essentially a diachronic process, in the sense that, to gain a full understanding of any given reversal, or set of reversals, we must consistently reground, or reimmerse, the dialectic in history itself. Dialectical thought, therefore, is thought to the second power: it is thought at once about its object and about its own operation and status as thought; it seeks to be both conscious and self-conscious simultaneously. It is that movement that Hegel described as *Aufhebung* or 'sublation', which at once cancels and preserves its object by lifting it to a higher level of analysis. The classical dialectic operates through this double movement or double negation: first, as we have already seen, by passing over into its opposite, and then by negating this first movement, transcending it and incorporating both elements at a higher level of abstraction, whereby one can see not only what differentiates objects but also what unites them.

Dialectical thinking, then, is systematic thought, thought that not only reflects upon its object of study but also upon its own operations and conditions of possibility; dialectical thought is nothing less than the practice of the dialectical method itself, the perpetual generation and dissolution of its own categories. The dialectical method is inherently relational and comparative. The terms of the dialectic do not exist *a priori*, as pre-existing categories, but rather emerge from the dialectic's object or content. The dialectical method is not simply a formula or mechanistic operation that we can apply to resolve any given conceptual or textual contradiction; it is intrinsic to the object itself. Thus, argues Jameson, as a method of analysis and critique the dialectic is inseparable from the gradual working through of its own inner logic, through 'a sympathetic internal experience of the gradual construction of a system according to its inner necessity' (*MF*, xi). The system itself emerges from its object, and thus the whole system correspondingly remains implicit in any given object or indeed at any given moment of the process. Dialectical thought does not simply dismiss other modes of understanding but works through them, revealing them to be inadequate and incomplete, before moving on to a greater level of abstraction. According to Jameson, it is this very abstractness of the dialectical style that forces us to move beyond the individual and isolated phenomenon and apprehend it as part of a network of relations; abstract terminology, he writes, 'clings to its object as a *sign* of the latter's incompleteness in itself, of its need to be replaced in the context of the totality' (*MF*, xiii).

Until a given object is situated in relation to the totality itself, it remains partial, fragmentary and incomplete. Herein lies the real difficulty of dialectical thinking and particularly of a dialectical style of writing, 'its holistic totalizing character' (*MF*, 306). Dialectical thought is totalizing thought, exhibiting an inherent 'preference for the concrete totality over the separate abstract parts' (*MF*, 45); it consistently makes connections, drawing together the most disparate phenomena and historical moments. This tendency to draw everything together accounts for some of the complexity and density of dialectical prose as well as its breadth, as it ranges over what we had always accepted as distinct and specialized areas of study, revealing hitherto unnoticed connections. At its best this creates what Jameson calls a 'dialectical shock' as the reader is forced into a new perception through the yoking together of what we had previously perceived as utterly distinct phenomena. Such a shock, suggests Jameson, is 'constitutive of and inseparable from dialectical thinking', signalling 'an abrupt shift to a higher level of consciousness, to a larger context of being' (*MF*, 375); its presence will be the mark of any genuine Marxist criticism.

Dialectical thought, as I have indicated above, is nothing less than the practice of the dialectical method itself, in other words, the elaboration of dialectical sentences. For Jameson, there is an ultimate obligation to 'come to terms with the shape of the individual sentences themselves, to give an account of the origin and formation' (*MF*, xii) if any concrete description of a literary or philosophical phenomenon is to be complete. Each sentence stands as a figure for the process as a whole, but at the same time we can only grasp the full import of an individual sentence when we situate it in relation to that more elusive and problematic concept of 'totality'. A concrete description of Jameson's own oeuvre, therefore, will sooner or later be obliged to give an account of what Terry Eagleton has called Jameson's 'magisterial, busily metaphorical' sentences.[5] This most palpable feature of Jameson's texts, their particularly dense and rhetorical style, has frequently been passed over 'in polite silence or with a shyly admiring phrase'.[6] Alternatively, Jameson's style has been interpreted as a sign of a more fundamental and inherent weakness in his work and thought. I will return to this latter criticism below; first, I consider Jameson's own particular style, taking as my initial unit of analysis the sentence and then progressively considering the larger units of composition – the example, the essay and the book.

If we take a sentence from Jameson's analysis of Adorno, we can see how the dialectical system begins to unravel itself from a given point of departure. Jameson describes a passage from Adorno's *Philosophie der neuen Musik* as an object lesson in dialectical thinking and a poetic object in its own right, a status Jameson's own prose can be said to emulate:

> What happens is . . . that for a fleeting instant we catch a glimpse of a unified world, of a universe in which discontinuous realities are nonetheless somehow implicated with each other and intertwined, no matter how remote they may at first have seemed; in which the reign of chance briefly refocuses into a network of cross-relationships wherever the eye can reach, contingency temporarily transmuted into necessity. (*MF*, 8)

In a single sentence Jameson momentarily holds together the 'fleeting instant' and the 'unified world', a 'discontinuous', fragmented reality and an intrinsically interrelated universe; each subordinate clause moves from the particular to the universal, from the disparate to the unified, from the part to the whole. Moreover, the sentence does not simply enumerate these moments as a set of static binary oppositions, but grasps them as moments in flux, in process. The sentence rhetorically carries us forward through a series of expanding horizons: an instance, a world, a universe, and simultaneously higher levels of abstraction: a 'fleeting instant', 'discontinuous realities', 'the reign of chance'. There is what Clint Burnham describes, following Sartre, as a certain *seriality* and *inflation* to Jameson's discourse, as he takes up examples from other texts and incorporates them into his own, at the same time transforming and amplifying the example, as though through the seriality of discrete images the totality as a whole emerges.[7]

As so often with a Jamesonian sentence, it pivots on the semi-colon, veering round upon itself. In its first movement, the dialectic of the sentence passes over into its opposite as the ephemeral and contingent comes face to face with the brute fact of necessity. The semi-colon signifies that a shift of the dialectical gears has taken place, at once differentiating and binding together the two distinct but dependent halves of the sentence; a connection has been made but these remain determinate parts. Dialectical thought is more than simply a unity of opposites, however, it is thought to the second power, that is to say, it is both reflexive and self-reflexive simultaneously. Thus Jameson's sentence can be seen to provide us with an analysis of Adorno's dialectical style at the same time as it reflects back upon the totalizing nature of dialectical thought. The totality, of which the sentence can be no more than a fragment, is unrepresentable in itself; it can only be articulated in the content of the work as an empty and abstract category, and therefore it can only be realized in the form, in the very structure of the sentence. The transitory character of Jameson's lexis: 'fleeting', 'briefly', 'glimpsed' and 'implicated' foregrounds the very elusiveness of the concept, of our inability to visualize or conceive such a realm except in the most provisional and transitory manner, in the *connectedness* of it all. The sentence does not insist or belabour the necessity of totalizing thought, or the dialectical unity of part to whole, but operates as a gestalt in which foreground and background oscillate continually. The visual and spatial metaphor refocuses our perception as the eye moves from the isolated fragment to the farthest horizon. Just as Adorno's text for Jameson temporarily transmutes contingency into necessity, his own text transmutes the immediacy of textual analysis into a glimpse of the totality and its own object lesson in dialectical thinking.

Jameson insists on the dialectical imperative towards the concrete, although, contrary to empiricism or positivism, within Hegelian dialectics it is the totality that marks the concrete rather than isolated, individual phenomena. As I shall argue in later chapters, the fundamental misunderstanding of the 'concept of totality' in much poststructuralist and postmodernist thought derives from conflating the *concept* with the phenomenon itself. The concept of totality is taken to designate a specific entity which is empirically verifiable and ultimately representable. For Jameson, on the other hand, the concept of totality functions as a methodological standard, an unrepresentable horizon which marks the limits of our thought rather than a possibility to be realized. The concept of totality, therefore, is always already inscribed within our discourse as a limit. I have already alluded to one form that this limit takes in the discussion of abstract terminology above; alternatively, this particular limitation of discourse can be traced through the utilization of examples. The example, or rather the necessity of using examples, is a sign of thought imperfectly realized. Examples are 'always the mark of abstraction or distance from the thought process: they are additive and analytical, whereas in genuine dialectical thinking the whole process would be implicit in any given object' (*MF*, 338). With examples, however, the thought process is rent asunder, on the one hand providing us with a presentation of method, and on the other with a series of discrete objects as examples. It is the very essence of dialectical thinking to overcome this separation between form and content, between the thought process itself and its object of study.

As with the previous analysis of Jameson's sentence, however, we cannot simply wish away this separation by fiat. Jameson's discourse is no less caught up within the reifying logic of capital than any other, and thus the use of examples is unavoidable. To be fully dialectical, therefore, we must attempt to think not only about the specific problem to which we seek a solution but, at the same time, about the situation in which the recourse to examples is unavoidable. The use of an example may provide a shorthand solution to a given problem, as an answer to a specific question, but as a solution it in turn represents a problem in its own right, the necessity of using examples in the first place. At the very time when he is forced to use an example, therefore, Jameson foregrounds the limits of this necessity. Jameson's analysis of the example, by example, forces us to consider the formal procedures at work rather than addressing a specific question. The necessity of utilizing examples itself becomes exemplary of dialectical self-consciousness, of that dialectical imperative to think the limits of one's own position back into the situation under analysis. Jameson's use of the example, as an example of the example, is just one instance of the self-evident relish of his style I alluded to above; one could also cite the long footnote on the formal status of footnotes. Even at his most strenuously dialectical there is always a self-conscious pleasure in Jameson's writing.

I have suggested that, for Jameson, the presence of the dialectical shock is the mark of a genuine Marxist criticism. That is to say, the shock one is forced to acknowledge when what were previously perceived to be utterly distinct phenomena are yoked together through the dialectic. I would now like to extend this notion of the dialectical shock to larger units of composition, and specifically in conjunction with Adorno's conception of the scandalous and transgressive potential of the essay. If we exclude *Sartre: The Origins of a Style*, all of Jameson's major published works – *Marxism and Form, The Political Unconscious, Postmodernism, or, The Cultural Logic of Late Capitalism, Signatures of the Visible, The Geopolitical Aesthetic* and *The Seeds of Time* – are volumes of collected essays, while the shorter works, *The Prison House of Language* and *Fables of Aggression*, are essentially extended essays. In *The Jamesonian Unconscious*, Clint Burnham interestingly argues for a distinction between the essay as a form and the chapter of a book. Burnham observes that the essay evolves out of the demands of academic production as well as the managerial and economic forces of journal production. However, Jameson's essays, particularly in the later film and postmodern books, cannot be said to be 'collected' in the same way as the two volumes of his collected essays are. According to Burnham, we see in these later texts how 'the academic "book" and the scholarly "essay" both disintegrate into the postmodern chapter.'[8] The postmodern chapter is at once an autonomous unit and simultaneously a part of a larger whole, the book itself. While it is true to say that once an essay is collected in the form of a book different expectations arise, we begin to make formal links and connections between chapters that we may not previously have made between the separate essays. However, it will be my contention that much of Jameson's work operates at its best if we consider it as an essay in Adorno's sense of the genre.[9]

In 'The Essay as Form' Adorno reflects upon the characteristics of the essay, which rather than 'achieving something scientifically, or creating something artistically . . . reflects a childlike freedom that catches fire, without scruple, on what others have already done'.[10] The essay, argues Adorno, eschews traditional notions of method and enquiry, taking as its raw material objects already culturally and historically determined and 'treating what is normally held to be derived, without however pursuing its ultimate derivation'.[11] It thus has the freedom to commence and conclude where it chooses, has to draw no 'final' conclusions but rather gains its polemical and critical force through its capacity to reorder, or recombine, its pregiven material in a new and potentially disruptive way. The innermost form of the essay, according to Adorno, is heresy. The essay is essentially transgressive, seeking to make visible in the object that which orthodox thought would keep secret.

If we consider Jameson's much acclaimed essay 'Reification and Utopia in Mass Culture' we can see how, at his best, Jameson utilizes the transgressive potential of the essay and cuts through the often polarized and static positions of academic debate. Jameson commences his essay by defining the conventional polarity between 'mass' and 'high' culture, and indeed will retain and use these designations, albeit in a qualified and modified form. Critics who valorize mass culture, observes Jameson, need to account for its pervasive anti-intellectual and anti-theoretical stance, particularly as this position is largely propagated by intellectuals themselves who have as yet failed to provide an adequate method of study for those objects they valorize. On the other hand, the strong advocates of high art, specifically those in the tradition of the Frankfurt School, suffer from a corresponding overestimation of the positive value of high art, especially modernist art. What is immediately apparent is that Jameson is seeking to move beyond the sterile binary opposition which the debate between high and mass culture has all too frequently been locked into and which inevitably declines into ethical and value judgements. He insists on the need to replace such sterile debates with a more historical and dialectical approach, an approach which demands that 'we read high and mass culture as objectively related and dialectically interdependent phenomena, as twin and inseparable forms of the fission of aesthetic production under capitalism.'[12]

Jameson's primary rhetorical gesture is that of the dialectical reversal; at every twist and turn of the text we find ourselves attempting to look at the situation, as Jameson says, from both ways at once. If we take the concept of reification itself we can see how such reversals function. On the one hand, the theory of reification refers to that process under capitalism whereby all aspects of human life are fragmented and instrumentally reorganized to meet the demands of capital. In this sense, the quality or 'ends' of human activity are bracketed, as all human activity is ruthlessly reorganized in terms of efficiency and sheer 'means'. On the other hand, the notion of reification provides us with an alternative perspective, that of *consumption*. Reification not only transforms human activity into sheer 'means' but also into an 'end' in itself, the commodification of labour power turning it into a product, or commodity, to be 'consumed'. The cultural implications of reification are that while all cultural artefacts are turned into commodities to be consumed, at the same time all commodities within a consumer society take on an aesthetic dimension. One does not just buy the commodity itself,-the new car, the television set, clothes or food, but one also buys an image, or buys into what is often referred to as a 'lifestyle'. In this sense, argues Jameson, what we consume is less the thing itself than its abstract idea or image. Reification is a double-edged sword, therefore, which results not only in the commodification of culture but also in the aestheticization of the commodity.

By focusing on the historical specificity of high and mass culture, Jameson highlights not only what separates and differentiates these two realms but also what unites them. Both are products of commodity reification and the escalating fragmentation of capitalism, as it systematically dissolves the fabric of social and group cohesion. Both modernism and mass culture, therefore, can be said to have the same content (in the broadest sense of the term); what differentiates them is the way that each processes or transforms this raw material:

> Both modernism and mass culture entertain relations of repression with the fundamental social anxieties and concerns, hopes and blind spots, ideological antinomies and fantasies of disaster, which are their raw material; only where modernism tends to handle this material by producing compensatory structures of various kinds, mass culture represses them by the narrative construction of imaginary resolutions and by the projection of an optical illusion of social harmony.[13]

Thus in a final dialectical transformation of the essay we find Jameson bringing to bear on the artefacts of mass culture the analytical methods of the Frankfurt School and revealing that repressed utopian impulse that can be traced in even the most degraded forms of mass culture. I will consider the utopian impulse in greater depth in chapter 4.

In the essay, then, concepts gain their precision and weight not through their derivation and definition but in relation to one another. As Adorno puts it, 'concepts do not build a continuum of operations, thought does not advance in a single direction, rather aspects of the argument interweave as in a carpet.'[14] The fecundity of the ideas concerned will depend on the density of the texture achieved. Thus in 'Reification and Utopia in Mass Culture' Jameson weaves a rich texture which encompasses not only modernism and mass culture, the Frankfurt School and Hollywood but also Kierkegaard and pop music, genre theory and the Freudian unconscious, the writings of Guy Debord and Baudrillard. The conjunction of such discourses is not an end in itself, a mere display of erudition, but serves as a provocation to thought, gesturing towards potential areas of study and new ways of conceiving things. Jameson, for instance, offers a redefinition of modernism not as the solution to commodification but as a reaction to it. He also highlights the common ground between the Marxian concept of reification and post-structuralist notions of the materialization of the signifier. Jameson does not resolve these questions but leaves them open ended, while his own short analyses of the films *Jaws* and *The Godfather* (parts 1 and 2) illustrate just two possible options.

The essay is an inherently discontinuous form, a form which does not attempt to mask its fragmentary status but on the contrary accentuates it. The dialectical essay ought to be, according to Adorno, the critical form *par excellence*, at once more dynamic and more static than what Adorno designates as traditional thought. The unity of the essay is determined by the unity of its object; it does not attempt to abolish discontinuities but works through their fissures – there will always be a tension between presentation and what is presented, between form and content. Paradoxically, it is the very restrictiveness of the essay as a form that facilitates the release of the full potential of the dialectical imagination. The tension between form and content gives it an edge and intensity which is lacking in more discursive prose. The problem for the essayist-dialectician is how to link these fragments together, since, as Jameson himself observes, the fundamental problem for any dialectical writer is that of continuity. For the writer who has, suggests Jameson, 'so intense a feeling for the massive continuity of history itself is somehow paralyzed by that very awareness, as in some overloading of perception too physical to be any longer commensurable with language' (*MF*, 50–1). What binds together Adorno's essays is less their thematic content than their 'style' and their shared historical moment; the problem of continuity is resolved less through the writing of a narrative than the 'construction' of larger units.

As I indicated above, there is a similar question mark over what binds together Jameson's own texts. *Marxism and Form*, for example, is organized 'around the sign of Discourse itself' (*MF*, xii). It is Jameson's most self-consciously dialectical text and one feels at every moment that imperative to totalize: from the strenuous efforts of the individual sentence to his readings of other writers, Jameson constantly situates his text in history. *The Political Unconscious*, with its focus on narrative, is organized around a central narrative of Realism – Naturalism – emergent Modernism. *Postmodernism, or, The Cultural Logic of Late Capitalism*, on the other hand, drawing on the heterogeneity of its own object of study and reflecting the collapse of grand narratives in the postmodern age, lacks a core narrative, presenting a more copious and expansive text befitting its dominant organizational category of 'space'. It ranges over such disparate phenomena as architecture, economics, New Historicism, photography and De Manian deconstruction, which are bound together by the historical moment of the postmodern. And *The Geopolitical Aesthetic* is organized around the problematic of representing the totality. Burnham sees the later books, on postmodernism and film, not as books in the traditional sense at all but rather as 'sublime quilts', as almost postmodern simulacra of books.[15] The question mark is over how well these larger 'constructed' units work.

There is a certain 'waning of effect' (to adapt Jameson's own phrase) characteristic of Jameson's texts, that is to say, the initial spark that is ignited in the essays is often smothered by the sheer quantity of material in the longer works. There is a tendency with dialectical prose to try to say everything, to cover every angle and perspective, before one actually says what it is one wishes to say. This can lead to diffuseness, to the style becoming ever more convoluted and opaque as it draws in increasing amounts of raw materials. The price that is paid for this is often the loss of that dialectical shock which Jameson sees as the mark of genuinely Marxist criticism. This is by no means to dismiss or play down the significance of the longer discursive works but to suggest that what is most scandalous and transgressive in dialectical thought, its shock effect for the Anglo-American consciousness, is somehow lost. The polemical and critical cutting edge of the essay declines as it is incorporated into larger forms. As we read the longer texts we tend to slip back into more narrative or analytical frames of mind, and indeed this may be why *The Political Unconscious*, with its central narrative structure, is Jameson's most satisfying book to read.

In short, perhaps it is not only our unfamiliarity with thinking the concept of totality that presents difficulties with dialectical prose, but there may be a problem inherent in the style itself. For Jameson, the essay can be seen as 'fragments of or footnotes to a totality which never comes into being' (*MF*, 52), the parts never quite form a whole; they can never be more than yet another fragment. The essay can offer a glimpse of the totality, but it always remains out of reach. The more the ideas are fleshed out and elaborated, the greater the sense of repetition, and the feeling that we cannot actually get beyond the starting point. There is then, I would suggest, an initial anti-climax on reading Jameson's books, a sense of formal disappointment which must be offset against the sheer intellectual intensity of the individual fragments themselves. In the reified world of late capitalism the promise the dialectic aspires to, the unity of subject and object, of theory and practice, the attainment of the concrete, of the totality itself, can never be realized and the levels of abstraction and difficulty inscribed in theoretical texts stand as a mark of that failure.

This failure is also inscribed in the sentences themselves. Jameson argues for the priority of dialectical thought over and above analytical and positivistic modes of thinking because of its ability to make connections and to relate discrete and disparate phenomena. The exact nature of those connections, however, often remains oblique and uncertain. Jameson's texts are pervaded by lexical equivocations, most notably with such phrases as 'something like' and 'kind of'. In a review of *The Political Unconscious*, Robert Scholes lists thirty such equivocations, including 'something like', 'would seem', 'at some level', 'virtual' and 'one would imagine'.[16] The difficulty posed by such equivocations is that they indicate that an equivalence is being posited but leave the exact nature of that equivalence unclear. As Scholes points out, all writers occasionally fall back on the use of equivocal devices but with Jameson it is in danger of becoming 'the dominant principle of discourse'.[17] Scholes writes that the 'expression 'something like' is not only the weakest possible form of comparison, it logically implicates its own contradiction (something *un*like).'[18] In other words, it suggests an analogy or a relation and simultaneously cancels it. Thus the precise nature of the formulation or the mechanisms by which it operates remain unclear or contradictory. Furthermore, 'Jameson's text, which is full of serious thought and learning, is also astonishingly reluctant to emerge from its own web of textuality to make contact with the world.'[19] Paradoxically, for all Jameson's assertions of the need to reground texts in their social and historical contexts, his own texts remain strangely aloof.

Eagleton has also identified the paradox of Jameson's style, observing that his prose has a tendency to escape 'even his own most strenuously analytical habits' and slip 'through the very dialectical forms it so persuasively delineates'.[20] For Jameson, the dialectical style is not only a political imperative but a pleasure in its own right and it is this, suggests Eagleton, Jameson's own style, that represents the utopian impulse of his work rather than the discussions of Ernest Bloch or Herbert Marcuse. 'The duality of the Jamesonian sentence,' writes Eagleton, 'at once political message and play of signifier, seems to me an eminently dialectical figure of the relation between desire and its historical deferment, opening a space between these options in which the reader is suspended.'[21] Ultimately style represents a political deferment, a compensation for pleasures historically postponed and goals which are unrealizable, and to this extent it foreshadows, argues Eagleton, a bleak and politically instructive displacement.

The Logic of Content

In the preceding section, I argued that the ideological tendency of a work is inscribed in its form rather than merely in its content, but this should not be taken to imply that Jameson is, in any sense, a formalist. Formalism has a tendency to downgrade the content of cultural artefacts, seeing it as little more than the projection of the form. For Jameson, on the other hand, form is a historical phenomenon not regardless of its content but precisely because its content is social and historical in character. Form, he suggests, is nothing less than content working itself out in the realm of the superstructure; the evolution of forms, far from consisting of a self-motivating logic as the Russian Formalists saw it, represents the emergence of new types of content as they force their way to the surface and displace the older obsolete forms. In other words, literary change 'is essentially a function of content seeking its adequate expression in form' (*MF*, 328), a process Jameson designates as the 'logic of content'.

The logic of content entails what is for Jameson a fundamental dialectical law of form, that is, it dictates that the raw materials themselves shape and restructure the formal codes of presentation. It is the content itself, through its own inner logic, which 'generates those categories in terms of which it organizes itself in a formal structure, and in terms of which it is therefore best studied' (*MF*, 335). According to Jameson, this process necessitates the movement from the intrinsic to the extrinsic, that is to say, a gradual enlargement of the critical perspective from the individual work to that larger social reality from which it emerges. To fully understand Jameson's text, therefore, it will be necessary to move beyond the consideration of the work itself to that historical moment from which it emerged. That is, within the broader context of Marxist cultural criticism in the US academy in the late 1960s and early 1970s.

The specific dilemma raised by Jameson's text is that it must be seen in relation to not one, but two backgrounds simultaneously. Jameson's texts are always directed against at least two audiences simultaneously, to be broadly defined as an academic audience and a political one. I have already noted how Jameson's preface to *Marxism and Form* identifies a general intellectual antagonist or opponent as that of Anglo-American empiricism and logical positivism. This can be said to represent the negative or critical component of his text, its polemical edge. I should now like to consider its positive component. In situating his own text Jameson notes the absence of a Marxist cultural presence in academic and intellectual circles; indeed, in the early 1970s, when North American students thought of Marxism they only had recourse to the struggles and polemics of the 1930s, which bore little relation to their contemporary needs and aspirations. The few familiar Marxist critics still readily accessible, Christopher Caudwell or Ernst Fischer, no longer seemed adequate or applicable to current critical requirements, particularly with the shift of critical emphasis since the 1930s from content-based criticisms to more formally based methods. In his 1982 *Diacritics* interview[22] Jameson enlarged on this need for a Marxist cultural presence, suggesting that any real systematic change in American society required as a minimal first step the creation of a social democratic movement, but that this in turn entailed two preconditions: the creation of a Marxist intelligentsia, and creation of a Marxist cultural, or intellectual, presence. *Marxism and Form* was to play a key role in establishing that Marxist cultural presence.

In the mid to late 1960s there was no space within the US academy or its professional bodies for Marxist ideas to be seriously discussed and propagated. In 1968, Jameson and a group of his graduate students at the University of California, San Diego, sought to rectify this situation through the formation of the Marxist Literary Group. The group emerged out of the events of the 1968 Modern Languages Association conference in Chicago, as an affiliated organization of the MLA.[23] According to Dan Latimer, the group was originally a part of the Radical Caucus, a group associated with such figures as Louis Kampf and Florence Howe, both later presidents of the MLA. Latimer suggests that the two groups 'split, with great noise and pain, along the fault lines of theory and praxis, with on the one hand the Jameson group, constituted by a number of more patient, tenured members of high profile departments, addicted to the higher lucubrations of theory; and on the other hand the Radical Caucus remnant constituted by more imperilled inner city, community college activists, demanding more overtly disruptive tactics and abjuring the long term'.[24]

Latimer's account, however, is rather tendentious and misleading. While there was certainly a degree of tension between the two groups in the early years, it soon petered out and, contrary to the view of factional infighting, the two groups worked closely together within the MLA, as they have continued to do to the present. It is also inaccurate to characterize the split between the two groups along the lines of theory and practice, the former based in high profile institutions and the latter in community colleges. The development of theory, and specifically Marxist theory, was indeed a central, if not the central, aim of the Marxist Literary Group. As Jameson's programmatic statement in the preface to *Marxism and Form* makes clear, 'within the United States itself, there is no tactical or political question which is not first and foremost theoretical, no form of action which is not inextricably entangled in the sticky cobwebs of the false and unreal culture itself, with its ideological mystification on every level' (*MF*, p. xviii). A commitment to theory, however, does not preclude a concern with issues of practice, while to privilege a particular form of practice fails to acknowledge that the Marxist Literary Group itself represented a significant intervention within the academy with practical as well as theoretical consequences.

Furthermore, as Jameson's statement makes clear, the whole question of praxis in contemporary US society was itself perceived to be a theoretical problem. The issue is no longer, argued Jameson, simply 'whether the street fighter or urban guerrilla can win against the weapons and technology of the modern state, but rather precisely where the street *is* in the superstate, and, indeed, whether the old fashioned street as such still exists in the first place in that seamless web of marketing and automated production which makes up the new state' (*MF*, p. xviii). With respect to the Radical Caucus, it is true to say that it emphasized social activism rather than theoretical concerns, adopting a more broad-based radicalism than the specifically Marxist perspective of the MLG; however, it was not restricted to community colleges in the inner city and drew many members from 'prestigious' or high profile institutions.

It is perhaps more accurate to speak of a difference of emphasis and focus in the respective programmes of the Radical Caucus and the MLG rather than of a deep ideological rift. The activities of the Radical Caucus focused on pedagogical and professional issues, while the MLG focused on questions of theory. The Caucus put out a monthly journal, *Radical Teacher*, which, as its title indicates, was concerned with issues of teaching, language and composition. In short, the Caucus was primarily interested in questions of the canon, of recovering women's and other literatures, and the nature of the profession itself. The Marxist Literary Group, on the other hand, was concerned specifically with the development of Marxist theory in the academy. Through its programme of sessions at MLA conferences and its own Summer Institute on Culture and Society, the Marxist Literary Group helped to transform the status of Marxist cultural theory in the US academy from a largely outdated and marginal practice to one of the most vital currents of contemporary theoretical discourse. At its height in the 1970s the Marxist Literary Group was the largest affiliated organization of the MLA. This presence was reduced towards the end of the decade and in the early 1980s as much due to the success of the work of Jameson and the MLG as to any lessening of interest in Marxist cultural discourse. As Marxism increasingly gained a foothold in the academy, so the necessity declined for a specific arena within which Marxist cultural theorists could meet. Marxism was established as a core component, or at least an option, on many course curriculums.[25]

The significance of *Marxism and Form*, then, lies not just in its methodological formulations and theoretical insights but in the central role it was to play in creating a strong Marxist presence within academic circles. *Marxism and Form* was to make available to an American audience, for the first time, an alternative tradition of Marxist critical theory, a tradition which focused not on the content of works but on their form; it finally, unequivocally established 'the legitimacy of Marxist aesthetic theory among broad sections of the literary critical profession'.[26] But, as I suggested above, *Marxism and Form* also had its own esoteric or political audience. Marxism is not a homogeneous body of knowledge or a single doctrine but encompasses a diverse range of 'Marxist' perspectives. *Marxism and Form* can be seen to be engaged with its own dialogue within Marxism, asserting the priority of Hegelian Marxism over and above the more deterministic varieties of economic Marxism and dialectical materialism. Hegelian Marxism, according to Jameson, is the only theory adequate to the task in hand, through its ability to encompass the sheer quantity of raw materials and the complexity of late, or consumer, capitalism. Thus *Marxism and Form* delineates the tradition from which Jameson's ideas are evolving as well as addressing the perceived needs and priorities for a contemporary Marxist critical practice. Furthermore, *Marxism and Form* can be seen to map the conceptual parameters of some of the most central and recurrent themes of Jameson's theoretical career: Adorno on form, Benjamin as allegorist, Bloch on the utopian impulse, Schiller and Marcuse on the hermeneutics of freedom, Lukács on narrative, mediation and reification, and Sartre on the primacy of history and class struggle. I

will return to detailed consideration and analysis of each of these
ideas in subsequent chapters.

Metacommentary

Marxism and Form concludes with a long chapter outlining what a
contemporary theory of dialectical criticism would entail. This chapter essentially expands and develops Jameson's award-winning 1971
essay 'Metacommentary', which for reasons of space and conciseness
I will mainly draw on here. With the publication of Susan Sontag's
influential work *Against Interpretation* (1966), the process of interpretation fell somewhat into disrepute; Jameson takes Sontag's influential book as his starting point and argues that any genuinely
profitable discussion of interpretation will take place not around the
nature of interpretation but around the need for it in the first place.
Thus Jameson commences his study by recounting the historical
nature of the contemporary anti-interpretative tendency, noting that
in both philosophy and literature all the major twentieth-century
schools have shared a similar preference for method in place of
metaphysics or form over content. What is less often remarked on,
however, is the tendency of form to slide into content in the sense that
what is initially a preference expressed by the critic is then projected
on to the work itself, becoming an aesthetic in its own right.

Thus Sontag 'begins by denying the rights of *all* interpretation, of
all content, only to end up defending a particular type of (modern-
istic) art that cannot be interpreted, that seems to have no determinate
content in the older sense'.[27] Jameson observes that this is also the case
with the Russian Formalists, who inverted the traditional relationship between form and content, viewing 'the aim of all technique as
the production of the work of art itself'[28] rather than directing the
reader outside the work to some ultimate ground or meaning. But
what was initially an attempt to isolate the uniquely literary quality
of the work, what defined 'literariness' apart from everyday discourse, eventually resulted in a 'radical aesthetization of life'.[29] For, 'if
content exists in order to permit form, it follows that the lived sources
of that content – the social experiences, the psychological obsessions
and dispositions of the author – also come to be formally motivated,
to be seen as means rather than ultimate ends or meanings.'[30] Indeed,
even the author comes to be seen as merely one more device for
bringing the work itself into being.

As with Sontag's recourse to modern art, the Formalists' emphasis on the lyric and the short story can also be seen as a consequence of their own procedures. The Formalists identified literariness, or poetic language, with language that drew attention to itself, drew attention to its own status as language and as such renewed one's perception of the material quality of language. Literature achieves this through a process of 'defamiliarization' or 'making strange', in other words, literature retards perception, it causes one to dwell on its own status as an artefact. As a particular form once more becomes familiar, the method of defamiliarization must be renewed or rejuvenated in some way, to once again jolt one out of familiarity, and for the Formalists this process worked through the elevation of a new 'popular' form. In *The Prison House of Language* (1972) Jameson observes that there are two particular problems with the notion of defamiliarization. First, it is an ahistorical concept: Victor Shklovsky saw the process of literary change as 'a uniform mechanism the same at all times and all places', which militates against any genuine sense of literary history and 'ends up turning diachrony into mere appearance' (*PH*, 59). Secondly, there is the problem of events in time: does defamiliarization operate only on the isolated image or figure, or can it also deal with a series of events or narrative? For Shklovsky the technique remained the same in both cases; it was just a matter of a difference in scope.

But the problems of narrative cannot be solved by the simple enumeration of techniques and devices, by the exposition of how well a given work 'retards' its own progression. Following Lukács, Jameson proposes narration as a 'basic way of coming to terms with time itself, and with concrete history' (*PH*, 62). Narrative is a temporal experience and unlike the short story, myth or tale, 'there are no pre-existing laws that govern the elaboration of the novel as a form: each one is different, a leap in the void, an invention of content simultaneous with the invention of the form' (*PH*, 73). The very notion of retardation implies a separation of form and content, though, formalized as the dual concepts of 'fabula' (story) and 'szujet' (plot, or discourse). Shklovsky's method therefore is unable to deal adequately with narrative and this finds its correlative in his principal object of study: the short story.

Jameson attributes to formalism the paradoxical status of 'the basic mode of interpretation of those who refuse interpretation'.[31] At the very heart of its procedures is the notion of 'bracketing': if all content is merely the projection of form, then texts have no extrinsic referent, a given text speaking only of itself, of 'its own coming into being' (*PH*, 88). The bracketing of all extrinsic referents allows for the construction of an intrinsic system or model of literariness, but it also returns the content by the back door, as only 'pre-existing things – objects, institutions, units of some kind – can be defamiliarized; just as only what has a name to begin with can lose its familiar name and suddenly appear before us in all its bewildering unfamiliarity' (*PH*, 70). In other words, we must bring with us a sense of an original meaning, a knowledge of the content prior to its formal presentation, for it to be defamiliarized. An act of interpretation has initially taken place, in the sense that we now understand the 'defamiliarized' object as not being what we had previously taken it to be.

Similarly, French structuralism can be seen to be no less contradictory. Structuralism shares with Formalism Saussure's 'foundational distinction between *langue* and *parole*' (*PH*, 101), but whereas Russian Formalism concentrated on the individual artefact, structuralism attempted to describe the overall organization of the sign system itself. Structuralism, suggests Jameson, 'can best be grasped as a philosophical formalism' (*PH*, 195); it rejects notions of substantive thought and insists on the bracketing of the referent – there is no one-to-one correspondence between a sign and its referent. But this raises something of a dilemma for structuralists, as most do presuppose beyond the sign itself some ultimate ground or reality as referent. So while 'its concept of the sign forbids any research into the reality beyond it,' structuralism maintains the notion of some ultimate ground 'by considering the signified as a concept "of" something' (*PH*, 106). Structuralism, then, initially rejects any pretence to interpretation, rather 'proposing . . . to replace the substance (or the substantive) with relations and purely relational perceptions'.[32] But once it has mapped these relations as a set, or series, of binary oppositions, it invariably sets out (as with Lévi-Strauss's analysis of myth)[33] to interpret these patterns of oppositions: thus, writes Jameson, the 'most characteristic feature of structuralist criticism lies precisely in a kind of transformation of form into content, in which the form of structuralist research . . . turns into a proposition about content' (*PH*, 198–9). Therefore, we find that stories are about stories, narration about the act of narration, and ultimately the content of a given work is nothing less than language itself. In a characteristic dialectical movement, we once more find ourselves in the situation of being forced to interpret at the very moment we show most reluctance to do so.

For Jameson, though, the question of whether or not to interpret a given work is not really the issue. It is more a matter of history. What is required is to historicize the cultural artefact, to lay bare its conditions of possibility. It is not a case of making value judgements about the work or attempting to resolve its contradictions, but of historically situating the work so that those contradictions become meaningful in themselves. For Jameson every commentary must at the same time be a metacommentary, *it must include a commentary on its own conditions of existence* and direct its 'attention back to history itself, and to the historical situation of the commentator as well as of the work'.[34] Structuralism, therefore, can be seen to fall short of a genuine metacommentary to the degree that it is not self-reflexive and does not contain a commentary on its own procedure and conceptual instruments. Jameson likens metacommentary to the Freudian hermeneutic in that it is based on the 'distinction between symptom and repressed idea, between manifest and latent content, between the disguise and the message disguised'.[35] Such a distinction, he suggests, answers our initial question 'why does a work need interpreting in the first place?' because what is implicit in the latent–manifest distinction is the function of a censor of some kind.

Jameson does not directly spell out what this censor may be, or may entail, but a brief consideration of his concluding analysis of Sontag's essay 'The Imagination of Disaster' reveals the direction in which Jameson's thought is developing. Sontag analysed 1950s and 1960s science fiction films as an expression of 'the deepest anxieties about contemporary existence'.[36] Jameson agrees with this analysis as far as it goes, but argues that it only considers the films on their own terms, at the level of their manifest content and not in relation to their form. According to Jameson, this manifest content masks a deeper, or latent, content which is markedly different from Sontag's existential anxieties. Beneath the surface of these disaster movies, writes Jameson, we encounter the mystique of the scientist and a particular collective fantasy about the nature of work. What scientists do is not *real* work, in the sense of manual or physical labour, but rather intellectual activity. Moreover, monetary gain does not appear to be the main objective or motivation for their endeavours. Yet the scientist does attain power and social significance. The scientific environment, the laboratory and hierarchy of research assistants, also resonates with older forms of artisan and guild production. What we find in 1950s science fiction movies, therefore, is a specific male fantasy about the nature of alienated and non-alienated labour, 'a wish fulfilment that takes as its object a vision of ideal work',[37] or 'libidinally gratifying' work. The point that Jameson wishes to underscore is that this particular fantasy is not an element of the content of the work as such but of its form. The specific content of these movies is simply a pretext for this deeper underlying fantasy. This notion of a repressed fantasy structure, and in particular the effacing of any traces of labour from the surface of cultural artefacts, provides the thesis behind *The Political Unconscious* and will be the subject of the following two chapters.

2

History: The Political Unconscious

Throughout *Marxism and Form*, Jameson consistently recapitulates and enacts the movement of the dialectic from the intrinsic to the extrinsic, from the isolated, individual artefact to its ultimate ground in history. With its opening exhortation 'Always historicize!' *The Political Unconscious: Narrative as a Socially Symbolic Act* unequivocally announces itself as a continuation of this project. *The Political Unconscious*, in a sense, completes and subsumes the work of *Marxism and Form* and *The Prison House of Language* as Jameson moved beyond the critical surveys of his earlier work and engaged directly with the most advanced currents of contemporary theory. With Jameson's move from the University of California, San Diego, to Yale in 1977, he was associated, for a brief period in the early 1980s, with what were loosely termed the Yale Deconstructionists: Paul De Man, J. Hillis Miller and Harold Bloom, as part of the cutting edge of Anglo-American cultural theory. If *Marxism and Form* can be seen as forging a Marxist intellectual presence in the academy, the publication of *The Political Unconscious* in 1981 clearly marks its arrival and the emergence of Jameson as a major theoretician in his own right. In the words of Terry Eagleton, *The Political Unconscious* established Jameson 'as without question the foremost American Marxist critic, and one of the leading literary theorists of the Anglophone world'.[1]

The critical reception of *The Political Unconscious*, however, was by no means unanimous: in the United States Jameson's text was extremely influential, whereas in Britain its reception was rather muted. The publication of *The Political Unconscious* prompted a flurry of interest in Jameson's work in North America: the Miami University of Ohio held a symposium on his work in 1982, the proceedings of which were subsequently published in a special issue of *Critical Exchange*. *Diacritics* also devoted an issue to his work, as did the *New Orleans Review*.[2] James Kavanagh's opening panegyric sets the tone for many of the subsequent articles from the Ohio symposium; reflecting on the transformation of the American critical scene from the heyday of New Criticism to the present centrality of Marxist criticism, Kavanagh suggests that this has been brought about largely through the work of Fredric Jameson:

> I want to mark this transformation, this reopening, of a field of theoretical and ideological practice as a nontrivial *political* accomplishment of which this 'special issue' is but one more result. Yes, we must recognize the historical conditions of possibility – the constant irruption of revolution from Vietnam to Central America, the re-emergence of capitalism's social and economic crisis, etc. – that set the stage for the discursive subject 'Fredric Jameson' to be the bearer of a *possible* ideological project; and we must also recognize that this project was so effectively realized only because a lived subject (however fictional and precarious) made a disciplined, comprehensive, and immanent appropriation-critique of virtually every critical language issuing from the crevices of the Western ideological apparatus, persuasively turning the attention of each to Marxism, such that it is becoming almost unimaginable to do literary theory without taking Marxism sympathetically into account.[3]

In contrast the British critic Eagleton concludes his review of the Jameson work with the wry comment: 'For the question irresistibly raised for the Marxist reader of Jameson is simply this: how is a Marxist-structuralist analysis of a minor novel of Balzac to help shake the foundations of capitalism?'[4]

How then can we account for such a disparity in the text's reception, from equally sympathetic Marxist critics? Robert Young has identified three principal reasons for the extreme variance in the American and British receptions of the text. First, *The Political Unconscious* appeared in the US 'at a time when the tide of deconstruction seemed virtually unstoppable',[5] yet Jameson's Marxism seemed at once able to appropriate Derrida's insights and at the same time supersede deconstruction itself. In the UK, on the other hand, a more firmly established tradition of Marxist criticism felt less of a need to accommodate itself to the criticisms of deconstruction. Secondly, Jameson's Marxist criticism offered a return to a kind of ethical criticism which had previously dominated the US critical scene and which structuralism and deconstruction had effectively ruled out of debate. As Young writes, 'this appealed to a traditional understanding of criticism's value, as well as to male critics who felt increasingly upstaged by the forceful politics that feminism had made available to women.'[6] Again, in Britain, an alternative to the kind of ethical critcism embodied in Leavis and his followers has long been available in the tradition of socialist humanism exemplified in the work of Raymond Williams. Finally, and perhaps most significantly for the text's reception in Britain and Europe, *The Political Unconscious* was seen to herald what Jameson called the 'Althusserian Revolution', and yet the text was appearing in Britain in a post-Althusserian context. Jameson's British readership was already familiar with Althusser's work, and more specifically the Althusserian influence on literary theory through the work of Eagleton and Macherey.[7] Jameson thus appeared to be heralding a theoretical revolution that had already passed by and for which the critique was now firmly established within British Marxism. By the end of the 1970s, the impetus behind the Althusserian reconstruction of Marxism, and its impact in Europe, was already on the wane.[8] This by no means invalidates its incisive critique or polemical force but it does point again to the situated nature of Jameson's discourse and the priorities he highlights for a renewed Marxist cultural politics. I shall return to the issue of the situatedness of Jameson's theory in the conclusion of this chapter.

Jameson's theoretical wager was to present a version of Marxism which was at once open to the plurality of the new theoretical climate and at the same time able to maintain the priority of Marxist interpretation. In a long and closely argued opening chapter entitled 'On Interpretation', Jameson offers a sustained defence of his Hegelian-Marxist position, a critique of the limitations of post-structuralism and a reinvigorated method of Marxist interpretation. As with his earlier work, Jameson's rhetorical strategy remains one of inclusion and co-option, rather than exclusion and rejection. He seeks to retain the positive and useful elements of contemporary theory while simultaneously revealing its inconsistencies and aporias, which, he argues, can only achieve coherence in the context of an overriding Marxist analysis. Contrary to the emphasis in *Marxism and Form* on the diversity of Marxisms, however, *The Political Unconscious* proposes the primacy of Marxism from a more global and totalizing perspective, as a final untranscendable horizon: 'the absolute horizon of all reading and interpretation' (*PU*, 17). Marxism is no longer conceived of as a situationally specific discourse but rather as the one mode of thought which subsumes all other interpretative systems within its own historical narrative and assumes priority over other, secondary methodologies by its very density and semantic yield.

In this chapter I shall analyse Jameson's historicizing and incorporative strategy. Initially, I consider the relationship between Marxism and historicism, outlining Jameson's formulation of 'structural historicism', before examining this concept in more detail with respect to *The Political Unconscious*. My consideration of this text will take the form of an analysis of the two major propositions behind the title *The Political Unconscious: Narrative as a Socially Symbolic Act*, that is, history as a political unconscious, and history as narrative. Treatment of the former will reconsider the sense in which we are to understand the political as 'unconscious' or alternatively the unconscious as 'political'. Treatment of the latter will consider the suggestiveness of Jameson's reformulation of the Althusserian problematic of structural causality. These analyses will focus on Jameson's reading of the work of Jacques Lacan and Louis Althusser respectively. While the work of these two figures clearly helps Jameson's project and the formulation of the concept of *structural historicism*, the work of Lacan and Althusser also marks the limit of Jameson's strategy of subsuming diverse philosophical positions within his own Hegelian-Marxist narrative. In the following chapter I shall return to the efficacy of Jameson's attempt to subsume what would appear to be radically heterogeneous discourses within his own overarching Marxist historical narrative by focusing on his attempt to co-opt the work of Deleuze and Guattari into his own problematic.

Marxism and Historicism

Historicism is essentially concerned with the problem of 'our relationship to the past, and of our possibility of understanding the latter's monuments, artifacts and traces'.[9] In his essay 'Marxism and Historicism' Jameson highlights four traditional solutions to this problem: antiquarianism, existential historicism, structural typology and Nietzschean antihistoricism, while insisting that Marxism, as an 'absolute historicism', marks an advance over these more limited and ideological options. The first and last of these solutions are the least satisfactory, as essentially they both amount to a refusal of the problem itself, albeit from opposing directions. Antiquarianism seeks to solve the problem by in effect abolishing the present and dwelling in the past, while Nietzschean antihistoricism, with its notion of necessary forgetting, or forgetfulness, valorizes the present at the expense of any knowledge of the past. I shall not, therefore, be considering these options in any detail as Jameson is much more interested in the possibilities offered by the second and third approaches.

Existential historicism has its theoretical origins in the conception that 'every culture is immanently comprehensible in its own terms.'[10] Existential historicism does not, suggests Jameson, seek to reconstruct a linear, evolutionary or genetic history (immediately susceptible to charges of teleology) but rather designates a 'transhistorical event', 'by which *historicity* as such is manifested by means of the contact between the historian's mind in the present and a given synchronic cultural complex from the past'.[11] Existential historicism views 'the experience of history [as] a contact between an individual subject in the present and a cultural object in the past',[12] that is to say, as an aesthetic experience, and consequently its practitioners are predominantly within the humanities. For Jameson, the strength and value of existential historicism lies in the 'quality of rapt attention that [it] brings to the objects of its study',[13] but herein also lies its central flaw or weakness. The problem with existential historicism is that both the subject and object poles of this experience are open to infinite relativization, and if history is not to collapse into mere chronology, the simple succession of one thing after another, then it must, *a priori*, posit a notion of unity. This principle of unity is nothing less than human nature itself, which as Althusser reminded us is always already ideological. So while existential historicism can be seen to restore something of this richness of historical experience so woefully lacking in today's alienated and reified world, it does so at the expense of History in its fullest sense. There is clearly a fundamental imbalance between existential views of historical experience and a recognition of the larger, collective, historical forces at work and we must look elsewhere to restore this balance, in short, to structural typology.

Structural typology provides us with the dialectical counterpoint to our previous position. Whereas existential historicism follows the path of subjective experience as it orientates our relationship to the past, structuralist historiography follows the path of the object, focusing on the forces and events of history as the determinate reality of an objective historical process, and organizing this data around various forms of patterning or typologies. In other words, structuralist historiography is not concerned with our subjective experience or interpretations of history but with the 'deep' structures or patterns embedded within texts which construct or constitute both that history and our experience of it. Structuralist historiography does not seek to articulate a sequence of events as causally related, but rather the 'conditions of possibility' for the emergence of given phenomena. By privileging the synchronic system over diachronic constructs, structuralist historiography repudiates two 'related and essentially *narrative* forms of analysis':[14] what can be termed the *teleological*, or Enlightenment sense of progress, and the *genetic*, or imaginary construction of the past term as the evolutionary precursor of the present moment. Structuralist historiography does not reconstruct the past in this sense but rather builds 'a model of "transition" from one to the other, and this is no longer then a genetic hypothesis but rather an investigation of structural transformations'.[15] Contrary to existential historicism, then, we have a greater sense of the vast and impersonal movement of history, of processes beyond the control and influence of individual subjects, but we have also lost that vital and urgent sense of contact with the past that was the great virtue of existential historicism. What structuralist typologies lack, suggests Jameson, is reflexivity, that dialectical self-consciousness which would raise structuralism to a consideration of its own historical moment.

According to Jameson, Marxism, as an absolute historicism, provides the only solution to this dilemma, uniting the urgency and intensity of existential historicism with the articulation of collective forces in the manner of structural typologies. Indeed, Jameson goes so far as to suggest that structural historiography is not necessarily radically different from or incommensurable with existential historicism:

> On the contrary, semiotic analysis of such texts generally discloses the operation of 'deep' semic oppositions – a kind of historical *pensée sauvage* – which can usually be found to project a whole structural typology of cultures imperceptible at the surface of the text and disguised or displaced by the emphasis on the sensitivity of the individual historian-subject.[16]

Similarly, all 'deep' structures can be rewritten in 'something like' a narrative or teleological vision of history. Jameson's aim, therefore, is to formulate what he terms a *structural historicism*, which would do justice to both the insights of existential historicism and structural typology, which can accommodate both the subject and object poles of historical experience and finally provide a solution to the 'seemingly unresolvable alternation between Identity and Difference',[17] as the rock upon which all historicisms come to founder.

The Marxian concept of 'mode of production' facilitates just such a squaring of the circle in that it functions not as a narrative of emergence but genealogically, as 'the narrative reconstruction of the conditions of possibility of any full synchronic form'.[18] For Jameson, mode of production is a *differential* concept in that any given mode of production – for example, capitalism – presupposes all previous modes of production – feudalism, Asiatic mode, primitive communism, etc. – as well as anticipating a future mode of production. In this sense no mode of production exists in isolation as a 'pure' state but coexists, at any given moment, with other modes of production. To borrow Raymond Williams's distinctions, at present capitalism represents the *dominant* mode of production but sedimented within this are the *residual* forms of previous modes of production as well as the potentially *emergent* form of a properly socialist mode of production.[19] We are still in need, however, of a concept or category with which to think this *structural coexistence* of various distinct modes of production, as well as the process of transition from one mode to another. Jameson suggests the term *cultural revolution*, and I shall consider this concept in greater detail in the following section.

Mode of production would, therefore, appear to meet the requirements of the object pole, articulating the unity and identity of given historical periods while simultaneously acknowledging their difference from previous as well as subsequent historical moments and their intrinsic diversity. But we still need to identify the position of the subject in relation to the historical past. Jameson suggests that the present formulation allows him to reground the subject in history in three distinct ways. First, a subject's relationship to the past is no longer to be seen as a relationship between an individual subject and an isolated cultural artefact but as a mediation for a non-individual and collective process, 'the confrontation of two distinct social forms or modes of production' whereby individual acts of reading and interpretation are seen as 'allegorical figures for this essentially collective confrontation of two social forms'.[20] This in turn enables the second movement of regrounding to take place, as history now retains the urgency of the past in the sense that 'the past will itself become an active agent in this process and will begin to come before us as a radically different life form which rises up to call our own form of life into question.'[21] Finally, in that mode of production structurally implies a future just as fully as a past it allows for the articulation of the utopian impulse, 'the sense of a hermeneutic relationship to the past which is able to grasp its own present as history only on condition it manages to keep the idea of the future, and of radical and utopian transformation, alive'.[22]

I will now consider more fully the assumptions underlying Jameson's structural historicism, suggesting that a number of theoretical problems arise from his attempted synthesis of a synchronic structure, mode of production and diachronic process, the unending narrative of class struggle.

History as Political Unconscious

For Jameson the problems of historicism enumerated above can only be resolved by Marxism because Marxism alone grasps the essential *mystery* of the past as a single great human adventure. The events of the past, writes Jameson, 'can recover their original urgency for us only if they are retold within the unity of a single great collective story; only if, in however disguised and symbolic a form, they are seen as sharing a single fundamental theme – for Marxism, the collective struggle to wrest a realm of Freedom from a realm of Necessity; only if they are grasped as the vital episodes in a single vast unfinished plot' (*PU*, 19-20). The dilemma is how to restore these faint murmurings of the past and recover this single great story. It is this task that Jameson sets himself in *The Political Unconscious*, or more specifically, the attempt 'to restructure the problematics of ideology, of the unconscious and of desire, of representation, of history, and of cultural production, around the all-informing process of *narrative*' (*PU*, 13). What is required, suggests Jameson, is a mode of interpretation which can accommodate the notion of structural causality, in other words, a mode of interpretation which lays bare the 'conditions of possibility' rather than the 'causal' determinants of texts.

Jameson's interpretative system proposes a series of concentric circles, or 'semantic horizons', which he designates as the political, the social and the historical; each horizon dialectically transcends the previous one. The first horizon coincides with the individual text, which following the work of Lévi-Strauss is to be read as a *symbolic act*: 'the individual narrative, or individual formal structure, is to be grasped as the imaginary resolution of a real contradiction' (*PU*, 77). The value of such a formulation is that it inscribes a movement beyond the purely formal properties of the work itself, not in the sense of a movement to some abstract extrinsic criteria outside the text, but 'rather immanently, by construing purely formal patterns as a symbolic enactment of the social within the formal and the aesthetic' (*PU*, 77). Lévi-Strauss's formulation encapsulates both the imaginary and the real aspects of cultural practice and this shift of registers is inscribed in the very ambiguity of Jameson's term, a 'symbolic act'. Depending on which half of the term is emphasized, the operation is merely a *symbolic* act and its solutions imaginary, or it is a genuine *act*, albeit on the symbolic level. For Jameson, the ambiguity of this notion is fortuitous in that it not only dramatizes the situation (and dilemma) of art and culture in contemporary society but it also dramatizes the present status of the real itself. In Jameson's earlier work the presence of the 'dialectical shock' was seen as the mark of genuinely Marxist criticism; with *The Political Unconscious* that role falls to the notion of 'contradiction', and to the notion of the text as a 'determinate contradiction'. The 'methodological requirement to articulate a text's fundamental contradiction', writes Jameson, 'may then be seen as a test of the completeness of the analysis' (*PU*, 80), or, to put it another way, the text must be seen as the imaginary resolution of real historical contradictions.

Jameson's second horizon of interpretation moves beyond the text itself and operates at the level of class discourse. Following E. P. Thompson, Jameson defines 'class' as a relational concept; in other words, the notion of class represents a 'historical phenomenon, unifying a number of disparate and seemingly unconnected events, both in the raw material of experience and in consciousness'.[23] It should be noted at this point that, for Thompson, such a definition of class is incompatible with the sense of class as a 'category'; rather it entails a historical experience that is dependent on social traditions and culture. Class consciousness, according to Thompson's definition, designates 'the way in which these experiences are handled in cultural terms: embodied in traditions, value-systems, ideas and institutional forms'.[24] As with his conception of mode of production, Jameson emphasizes the relational characteristics of class, whereby each class can only be defined in its relationship with other social classes. Furthermore, class ideology or class consciousness is itself differential, in the sense that its values, ideas and traditions are not fixed and immutable but active and fluid in opposition to other class discourses. For Thompson, such a notion of class as one of historical process is incommensurable with the notion of structure; as I shall discuss below, this is a distinction that Jameson himself elides.

A relational and oppositional conception of class discourse facilitates Jameson's rewriting the categories and terms in which the text is understood as a 'dialogical structure', in so far as the dialogical relationship is understood as 'antagonistic'. The object of study at this second level, then, is what Jameson calls the *ideologeme* or 'the smallest intelligible unit of the essentially antagonistic collective discourse of social classes' (*PU*, 76). The ideologeme is not simply some kind of ideological slogan but is again intrinsic to the form of the text and in the structure of its language. Whereas the first level saw the text as an enactment, the imaginary resolution of a real social contradiction, immanent in the formal patterning and structure of the text, the second level treats the text as the *parole*, or individual utterance, of the *langue* of class discourse. The emphasis on the dialogic nature of class discourse entails that we not only listen to the hegemonic discourse but we also attempt to retrieve the silent and repressed voices against which dominant discourses struggle and define themselves. For Jameson, the value of the concept of the ideologeme resides in its 'amphibious nature' (*PU*, 87), which can manifest itself either as a pseudoidea, in the sense of a belief system or abstract value, or 'as a protonarrative, a kind of ultimate class fantasy about the "collective characters" which are classes in opposition' (*PU*, 87). But herein also lies the problem with Jameson's concept, which as he writes 'must be susceptible to both a conceptual description and a narrative manifestation all at once' (*PU*, 87). One could well ask: why must it? Particularly as Jameson goes on to say that ideologemes can be elaborated in either direction independently. As with so many of Jameson's formulations, its very flexibility, which in Jameson's own hands facilitates frequently brilliant and insightful readings, makes it difficult both to define and to utilize.

The final horizon of interpretation situates the cultural text in relation to history as a whole, whereby a given text is read in terms of the *ideology of form*. The previous horizon emphasized the distinctive and antagonistic nature of class discourses, drawing attention to the polyphonic rather than the monological character of discourse. But, suggests Jameson, the inverse operation is equally feasible in that 'such concrete semantic differences can on the contrary be focused in such a way that what emerges is rather the all-embracing unity of a single code which they must share and which thus characterizes the larger unity of the social system' (*PU*, 88). This single code provides a new object of study which transcends the previous two levels and can be designated as mode of production, as 'the symbolic messages transmitted to us by the coexistence of various sign systems which are themselves traces or anticipations of modes of production' (*PU*, 76).

I have already indicated how Jameson fends off accusations of linearity and teleology with regard to the notion of mode of production through a conception of structural coexistence, and I should now like to consider this in more detail. For Jameson, even the most schematic and mechanistic conceptions of historical 'stages' entail a conception of a cultural dominant, an ideological form specific to a given mode of production; however, this does not imply that mode of production designates a synchronic system. The problem with synchronicity is that it has become synonymous with notions of the 'total system' and as such implicitly excludes the function of the negative:

> In particular, everything about class struggle that was anticipatory in the older dialectical framework, and seen as an emergent space for radically new social relations, would seem, in the synchronic model, to reduce itself to practices that in fact tend to reinforce the very system that foresaw and dictated their specific limits. (*PU*, 91)

At the level of cultural production, any antisystemic or oppositional tendencies ostensibly inscribed within the work would also be seen as ultimately deriving from and reinforcing the system itself. This dilemma can only be resolved if we respect the various levels of historical abstraction, as, for instance, with Jameson's series of enlarging semantic horizons. Such a system allows one to respect the specificity of individual texts and also conduct a synchronic analysis in terms of the mode of production, while at the same time the system's projection of a longer view of history avoids the structural limitations imposed by notions of a total system. A second problem that arises with the notion of historical stages or periods is that the system tends to result in a purely typological or classificatory operation, whereby texts are simply slotted into their appropriate historical moment. Jameson insists that his system of expanding horizons avoids this pitfall through the identification of the specific form of 'contradiction' at each stage of the process rather than the slotting of texts into pre-existing historical categories.

No mode of production, I suggested above, exists in a pure form but always coexists with other modes of production. For Jameson, the implication of this is that while the concept of mode of production may be said to be synchronic, the actual moment of the coexistence of several distinct modes is, on the contrary, dialectically open to history. Any attempt to thereby classify texts according to their respective modes of production will inevitably be forestalled, as all texts will be seen to be 'crisscrossed and intersected by a variety of impulses from contradictory modes of cultural production all at once' (*PU*, 95). The object of study for this third horizon will be what Jameson terms 'cultural revolution'. The term has its strongest resonance with the Chinese experience of the 1960s and indeed Jameson does not dismiss or foreclose on such associations, particularly in the sense of revivifying the revolutionary process from the bottom up.

The concept, however, has much wider connotations. In its broadest sense cultural revolution defines the process of transition from one mode of production to another and, as every concrete historical society is a coexistence of several distinct modes of production, 'cultural revolution will therefore be a moment of "nonsynchronous development" . . . a moment of overlap, of the struggle in coexistence between several modes of production at once'.[25] The Western Enlightenment can be seen as just such a moment of struggle and as part of the bourgeois cultural revolution. In other words, cultural revolution designates the process through which social formations retrain or reprogram subjects for new modes of social life, the process through which subjects acquire new habits, new modes of consciousness and transform human practices.

In terms of literary and cultural studies, Jameson sees the notion of cultural revolution opening up a whole new framework for the humanities, in the sense that the cultural practice of a given mode of production 'has as its essential function to recreate at every moment the life world of that particular mode and to keep it in being at every moment'.[26] This process of cultural reproduction is not merely a secondary, superstructural activity dependent on the primary process of material production, but rather 'a single immense process on all these levels'.[27] Thus, maintains Jameson, cultural producers are 'ideologues', although ideologues of a very special sort, and all cultural texts are the sites for class struggle through the confrontation of their various ideologies:

> The task of cultural and social analysis thus construed within this final horizon will then clearly be the rewriting of its materials in such a way that this perpetual cultural revolution can be apprehended and read as the deeper and more permanent constitutive structure in which the empirical textual objects know intelligibility. (PU, 97)

In this sense cultural revolution designates the 'nonsynchronous development' of culture and social life; it is, suggests Jameson, beyond the synchronic/diachronic dichotomy. The ideology of form therefore defines 'the determinate contradiction of the specific messages emitted by the varied sign systems which co-exist in a given artistic process as well as in its general social formation' (*PU*, 98-9).

We should note though that at this level a dialectical reversal has taken place and 'form' must now be apprehended as 'content' in the sense that the formal processes are now grasped as sedimented content in their own right; in other words they carry 'ideological messages of their own, distinct from the ostensible or manifest content of the works' (*PU*, 99), for example, through literary genre. I will now assess some of the presuppositions that underlie Jameson's system of dialectically expanding horizons.

The notion of a *political* unconscious clearly involves an initial broadening of the concept beyond its conventional usage. For Jameson, the political unconscious is a 'collective' unconscious rather than a site of repressed desires and drives associated with an individual psyche. Jameson's collective unconscious, however, is not a Jungian one in the sense of a repository for mythical archetypes, but rather Walter Benjamin's nightmare of history:

> As in all previous history, whoever emerges as victor still participates in that triumph in which today's rulers march over the prostrate bodies of their victims. As is customary, the spoils are borne aloft in that triumphal parade. These are generally called the cultural heritage. . . . There has never been a document of culture which was not at one and the same time a document of barbarism.[28]

For Jameson, this heritage of violence and barbarism remains sedimented within our cultural texts, not in their content, in the sense of proletarian novels or socialist realist art, but rather through the form, through what we have identified as the various levels of 'contradiction' within the text. History is not so much the 'context' within which literary texts are reinserted, but a 'subtext', in the sense that each text itself is a rewriting or restructuration of prior historical material. This subtext, however, is nowhere immanently available to us as a thing-in-itself; it must always be '(re)constructed after the fact' (*PU*, 81). The literary text is always in an active relationship with the real, not in the sense that its content 'reflects' reality but in the way that the real is drawn into its own formal structures. The whole paradox, writes Jameson, 'of what we have here called the subtext may be summed up in this, that the literary work or cultural object, as though for the first time, brings into being that very situation to which it is also, at one and the same time, a reaction' (*PU*, 81–2). History, then, is only accessible to us through texts, it 'can be approached only by way of prior (re)textualization' (*PU*, 82). To put it another way, like the unconscious, history cannot be known in itself but only through its effects.

Jameson's primary mediation between cultural texts and their social and historical situation is that of reification. In chapter 6 I argue that Jameson's uncritical employment of a Lukácsian conception of reification raises a number of theoretical and political difficulties, but for the present I will follow Jameson's usage. A formal difficulty of

Jameson's deployment of the term is related to the lack of any precise definition within his text. Indeed, the fullest definition of reification comes within a consideration of rationalization:

> For the dynamic of *rationalization* – Weber's term, which Lukács will strategically retranslate as *reification* in *History and Class Consciousness* – is a complex one in which the traditional or 'natural' . . . unities, social forms, human relations, cultural events, even religious systems, are systematically broken up in order to be reconstructed more efficiently, in the form of new post-natural processes or mechanisms; but in which, at the same time, these now isolated broken bits and pieces of older unities acquire a certain autonomy of their own, a semi-autonomous coherence which, not merely a reflex of capitalist reification and rationalization, also in some measure serves to compensate for the dehumanization of experience reification brings with it, and to rectify the otherwise intolerable effects of the new process. (*PU*, 62–3)

With a characteristic Jamesonian sentence one is overwhelmed with the density and complexity of the sentence itself, as the seemingly relentless and ruthless process of rationalization – or is it reification? – proceeds, turns back upon itself and finally provides its own compensation. But what exactly is meant by 'post-natural processes or mechanisms'? And what is the status of a 'certain' autonomy or 'some measure' of compensation? How far does autonomy stretch here and what exactly is becoming autonomous from what? Jameson's description appears to simultaneously explain all and nothing.

The concept of reification is highly versatile in Jameson's prose and to attempt a simple definition is in itself misguided: meaning is more fluid than this and the full import of Jameson's terms can only be derived from their context and usage. While it may remain unclear exactly what Jameson means by reification, its mediatory function is quite explicit. Reification at once accounts for the historical processes of differentiation, separation and division under capitalism and at the same time for the psychic fragmentation at the individual experiential level. For Jameson, the traces of human labour are gradually effaced from the products of commodity production as the levels of specialization and division increase, although these traces can never be completely erased since all commodities remain, in the last instance, produced. Using the analogy of Freudian psychoanalysis, Jameson suggests that these traces have been repressed through the processes of commodity production and the structure of commodity fetishism. Pursuing the analogy further, if we analyse the mechanisms by which this repression takes place, it will be possible to retrieve and restore those latent traces of production to the manifest content of the text. Jameson finds textual justification for this semantic expansion of the concepts of the unconscious and repression through Lévi-Strauss's analysis of myths as imaginary resolutions of real social contradictions and Northrop Frye's conception of literature as a symbolic meditation on the destiny of community. There is, however, a more significant presupposition in *The Political Unconscious* upon which this widening of the concept of the unconscious would seem to rest and which Jameson never fully elucidates: that is to say, an equivalence between his own conception of History and the Lacanian conception of the 'Real'.

Jameson uses Lacan's capitalized Real consistently throughout his text, associating it directly with Althusser's notion of 'absent cause' and consequently aligning it with his own conception of History. I shall discuss Althusser's notion of structural causality in greater detail in the following section; for the present I shall restrict myself to an analysis of the Lacanian notion of the Real. In his essay 'Imagining the Real: Jameson's Use of Lacan', Michael Clark highlights the parallels between Lacan's concept of the Real as inaccessible except through its effects on the symbolic, and Jameson's view of History as inaccessible except through textual form, 'most notably, the narratives that encapsulate and dramatize the various ideological fantasies operating at any particular period'.[29] Clark writes:

> Lacan's transposing the ground of consciousness from what Freud calls the 'other scene' of the unconscious to the mechanisms of symbolic structures opens the unconscious to the determination of history as it functions at the material and social levels on which symbolic structures exist for Marxism.[30]

Clark's claim is essentially that Lacan's reformulation of the concept of the unconscious and its relation to the Real enables Jameson to ground the text in History and retain access to History without recourse to a naive realism or vulgar materialism. At the same time, Lacanian theory facilitates a conception of the unconscious and subjectivity which does not fall into the errors of either humanism or anti-humanism but allows for the articulation of the relationship between individual experience and trans-individual processes. The question is whether or not such a claim is sustainable.

First, we must dismiss the notion that Lacan's conception of the Real has anything to do with empirical reality. For Lacan, the Real is unknowable, it is that which is beyond language and resists symbolization absolutely. As a concept it is inextricably entwined with Lacan's notion of the three orders or registers: the Imaginary, the Symbolic and the Real.[31] The Real is essentially that which resists mirror reflection and symbolization, it is beyond representation and linguistic expression. Not surprisingly, therefore, it is an area of Lacan's work that exponents say least about. For example, in his influential essay 'The Imaginary and Symbolic in Lacan' Jameson commences his discussion of the three orders with the observation, 'If the notion of the Real is the most problematical of the three – since it can never be experienced immediately, but only by way of the mediation of the other two – it is also the easiest to bracket for the purposes of this presentation.'[32] For my purposes, however, it is necessary to say a little more than this. The Real functions as the limit of the Symbolic and Imaginary; it cannot be assimilated to either of the other two orders. The Real of trauma, for example, is that which it is impossible to assimilate and the Real of repression is that which it is impossible to say. The Real, in other words, is that which it is impossible for the subject to bear and 'which can be known only through the effect of a shock and about which nothing can be said, which is why the characteristics of the Real are all negative. The Real is a limit you run up against; it is the void, the impossible, an impasse.'[33]

This purely negative conception of the Real, however, would not appear to accord with what Slavoj Žižek calls the radical ambiguity of the Real, as something that at once erupts within the Symbolic as trauma, while simultaneously acting as the support for this Symbolic structure:

> The ambiguity of the Lacanian real is not merely a nonsymbolized kernel that makes a sudden appearance in the symbolic order, in the form of traumatic 'returns' and 'answers'. The real is at the same time contained in the very symbolic form: the real is *immediately rendered* by this form.[34]

Žižek, therefore, draws a distinction between our *social* reality, that is to say, the Symbolic order and the Real itself. The Real at once serves as support for that social reality and at the same time radically disrupts its balance with its appearance. For Jameson, the Real is simply History itself: 'it is not terribly difficult to say what is meant by the Real in Lacan,' he writes. 'It is simply History itself.'[35] Jameson, however, does acknowledge that for psychoanalysis the history in question is the history of the subject, which is not quite the same thing as Jameson's 'History itself'. Indeed, it is rather the resonance of the word that suggests to Jameson that a confrontation between the materialism of psychoanalysis and historical materialism is long overdue. I will return to this rapprochement of psychoanalysis and Marxism in the final section of the following chapter.

As I have already observed, what makes Jameson's system dynamic rather than merely classificatory is his insistence on the role of contradiction. The presence of History in a particular text manifests itself as a particular form of contradiction at each specific horizon of interpretation. Clark observes that within Jameson's schema contradiction serves 'as the measure of the effect of History on its "narrativization"' and functions in much the same way as that of desire for Lacan, that is, as 'an "anchoring point" that orients the symbolic toward the Real'.[36] This parallel between the functions of desire and contradiction is further reinforced through Jameson's identification of the relationship between desire and the Real with his own conception of the relationship between desire and History, in the sense that History is that which resists desire. Just as the Real, for Lacan, is that which it is impossible to bear, History, for Jameson, is 'what hurts' (*PU*, 102). For Lacan the desire of a subject is inextricably bound up with the desire of the other, both in the sense of the desire *for* the other and the desire *of* the other. Thus, argues Clark:

> in addition to marking the effect of the Real on the Symbolic, desire also marks the threshold between the individual and the social, a connection that suggests an extension of desire beyond the individual subject – the very task that Jameson says must be achieved if the Freudian model of the unconscious is to function within a Marxian perspective.[37]

According to Clark, Jameson's text marks a significant advance over prior efforts to adapt Lacanianism to Marxism – although, in a previous essay, he also highlighted a number of difficulties with the text.[38] There are clear parallels between Lacan's three orders, the Imaginary, the Symbolic and the Real, and Jameson's three horizons of interpretation, text, society and History, or to put it another way, text as imaginary resolution, socially symbolic act and History as non-representable. These parallels, however, are never made explicit in *The Political Unconscious*. Jameson's refusal to acknowledge the analogy should perhaps be read as an indication that we should not be too ready to assimilate one system to the other, respecting the specificity of the object of both, desire for Lacan and History for Jameson. Especially as Jameson insists that while presenting 'striking analogies of structure',[39] Marxism and psychoanalysis are not superimposable on each other, and we must respect the specificity of each discourse and its distinct object of study.

Jameson's practice at times appears to belie this warning, however, presenting the concepts of Marxism and psychoanalysis as apparently interchangeable and even equivalent. This confusion can be traced to the conflation of Althusserian and Lacanian discourses within *The Political Unconscious*. Althusser himself liberally appropriated terminology from psychoanalysis, his most familiar appropriations being the Freudian concept of 'overdetermination' and his reformulation of the concept of ideology through the Lacanian notion of the mirror phase. As Ted Benton has pointed out, though, Althusser's use of Lacanian psychoanalysis was seriously undertheorized and left as many unresolved questions as he sought to answer.[40] For Althusser, ideology 'is the expression of the relation between men and their "world", that is, the (overdetermined) unity of the real relation and the imaginary relation between them and their real conditions of existence'.[41] In short, ideology is the subjects' imaginary relation to their real conditions of existence. Individuals are constituted as subjects through ideology by a process of interpellation or hailing. Very briefly and schematically, this process, according to Althusser, is a specular or mirroring process whereby ideology hails 'individuals as subjects' who thereby recognize themselves in the image of the dominant ideological 'Subject' which in turn enables 'the mutual recognition of subjects and Subject' and finally 'the subject's recognition of himself'.[42] Althusser's use of psychoanalytic theory for his own theory of ideology is stated most explicitly in the conclusion to his short essay 'Freud and Lacan':

> Freud has discovered for us that the real subject, the individual in his unique essence, has not the form of an ego, centred on the 'ego', on 'consciousness' or on 'existence' – whether this is the existence of the for-itself, of the body-proper or of 'behaviour' – that the human subject is de-centred, constituted by a structure which has no 'centre' either, except in the imaginary misrecognition of the 'ego', i.e. in the ideological formations in which it 'recognizes' itself.[43]

Althusser goes on to say that this *structure of misrecognition* is the concern for all investigations into ideology. As Michèle Barrett points out, Althusser's vocabulary trails Lacanian resonances but does not reproduce Lacan's theories in a precise way, and indeed uses Lacan's concepts in very different senses. For example, Althusser's use of the term imaginary 'might be reduced to "lived": it is the domain of emotion, affect, will and experience';[44] this is not an everyday usage of the term, writes Barrett, but neither is it Lacan's. Similarly, Althusser's specular theory of ideology speaks of misrecognition but, as my overly schematic description of the process above makes clear, 'his entire approach is cast in terms of the process of recognition as the means by which the subject is constituted to itself and to others.'[45]

The very cornerstone of the Lacanian theory of the subject, however, rests on an initial identification with an image outside itself; the infant recognizes itself in the place of an-other and therefore is fundamentally alienated from itself. For Lacan, the subject is inherently a divided subject. Althusser's theory of ideology, on the other hand, is primarily concerned with how subjects recognize themselves and are confirmed in that identity through the dominant ideology – although, in defence of Althusser, this recognition is always an *imaginary* recognition and therefore at once a fundamental (mis)recognition. For Althusser, there is no such thing as a divided subject, there is only the subject and, what he calls, the abyss alongside it, but the subject itself is always unified.

Barrett suggests that this is not simply a question of emphasis or of whether or not Althusser understood Lacan properly, but 'whether he (or anyone else, indeed) could integrate such an argument into an account whose backdrop was the Marxist theory of reproduction of the relations of production'.[46] Reflecting on Althusser's conclusion to the essay 'Freud and Lacan' – quoted above – Barrett acknowledges that here Althusser comes closer to Lacan than in any of his other writings. But when Althusser comes to investigate ideology the social categories through which subjects recognize themselves 'may fit the Marxist framework in which Althusser was operating . . . but they do not correspond at any meaningful level with the content of Lacan's arguments about the ego and its identifications.'[47] Barrett concludes: 'with the advantage of hindsight, the gulf between Althusser and Lacan appears now as completely unbridgeable.'[48]

This gulf can also be detected in Jameson's text in the equally imprecise way he uses Lacanian terminology. Jameson borrows the concept of the symbolic act from the work of Kenneth Burke (*PU*, 81) and when discussing the notion in relation to Burke uses a lower case 'r' in relation to the 'real'. We may surmise, as there is no definition of the term, that 'real' designates a realist conception of reality as independent of human perception and activity. In the following exposition of the symbolic act, however, there is a significant slippage in register: 'The literary or aesthetic act therefore always entertains some active relationship with the Real; yet in order to do so, it cannot simply allow "reality" to persevere inertly in its own being, outside the text and at a distance' (*PU*, 81). The lower case 'real' has now been replaced by a capitalized Real, while the use of the semi-colon links this capitalized Real with the 'reality' in quotation marks, yet, as I have argued above, the Lacanian Real does not refer to reality (in quotation marks or otherwise). How, then, are we to read this relationship between cultural artefacts, the Real and reality? Following Barrett, we may say that Jameson's horizons of interpretation trail Lacanian resonances but there is no correspondence between them in any meaningful sense; Jameson does not reproduce Lacanian categories in a precise sense and this serves to obfuscate the specific nature of the analogy being made.

The unresolved question of the relationship between the different theoretical systems that Jameson deploys also has implications for his own textual analysis. For instance, what precisely is the relationship between his three horizons of interpretation and what is the mechanism of transition from one to another. Jameson's own practice does little to resolve the dilemma since he focuses on each particular object of study – the symbolic act, the ideologeme and the ideology of form – individually and each in relation to a different text, suggesting that Jameson himself may remain uncertain on this point. As James Iffland puts it, 'I do not wish to suggest that the text cannot be all three of these differently formulated objects of study. Rather my question is *how* is it all three?'[49] On the one hand, Jameson's reluctance to provide answers underlines once again that he is not simply producing a model of interpretation: the three concentric horizons of interpretation do not provide us with a template which we can lay over texts to identify particular ideologemes etc. On the other hand, it simply leaves the problems unresolved.

In concluding this section, I should like to pose one further question: to what extent is History repressed in cultural texts and operates as a textual unconscious? Jonathan Arac foregrounds the dilemma of political (un)consciousness in Jameson's text through a critique of Jameson's reading of Conrad.[50] Arac does not offer an alternative reading but rather through a juxtaposition of Jameson's text with that of a previous generation of left criticism (Irving Howe's reading of *Nostromo* in *Politics and the Novel*) highlights what Jameson actually leaves out, that is to say, 'the historical-political consciousness actually available in the work'.[51] Taking the opening paragraph of *Nostromo*, Arac reveals a scene not empty of people but, on the contrary, replete with traces of human presence, human labour and a 'historical consciousness wholly suppressed by Jameson's reading'.[52] In other words, in order for the geiger counter of the political unconscious to unveil the repressed and buried reality of history it must first repress and bury it. I shall now consider at greater length the status of History itself and the sense in which we can say that History is a narrative.

History as Narrative

As I indicated above, Marxism for Jameson is an 'absolute historicism' in the sense that it simultaneously historicizes its object of study
and its own conditions of possibility. In other words, it constantly
underscores the historicity of its own conceptual operations and
categories; thus 'Marx's method ... excludes from the outset any
possibility for theory to *alienate itself speculatively* in its own ideational
products by presenting them either as ideal realities without a history
of their own or as idealities that refer to a reality that would itself be
nonhistorical.'[53] The view that Marxism is a historicism, 'absolute' or
otherwise, received its most stringent critique through the work of
Althusser, and *The Political Unconscious* represents Jameson's most
sustained engagement with Althusserian antihistoricism. For
Althusser the inevitable outcome of reading Marxism as a historicism
is that it conflates the various distinct levels of society (the economic,
the political, the ideological, etc.), reducing and flattening the social
totality into a version of the Hegelian conception of totality, thus
eliding their real differences. The index of this theoretical lapse,
according to Althusser, is that it 'precipitates the theory of history
into real history; reduces the (theoretical) object of the science of
history to real history; and therefore confuses the object of knowledge with the real object'.[54]

Jameson subjects Althusser's three forms of historical causality or
effectivity – mechanical, expressive and structural – to a thorough re-
examination, arguing not only that Marxism is a historicism but also
that as an absolute historicism it can accommodate the Althusserian
critique. The first form of historical causality, mechanical causality –
or the billiard ball effect – would appear to have been conclusively
refuted by modern physics, and for Althusser it lacks the capacity to
think the effectivity of the whole on its parts. Jameson, however,
suggests that the concept has a 'local validity', citing the example of
'the crisis in late nineteenth-century publishing, during which the
dominant three-decker lending library novel was replaced by a
cheaper one-volume format, and the modification of the "inner form"
of the novel itself' (*PU*, 25) as just one instance where it retains a
certain explanatory force. Although, on balance, it remains an inadequate and unsatisfactory category for a greater understanding of the
historical process, mechanical causality can be said to have a provisional value in cultural analysis through its assertion that material
and contingent accidents can have an effect on the structure and tone

of our narrative paradigms. For Jameson, therefore, mechanical causality is less a concept that can be 'evaluated on its own terms, than one of the various laws and subsystems of our peculiarly reified social and cultural life' (*PU*, 26).

The full weight of Althusser's critique of historicism, however, is reserved for the second category of expressive causality, which he identifies with the Hegelian conception of history. History, for Hegel, 'is mind clothing itself with the form of events or the immediate actuality of nature'.[55] In other words, history is mind, or spirit, as it manifests itself in nature, in the external world. As with the philosophy of mind, Hegel's philosophy of history can be seen in terms of the growth and progress of 'world-spirit' as it attains ever greater self-realization, or self-awareness. The progress of world-spirit therefore can be described as a historical narrative in which the journey of world-spirit is divided into chapters or historical periods as the 'world spirit passes through stages at each of which it possesses a more adequate awareness of what it is'.[56] According to G. A. Cohen, the ideas of spirit and freedom are simply two ways of describing the same thing: he writes, 'the idea of spirit *is* freedom.'[57] In short, history is spirit's biography with freedom as its telos. Jameson reminds us, though, that we should not view the attainment of 'Absolute Spirit' as the final stage of history; rather, as with absolute knowledge, it 'is meant to describe the historian's mind as it contemplates the variety of human histories and cultural forms'.[58]

For Althusser, the two essential characteristics, or errors, of the Hegelian conception of history are its positing of a *homogeneous continuity* of time and its *contemporaneity*. The former is a direct consequence of the continuity of the dialectical development of the Idea in Hegel's philosophy. In other words, just as the growth of consciousness is punctuated by stages as consciousness dialectically transcends unsatisfactory and inadequate levels·of awareness, 'the science of history would consist of the division of this continuum according to a *periodization* corresponding to the succession of one dialectical totality after another.'[59] For Hegel, the structure of historical existence, writes Althusser, 'is such that all the elements of the whole always co-exist in one and the same time, one and the same present, and are therefore contemporaneous with one another in one and the same present'.[60] Furthermore, the Hegelian conception of history constitutes itself as the *absolute horizon* of all knowing, thus effectively ruling out any anticipation of an alternative future – while it is Marxism's capacity to entertain such a future that sets it apart from other theories of history. Finally, the Hegelian model, observes

Althusser, leads to a fallacious separation of synchrony and diachrony, whereby the diachronic is merely the development of this contemporaneous present in 'the sequence of a temporal continuity in which the "events" to which "history" in the strict sense can be reduced . . . are merely successive contingent presents in the time continuum'.[61]

Althusser's second point of critique is directed against Hegel's conception of totality itself. The most serious misconception deriving from Hegel's view of history, observes Althusser, is its formulation of the social whole, or totality, as an *expressive whole*, in the sense that 'it presupposes in principle that the whole in question be reducible to an *inner essence*, of which the elements of the whole are then no more than phenomenal forms of expression, the inner principle of the essence being present at each point in the whole.'[62] In other words, the notion of an inner essence and outer phenomena presupposes that the totality, if it is to be applicable everywhere and at every moment to each of the phenomena arising in the totality, must have a certain nature, which the parts are merely the outer expression of. This again reduces the heterogeneity of historical time to a homogeneous continuum and the specificity and relative autonomy of the distinct levels of the social totality to a contemporaneous or homogeneous present. Therefore, contrary to mechanical causality, expressive causality allows us to think the determination of the whole on the parts but it does so only if we conceive of the whole as a totality in a spiritual or metaphysical sense.

Althusser's own conception of totality is that of a structure within which subordinate or regional structures exist. The social totality is of a structural whole within which distinct and relatively autonomous levels coexist, and which is determined 'in the last instance by the economy'. Thus the economic structure exists as one level or region of the structure as a whole. Such a conception of a complex structural unity presents Althusser with a number of theoretical problems, however, specifically the lack of concepts with which to think the determination of phenomena by a structure, or the determination of one structure upon a subordinate one, and finally the relations that exist between structures. In other words, '*how is it possible to define the concept of structural causality?*'[63] Althusser's answer to this problem is to propose a theory of 'overdetermination', or multiple causality.

As Jameson points out, Althusser's critique of Hegelianism is in fact a coded critique of Stalinist tendencies within the French Communist Party (*PU*, 37), and more specifically of Stalin's version of dialectical materialism, or diamat, which produced 'a unilinear vision of history as the evolution in fixed sequence of progressive modes of production'.[64] Althusser opposed what he saw as the simple contradiction of the Hegelian dialectic and its Marxian variant – that is, the reduction of all contingent contradictions to a generalized contradiction between the forces and relations of production – with a new conception of complex contradiction and overdetermination. To think this new concept of structure and overdetermination Althusser employs the category of *Darstellung* (or presentation). *Darstellung* is used to designate 'the mode of *presence* of the structure in its *effects*, and therefore to designate structural causality itself'.[65] In other words, 'the structure is immanent in its effects, a cause immanent in its effects in the Spinozist sense of the term, that *the whole existence of the structure consists of its effects*, in short that the structure, which is merely a specific combination of its peculiar elements, is nothing outside its effects.'[66] History, therefore, is what Althusser calls an 'absent cause', something that we know, not as the thing-in-itself, but through its effects; indeed the very notion of the concrete is the product of thought and not empirical existence itself. We cannot know history itself, but only have knowledge of it as the concept of history, and must therefore maintain at all times the distinction between the object of Knowledge (the concept of history) and the real object (the empirical events of history).

Jameson concedes that on its own terms the Althusserian critique is 'quite unanswerable' (*PU*, 27), but then in a characteristic rhetorical gesture suggests that this is to miss the point, that Althusser is not attacking historicism as such. What is really at issue here, suggests Jameson, is a dual problem around the nature of periodization and the representation of History. First, there is a synchronic dimension to the problem in which the concept of a historical period presents everything as 'a seamless web of phenomena each of which, in its own way, "expresses" some unified inner truth' (*PU*, 27). And secondly, there is a diachronic dimension 'in which history is seen in some "linear" way as the succession of such periods, stages, or moments' (*PU*, 28). For Jameson the second problem represents the prior one, for the reason 'that individual period formulations always secretly imply or project narratives or "stories" – narrative representations – of the historical sequence in which such individual periods take their place and from which they derive their significance' (*PU*, 28). What Althusser is really attacking under the rubric of expressive causality, and historicism generally, suggests Jameson, is in fact allegorical interpretations which seek to rewrite given sequences or periods in terms of a hidden master narrative.

However, if we understand allegory not as the reduction of the heterogeneity of historical sequences to a predetermined narrative but as an opening up of multiple horizons, then the concept of a historical narrative can be rehabilitated. Indeed, Jameson proposes that his conception of the political unconscious can resolve this dilemma, of accommodating the Althusserian critique within a teleological, or more accurately *narrative*, vision of history, by relocating it in the object. This would then allow for a defence of expressive causality along the lines of the case made for mechanical causality in that it has a local validity:

> if interpretation in terms of expressive causality or of allegorical master narratives remains a constant temptation, this is because such master narratives have inscribed themselves in the texts as well as in thinking about them; such allegorical narrative signifieds are a persistent dimension of literary and cultural texts precisely because they reflect a fundamental dimension of our collective thinking and our collective fantasies about history and reality. (*PU*, 34)

Our task as critics is not to abolish these faint murmurings of history and reality from texts but to retain them and open ourselves up once more to the reception of history through our cultural texts. We can, suggests Jameson, reformulate Althusser's conception of history, taking account of both his critique of expressive causality and interpretation generally while at the same time retaining a place for these operations, if we acknowledge that 'history is *not* a text, not a narrative, master or otherwise, but that, as an absent cause, it is inaccessible to us except in textual form, and that our approach to it and to the Real itself necessarily passes through its prior textualization, its narrativization in the political unconscious' (*PU*, 35). As with the Althusserian conception of structure, History is not immediately present, not graspable in itself but is something we know through its effects or textualizations. Before examining Jameson's synthesis of Althusserian antihistoricism with his own absolute historicism in more detail, I will consider his second critique of structural causality.

Jameson observes that if Althusserian Marxism is to be classified as a structuralism then it must be with the proviso 'that it is a structuralism for which only *one* structure exists' (*PU*, 36), that is to say, the mode of production. While Althusser on the one hand effectively discredited all teleological views of history, on the other he also served to restore the concept of mode of production as the central organizational category of Marxism. Althusser identified the mode of production with the structure as a whole, with the total system of social relations and relationships between levels. Thus the concept of mode of production takes on something of an eternal character, while at the same time the emphasis on the semi-, or relative, autonomy of distinct levels served to legitimate 'a renewed defence of the reified specializations of the bourgeois academic disciplines' (*PU*, 38). This ambiguity, according to Jameson, is a consequence of Althusser's rejection of 'mediation'. Mediation, or as Jameson now terms it transcoding, is the traditional way in which Marxism makes connections between disparate phenomena and social life generally, and between distinct levels of the totality. Althusser rejected mediation on the grounds that it posited an identity between phenomena and conflated distinct social levels. Jameson again takes Althusser on his own terms to reveal the inconsistency of his position and to show that what Althusser may rule out in theory, he does in practice. In other words, Althusser's notion of semi-autonomy can be seen to *relate* distinct phenomena just as much as it *separates*.

Moreover, if we are to define *difference*, then we need a prior concept of *identity* to define it against. Mediation is just such a process in that it 'undertakes to establish [an] initial identity against which then – but only then – local identification or differentiation can be registered' (*PU*, 42). This is not to affirm an identity between the phenomena concerned but to register a *relationship* between them, and for Jameson:

> Such momentary reunification would remain purely symbolic, a mere methodological fiction, were it not understood that social life is in its fundamental reality one and indivisible, a seamless web, a single inconceivable and transindividual process, in which there is no need to invent ways of linking language events and social upheavals or economic contradictions because on that level they were never separate from one another. (*PU*, 40)

Just as historicism was not Althusser's real target, Jameson contends that mediation is simply a code for the practice of 'homologies', which all too easily tend to posit solutions and forestall the laborious work of theory.

At this point Jameson is ready to reappraise the work of Althusser, drawing the conclusion that structural Marxism is not so much a radical break with traditional Marxisms as a modification within the dialectical tradition, and that 'Althusserian structural causality is therefore just as fundamentally a practice of mediation as is the "expressive causality" to which it is opposed' (*PU*, 41). Indeed, we discover that Althusser is in accord not only with Hegel but also with

Lukács. According to Jameson, Lukács's notion of totality is one of a methodological standard, 'an essentially critical and negative, demystifying operation' (*PU*, 52) and as such is 'non-representational'. Thus it can be seen to rejoin Althusser's notion of 'absent cause'. Jameson's appraisal and reformulation of Althusserian Marxism is nothing less than a virtuoso performance of dialectical subtlety and rhetorical ingenuity. His assimilation, however, of structural Marxism back into his own Hegelian paradigm seems just a little too neat; everything falls into place a little too readily. Even acknowledging Jameson's criticisms of Althusserian theory, Althusserianism and Hegelianism would still appear to remain radically incommensurable.[67] In a persuasive critique of Jameson's position Robert Young suggests that Jameson is attempting to bring about 'something which from a perspective of European Marxism is truly scandalous, namely a rapprochement between the two antithetical traditions of Sartre and Althusser, incorporated within a larger Lukácsian totality'.[68] Jameson's recourse to Lukács and Sartre is less pronounced in *The Political Unconscious* than in his earlier texts but it remains implicit in his conception of History – and yet it is this very question of history that so divides these two figures, who cannot be simply synthesized together as Jameson attempts to do.

History as Whose Narrative?

The locus of Jameson's dialectical recuperation of expressive causality is to relocate the problematic in the object, situating the traces of a historical master narrative in the texts themselves; but this does not resolve the problem, it simply relocates it. According to Young, Jameson's synthesizing strategy completely misses the substance of Althusser's critique of Sartre, namely that for Sartre consciousness remains the basis for the structure of the totality. The very real differences between Althusser's and Sartre's respective views of history are simply elided as Jameson relies more on 'the persuasive rhetoric of a rough argument than a theory whose logical premises and moves have been demonstrated in detail'.[69] Such a strategy, which consistently eradicates theoretical differences, Young observes, would be impermissible in a European intellectual climate strongly influenced by post-structuralism and deconstruction. Jameson's sweeping, all-inclusive, theoretical gestures, therefore, can be seen as a consequence of his position as a Marxist within the United States and more specifically as an academic Marxist. As Young indicates,

'*The Political Unconscious* remains noticeably circumspect in spelling out the politico-theoretical implications of what it is trying to do.'[70] Indeed, the one reflection on the kind of politics Jameson's theorizing implies is a footnote on alliance politics (*PU*, 54). Jameson's strategy and his view of History as a single great adventure appears to be a particularly North American perspective, tending overhastily to assimilate cultural and historical diversity to a single master narrative.

Althusser forcefully argued that the 'inversion' of a problematic does not resolve it but rather retains the same structure as the initial problematic in inverted form. It will not therefore be surprising, in a kind of return of the repressed, to find the same dilemmas arising in Jameson's inversion of expressive causality – something he wished to banish in the first place. Thus his defence of mediation against the overhasty positing of an identity between phenomena and the conflation of distinct structural levels finds its theoretical justification in just such a conflation, in the sense that mediations will remain purely a fiction unless we grasp social life as 'in its fundamental reality one and indivisible, a seamless web, a single inconceivable and transindividual process' (*PU*, 34). Equally, Jameson's strenuous efforts to define History as a single great adventure, as the great unfinished narrative of the collective struggle to wrest the realm of freedom from the realm of necessity, rest on the positing of a single unified and homogeneous time. For Jameson, this is the time of class struggle, or rather of North American capitalism. In a series of contentious essays on 'Third World' literature Jameson proposed that:

> Third-world texts, even those which are seemingly private and invested with a properly libidinal dynamic – necessarily project a political dimension in the form of national allegory: *the story of the private individual destiny is always an allegory of the embattled situation of the public third-world culture and society.*[71]

To substantiate this claim Jameson offers a reading of a work by the Chinese writer Lu Xun and *Xala* by the Senegalese writer Ousmane Sembsne. Jameson's readings are, as always, illuminating and provocative, but can we really reduce the diversity and heterogeneity of 'all' Third World literature to the examples of two writers, and on the basis of such a reduction can we seriously argue that Third World literature *always* constitutes national allegories? The unease one feels with such a sweeping, overgeneralizing statement is only heightened by the insertion of a clause on 'a properly libidinal dynamic'. What, one may ask, would be an 'improper' libidinal dynamic? And who is to decide what is proper and improper in such a case, the writer, the indigenous critic or the First World cultural theorist? Reflecting on his increasing discomfort on reading Jameson's essay Aijaz Ahmad writes:

> when I was on the fifth page of this text (specifically, on the sentence starting with 'All third-world texts are necessarily . . .' etc.), I realized that what was being theorized was, among many other things, myself. Now, I was born in India and I am a Pakistani citizen; I write poetry in Urdu, a language not commonly understood among US intellectuals. So, I said to myself: '*All? . . . necessarily?*' It felt odd. Matters got much more curious, however. For, the farther I read the more I realized, with no little chagrin, that the man whom I had for so long, so affectionately, even though from a physical distance, taken as a comrade was, in his own opinion, my civilizational Other.[72]

Jameson's totalizing logic treats the whole 'Third World', a problematic concept in itself, as a homogeneous entity in which the Other is constituted as the same. In Jameson's text, the Third World is defined 'solely in terms of its experience of colonialism',[73] and simply reduplicates the history of European colonialism. As I shall discuss in chapter 6, the Third World plays an increasingly ambiguous, or more precisely an 'amphibious', role in Jameson's theorizing, providing a dialectical contrary to the First World as an absent centre within postmodernism and as a sign of the final globalization of late capitalism. In terms of *The Political Unconscious*, however, it facilitates an answer to that recurrent question of what 'History itself' is and whose single great adventure it is. It is, in short, the history of the West, that is, of modernization and the rise of capitalism, and no one, notes Young, is apparently 'allowed a history outside of "us" – that is Western civilization and the Western point of view, which for Jameson seems to mean the USA'.[74] Jameson would not appear to have accommodated the Althusserian notion of structural causality within his own conception of structural historicism so much as to have annulled the former through a revamped Hegelianism in the shape of the latter.

The Althusserian conception of structural causality cannot be so easily folded back into a narrative vision of history with its continuum of time – for Jameson, the time of class struggle. For Althusser there is no single continuum of time but different times deriving from the possibility of different histories corresponding to the different levels of the social whole. Each of these different 'levels', writes Althusser, 'does not have the same type of historical existence. On the contrary, we have to assign to each level a *peculiar time*, relatively

autonomous and hence relatively independent, even in its depend-
ence, of the "times" of the other levels.'[75] In short, for each mode of
production there is a particular time and history, punctuated in a
specific way by the development of the productive forces. This is not
the lesson, however, that Jameson draws from Althusser. Criticizing
Jameson's Eurocentrism, which it would perhaps be more appropriate to describe as US-centrism, Young writes: 'Such an arrogant and
arrogating narrative means that the story of "world history" not
only involves what Fredric Jameson describes as the wrestling of
freedom from the realm of necessity but always also the creation,
subjection, and final appropriation of Europe's "others".'[76]

In conclusion I will consider two further difficulties raised by
Jameson's conception of a political unconscious: the nature of the
relationship between history and text, and the role narrative plays
here; and finally Jameson's 'solution' to the problem of diachrony
through the non-synchronous development of modes of production.

Jameson emphasizes that History, in the sense that he aligns it with
Althusser's 'absent cause' or Lacan's 'Real', is fundamentally non-
narrative and non-representable. Furthermore History is not a text
but it remains inaccessible except through its prior (re)textualiz-
ations. John Frow poses the question, 'if history is accessible only
through discursive or epistemological categories, is there not a
real sense in which it therefore has only a discursive existence?'[77]
Jameson is rightly at pains to avoid such a conclusion since this
would lead down the post-structuralist and postmodernist path of
relativism and the reductive notion that there is nothing outside the
text – what the critical realist philosopher Roy Bhaskar calls the
'epistemic fallacy' or the reduction of 'being' to 'knowing'.[78] Unfortunately, Jameson's defence of an independent reality seems to amount
to little more than a single sentence. One does not have to argue the
reality of history, he writes, 'necessity, like Dr Johnson's stone, does
that for us' (*PU*, 82). History, for Jameson, is the experience of
necessity: it is not a narrative in the sense that it represents the
content of a story, but rather the form through which we experience
necessity; the formal effects of an absent, non-representational cause.

We find ourselves then in the paradoxical situation that Jameson's
justification for History as a 'properly narrative political unconscious' (*PU*, 102) is that it needs no justification:

> Conceived in this sense, History is what hurts, it is what refuses desire and
> sets inexorable limits to individual as well as collective praxis, which its
> 'ruses' turn into grisly and ironic reversals of their overt intention. But this
> History can be apprehended only through its effects, and never directly as

some reified force. This is indeed the ultimate sense in which History as
ground and untranscendable horizon needs no particular theoretical justification: we may be sure that its alienating necessities will not forget us,
however much we might prefer to ignore them. (*PU*, 102)

History is not so much a thing, or a process we can know, but a
structural limit on consciousness and agency, a limit we constantly
come up against whether we intend it or not. It would seem, though,
that after having painstakingly worked through the Althusserian
strictures against historicism we are back where we started, that is to
say, the precipitation of the theory of history into real history, or the
conflation of the object of Knowledge with the real object. In other
words, the reduction of the theory or science of history to history itself
is a reduction which, as Michael Sprinker has pointed out, 'risks
collapsing into empiricism'.[79]

We need not, however, completely abandon the concept of history
as essentially narrative, or, indeed, the narrative of class struggle.
Paul Ricoeur argues that 'if history were to sever its links with
narrative it would cease to be historical,'[80] but the insistence on the
essential narrative character of history is not to be confused with the
defence of narrative history. What Jameson appears to overlook in his
conception of a political unconscious is the gap inscribed between the
historical narrative and history itself by the very act of narration, 'the
distance introduced by narrative between itself and lived experience
. . . Between living and recounting, a gap – however small it may be
– is opened up. Life is lived, history is recounted.'[81] Narrative's
particular value lies in its 'intelligibility', in its ability to organize the
bewildering mass of historical data into a form that is readily understandable. While both human experience and narrative share a
temporal quality, temporality in itself does not constitute a narrative. Thus our experience of life does not necessarily have the form of
narrative, except in so far as we give it that form through processes of
selection and organization, what is known as 'emplotment'.[82]

The notion of emplotment has the advantage of foregrounding the
inherent ideological component of history. Our historical narratives
are not neutral or scientifically objective but rest on certain ideological presuppositions. For instance, the notion of the plot is that it has
a beginning, a middle and an end, yet history is necessarily selective,
not only in the events and actions it chooses to recount but in where
it chooses to begin and end and the point at which it decides that a
given narrative is coherent and complete. This does not necessarily
imply that history is anything we choose it to be. One can still put a
case for an independent reality subject to veridical criteria, while

acknowledging the mode of presentation as itself an important signifier of meaning. We can, therefore, perhaps reformulate Jameson's conception of History and Narrative to take account of both Althusser's notion of the specificity of historical times and the recent reflections of historiography and suggest that History is not a narrative, master or otherwise, but remains inaccessible to us except through its prior (re)narrativizations, which always presuppose an implicit political unconscious.

If Jameson's project exhibits a tendency towards an overly homogeneous conception of time, it also falls prey to the charge of 'contemporaneity'. Jameson's use of mode of production as the final determining instance seeks to avoid the charge of economism or vulgar Marxism by designating it as the unity of both the forces and relations of production, and then identifying the mode of production, following Althusser and Balibar, with the social totality as a structure. Gregory Elliott summarizes Balibar's thesis thus: '[as] a conceptual object, a mode of production was conceived by Balibar as a self-reproducing totality which reproduced both the relations and the forces of production and the non-economic conditions of existence, i.e. the requisite conditions of the other instances.'[83]

The problem with such a definition, Elliott points out, is that it cannot account for the transition from one mode of production to another, as each mode of production becomes a self-enclosed totality. Balibar thus proposed a general law of transition based on the postulate of transitional modes of production 'characterized by a "dislocation" between the forces and relations of production'.[84] According to Elliott, this solution is ruled out on at least three counts. First, it requires a distinction between the synchronic and the diachronic, which Althusser's epistemology rules out. Secondly, it restores the very teleological representation of history Althusser's strictures again ruled out. And finally, it still cannot account for the transition between a transitional and a non-transitional mode of production. Balibar, therefore, proposed a second solution to the problem of transition from one mode of production to another. As Elliott describes it:

> Periods of transition, he conjectured, are 'characterized by the *coexistence* of several modes of production'. The non-correspondence between the two connections of the economic structure and between the different social levels during them, 'merely reflects *the coexistence of two (or more) modes of production in a single "simultaneity", and the dominance of one of them over the other*'.[85]

This would certainly appear to accord with Jameson's theorization of dominant, residual and emergent modes of production and non-synchronous development as I outlined it above. Elliott, however, identifies a number of presuppositions (again not all of which are consistent with Althusserian epistemology), but of 'greatest salience here was the distinction made . . . between *mode of production* and *social formation*.'[86] According to Elliott, the fruitfulness of this distinction 'is to differentiate between the theoretical Marxist concepts (themselves of different degrees of abstraction) employed in the analysis of any given historical/social reality and the particular realities . . . under analysis'.[87] However, it is precisely such a distinction which Jameson's theorization wishes to forestall, arguing that it is inadequate and misleading 'to the degree that it encourages the very empirical thinking which it was concerned to denounce, in other words, subsuming a particular or an empirical "fact" under this or that corresponding "abstraction"' (*PU*, 95). What we can take from the notion of social formation, suggests Jameson, is the concept of the structural coexistence of several modes of production simultane-ously, and this at a stroke resolves the problem of the synchronic and diachrony. What is synchronic, writes Jameson, is the 'concept' of the mode of production: 'The moment of the historical coexistence of several modes of production is not synchronic in this sense, but open to history in a dialectical way' (*PU*, 95).

It takes more than an act of fiat, though, to resolve this dilemma, and Jameson's response does not really seem to be a solution. First, Jameson insists that there can only be one totality, which he identifies with the mode of production, but if there is a structural coexistence of more than one mode of production would this not imply the structural coexistence of more than one totality? For Balibar, this was one of the logical outcomes of his theory of transitional modes of production. Secondly, Jameson argues for the necessity of a structural dominant, so that we can distinguish between the various historical modes of production, and the transition between these various dominants is accounted for with the concept of cultural revolution. But is there not a sense in which, if a mode of production does not exist in a pure state but always in coexistence with other modes of production, history can thus be said to be in a state of permanent cultural revolution? If we take Jameson's example of the Enlighten-ment, there is a sense, as Habermas argues, that this is an unfinished project, that postmodernism, far from signalling the end of the Enlightenment, signals that it has yet to be completed. This in itself does not undermine Jameson's thesis but it does raise serious questions about the explanatory force of the concept. At which point can one particular cultural revolution be said to be the dominant one and how does one define this dominance? Furthermore, if the transition between modes of production is defined in terms of cultural revolution and, as I have stated, this appears to be the permanent state of affairs, are we not in exactly the same position as Balibar, whereby all modes of production thus appear to be transitionary modes, and how do we therefore explain the transition between these transitionary modes? Alternatively, how do we explain the transition from one cultural revolution to the next?

In *Karl Marx's Theory of History: A Defence*, G. A. Cohen writes, as Balibar also acknowledges, that *mode* refers to a *way* or a *manner* and not a set of relations.[88] The economic structure, insists Cohen, is just that, a *structure*, 'a framework of power in which producing occurs', while the mode of production is a process, 'a way of producing'.[89] Following Cohen we can distinguish three senses in which Marx used the concept of mode of production: first, the material mode, or the way in which individuals work with their productive forces; second, the social mode as the social properties of the productive processes; and finally, the mixed mode as the designation of both the material and social properties of the way production proceeds. It is in this final sense that Jameson uses the term, but this does not accord with a conception of the mode of production as a structure. Although every structure is subject to process, this does not make it a process itself: as Cohen writes, the 'economic structure is . . . variously implicated in movement and process, but to represent the structure as itself a process is to violate both the concept of structure and the intent of historical materialism.'[90] Jameson's conception of a *structural historicism*, therefore, would appear to leave unanswered as many questions as it sought to resolve.

3

The Politics of Desire

In the previous chapter I considered Jameson's strategy of appropriating radically antithetical discourses within his own Marxist conceptual framework and suggested that this tended to elide theoretical differences. Thus, rather than resolving the dilemmas of historicism, Jameson's conception of *structural historicism* simply reproduced the problems in 'inverted' form. In this chapter I will extend this analysis through an examination of Gilles Deleuze and Félix Guattari's *Anti-Oedipus*. The *Anti-Oedipus* achieved a certain notoriety on publication and has subsequently been celebrated and disparaged in equal measure. Jameson sees the text as a major work of probably France's most important contemporary philosopher. Perry Anderson, on the other hand, has described it as 'the expression of a dejected post-lapsarian anarchism'.[1]

For Jameson, Marxism's theoretical primacy rests on its ability to appropriate other critical discourses, such as Deleuze and Guattari's, through historicizing their procedures. In this chapter I examine Jameson's own procedure and question just how successful this manoeuvre is. I initially consider the problematic relationship between pleasure, desire and politics and explicate the distinction between pleasure and desire in post-structuralist discourse. I situate the post-structuralist celebration of desire and *jouissance* in relation to the events of Paris, May 1968, before outlining Deleuze and Guattari's conception of desiring-production. While Jameson's historization of the *Anti-Oedipus* reveals it to be predicated on those very concepts of identity and totality that it seeks to undermine, I contend that his very selective and partial reading of the *Anti-Oedipus* seriously brings into doubt its affinity to his own doctrine of a political unconscious and consequently of the strategy of appropriating radically distinct discourses in general. In the concluding sections of this chapter I sketch Jameson's own formulation of a libidinal apparatus, and finally address the question of the subject and ideology through the dialectic of ideology and Utopia.

Ideologies of Pleasure

The relationship between pleasure and politics, indeed the question of pleasure itself, has always been a problematic one for the left. The left is traditionally portrayed as puritanical and aridly intellectual, while the right is cast as hedonistic and decadent. In 'Pleasure: A Political Issue' Jameson examines the resistance on the part of the left to issues of pleasure, particularly the 'class' dimension of sexual politics:

> The conception of the primacy of class issues and class consciousness suggests that from a working-class perspective, issues of sexual liberation may be grasped, not on their own terms, but rather as so many class ideologies and as the collective expression of groups (such as middle-class youth) that working-class people identify as the class enemy.[2]

Similarly for women the politics of pleasure is by no means merely an existential issue, or, as I shall suggest below, an ethical question of one's relationship to one's own body. The politics of pleasure is first and foremost a collective concern, inextricably bound up with questions of male power and domination. Therefore, writes Jameson, 'if it begins to turn out that the value of 'pleasure' as a political slogan is not merely unattractive to working-class people but also to women, then its ideological effectivity is evidently a rather diminished one.'[3]

This is not to advocate, however, that the left simply resign itself to the situation, accepting the mythology that surrounds pleasure and in effect abandoning the terrain to the right; on the contrary, Jameson insists on the need to reformulate our conception of pleasure and define, what he terms, its 'proper' political use. According to Jameson, there is no such thing as pleasure in its own right, 'only pleasurable activities, or something like a fading effect of pleasure after the fact',[4] and what is really at stake in the polemics over pleasure is not so much the experience itself but rather the '*idea* of pleasure, the ideologies of pleasure'.[5] I will briefly explicate two such ideologies in order to distinguish between issues of pleasure and desire.

According to Foucault, pleasure is essentially an ethical problem, in the sense of the way we constitute ourselves as moral agents, in other words, it is a relation of one to one's self, to one's own body.[6] Pleasure is thus characterized by Foucault as a practice of the self. Desire, on the other hand, is not simply a question of personal ethics; it is not reducible to the subject in the sense that it is a practice of the self but is rather at the very heart of our constructions of subjectivity. We think of ourselves not merely as subjects that desire but as desiring subjects; desire is what drives us forward, and it is also part of the unconscious structures of society, the social nexus within which our subjectivity is constituted. In short, desire is a force or drive that is greater than its individual manifestations.

The dissociation of pleasure and desire within theoretical discourse is visibly marked in the publication of two seminal texts in the early 1970s: Roland Barthes's *The Pleasure of the Text* (1973) and Deleuze and Guattari's *Anti-Oedipus* (1972). As his title indicates, Barthes is concerned with 'pleasure' and he shares with Foucault a certain antipathy to the theoretical value attributed to desire: 'we are always being told about Desire,' writes Barthes 'never about Pleasure; Desire has an epistemic dignity, Pleasure does not.'[7] Deleuze and Guattari, on the other hand, focus on 'desire' and have nothing substantial to say about pleasure at all. Both *The Pleasure of the Text* and *Anti-Oedipus* conclude with a celebration of immanence and the intensity of the moment, but each text reaches this terminus by very different routes. Moreover, while each text, ostensibly, advocates radically differing conceptions of politics, both can be seen to undermine the preconditions on which any meaningful politics can be conceived and practised.

The Barthesian ideology of pleasure renounces all political commitment in favour of an individualistic hedonism of the text, or as Barthes eloquently puts it, the 'text is (should be) that uninhibited person who shows his behind to the *Political Father*.'[8] For Barthes the pleasure of the text consists of an erotics of reading, a surrendering of oneself to the flux of language, its contradiction and difference, to its plurality of voices or what Barthes calls a 'sanctioned Babel'. The precondition for such an eroticism of the text is essentially its excess: its repetition to excess and its unexpectedness, in the sense that it is 'succulently new'. In other words, the pleasurable text is that which goes beyond representation, that undoes nomination through its own excess, it is something we can say nothing about and only surrender ourselves to the polymorphous perversity of *jouissance*:

With the writer of bliss (and his reader) begins the untenable text, the impossible text. This text is outside pleasure, outside criticism, *unless it is reached through another text of bliss*: you cannot speak 'on' such a text, you can only speak 'in' it, *in its fashion*, enter into a desperate plagiarism, hysterically affirm the void of bliss (and no longer obsessively repeat the letter of pleasure).[9]

Barthesian bliss is what Jameson defines as a narrow, culinary, bourgeois sense of pleasure, a perspective we need to move beyond in order to reflect upon what he calls the 'deeper subject', the libidinal body itself. This, I suggest, is to move from the terrain of 'pleasure' to 'desire' and to see that pleasure, or more precisely what I will now define as desire, as a figure, an allegory, for a broader process of transformation. As Jameson writes, 'the thematization of a particular pleasure as a political issue . . . must always involve a dual focus, in which the local issue is meaningful and desirable in and of itself, but is also *at one and the same time* taken as the *figure* for Utopia in general, and for the systematic revolutionary transformation of society as a whole.'[10] I return to the issue of Utopia and desire in the concluding section of this chapter. First I shall examine the radically different conception of desire advocated by Deleuze and Guattari.

Ideologies of Desire

Subtitled *Capitalism and Schizophrenia*, the *Anti-Oedipus* provides, claim its authors, the first genuinely materialist form of psychiatry; what they term 'schizoanalysis':

> Schizoanalysis foregoes all interpretation because it foregoes discovering an unconscious material: the unconscious does not mean anything. On the other hand the unconscious constructs machines, which are machines of desire, whose use and functioning schizoanalysis discovers in their immanent relationship with social machines.[11]

With this unambiguous rejection of interpretation, latent unconscious material and mediation in favour of an immanent relationship between desire and the social field, it would seem a little strange, if not perverse, for Jameson to claim in *The Political Unconscious* that the 'thrust of the argument of the *Anti-Oedipus* is, to be sure, very much in the spirit of the present work' (*PU*, 22). Indeed, this most transgressive and fluid of texts would appear to resolutely resist just the kind of recuperative strategy that Jameson proposes and therefore provides something of a litmus test for Jameson's strategy in general.

For Jameson the usefulness of the *Anti-Oedipus* lies initially in its reintroduction of questions of history into those otherwise resolutely anti- or ahistorical moments of structuralism and post-structuralism. However, in *The Political Unconscious* he is more specific in identifying particular affinities between his own doctrine of a political unconscious and the work of Deleuze and Guattari, that is, an intention 'to reassert the specificity of the political content of everyday life and of individual fantasy-experience and to reclaim it from that reduction to the merely subjective and to the status of psychological projection which is even more characteristic of American culture and ideological life today than it is of a still politicized France' (*PU*, 22). Jameson, then, claims a threefold kinship with the *Anti-Oedipus*: first, that it reinstates the political nature of our everyday experience; secondly, that it re-asserts the collective or political dimension of our fantasy-experience; and finally, that the situation Deleuze and Guattari are describing is even more characteristic of the experience of the subject within North American culture than it is of the more politicized climate of con-temporary France. Situating the *Anti-Oedipus* in its own historical moment I shall critically examine the first two of these claims before suggesting that the third is crucial for Jameson's attempt to resite the *Anti-Oedipus* as a second-degree critical philosophy.

The *Anti-Oedipus* emerged from that period of 'euphoria and dis-illusionment, liberation and dissipation, carnival and catastrophe'[12] we now know as May '68. For a brief and dramatic moment in the spring of 1968, writes Terry Eagleton, it appeared that the combined forces of the French student protests and workers' strikes would rock the French state to its very foundations. With hindsight, the strikes and protests of May 68 can be seen to have been less the harbinger of a new revolutionary movement than the end of an older form of revolutionary politics. The traditional working-class organizations, the French Communist Party and the unions, stood condemned in the eyes of many militants as complicit in the maintenance of the existing social structure. Rather than acting as the vehicle of revol-utionary change the Communist Party proved to be an obstacle and block at the very moment social transformation appeared to be imminent. No less a figure than Althusser himself has provided one of the most eloquent and succinct analyses of the Communist Party's failings at this crucial juncture.

Although Althusser did not break with the Communist Party after May '68 his critique of the party apparatus, when it finally came a decade later, was incisive. In a tone markedly different from that of his path-breaking works two decades earlier, Althusser now wrote:

Behind [the] view of a scientific theory produced by bourgeois intellectuals, and 'introduced . . . from without' into the working-class movement,
lies a whole conception of the relations between theory and practice,
between the Party and the mass movement, and between party leaders and
simple militants, which reproduces bourgeois forms of knowledge and
power in their separation.[13]

According to Althusser, Marxist theory could be seen to have re-
gressed from the work of Marx himself and, more specifically, Marxism was lacking in fully developed theories of the state, of
superstructures and of political organizations. Historically this has
meant that the working-class movement has tended to reproduce
bourgeois structures of power and organization. Thus the party itself
can be seen to reproduce the dominant ideology through its own
structure and organization and in particular through 'the difference
between its leaders and its militants' which replicates 'the structures
of the bourgeois State'.[14]

The problem of the working-class movement reproducing a reactionary ideology, then, is not merely a question of the level of class
consciousness, of inadequate theory or deviating from the party line,
but it is inherent in the organizational structure of the party and
movement itself. In tones that echo his old adversary Sartre, Althusser
observes that the separation of militants from the party leadership
and a reliance on bourgeois forms of organization simply replicate
bourgeois structures of power and modes of politics. The revolutionary group tends to ossify and the maintenance of its own structures
and organization takes precedence over revolutionary change.

For many French intellectuals, radicalized through May '68, the
lessons they drew were that revolutionary transformation was no
longer only a question of the seizure of state power but rather of
challenging all the existing structures and organizations that maintained state power in the first place. As Peter Dews puts it, if 'the
embodiment of the worker's movement could act as simply one more
apparatus of repression, then the real struggle seemed to be no longer
between worker and capitalist, but between institutionalised power
and resistance'.[15] After May '68 sections of the student movement and
far left sought to redefine the terms of political struggle around
notions of 'molecular' politics: in other words, the politics of autonomous groups which eschewed identifiable goals and focused on
more local and less global strategies of political change, what Dews
identifies as *enragé* politics. As Dews observes, there was a recognition that 'social systems are both imposed by force from above –
they embody relations of *power* – and are adhered to or rejected from

below – they are invested or disinvested with *desire.'*[16] The immediate political task, post-May '68, was not to challenge the coercive and repressive structures of the state, argued the militants, but rather to analyse and disinvest those structures and to reconceptualize non-repressive forms of political organization and activities. In short, subjects were seen to be complicit in their own subjugation through support and investment in the existing political structures and organizations. Thus, in the words of Foucault, we need to rid ourselves of that 'fascism in us all, in our heads and in our everyday behaviour'.[17]

Terry Eagleton, however, has provided a rather more sober analysis of the situation. From a position of defeat and disillusion, he argues, evolved the post-structuralist critique of totalizing thought and the rejection of 'all forms of political theory and organization which sought to analyze, and act upon, the structures of society as a whole'; unable 'to break the structures of state power, post-structuralism found it possible instead to subvert the structures of language.'[18] From the subversion of political structures to the subversion of structure *per se* seems to have been a very short step and the project of molecular politics to disinvest traditional forms of oppositional politics and formulate new political structures migrated into a general disinvestment of all forms of structure, since the uninhibited release or realization of desire was perceived as *in-itself* revolutionary and emancipatory.

The Production of Desire

Unlike Barthes's retreat into a hedonism of the text, Deleuze and Guattari's politics of desire seeks to reclaim some form of collective subject or historical agency. As Jameson points out, their principal theoretical antagonist is not so much Marx as Freud. For Deleuze and Guattari, Freud is at once the discoverer of that realm of free synthesis where anything is possible and is subject only to the motivation of desire – the polymorphous perversity of the pleasure principle – while at the same time the punitive father who sought to restrict this liberating force through the law of the Oedipus complex. The Oedipus complex, they argue, is not so much a psychic crisis as a structure imposed on unconscious desire by social forces, channelling the free flows of desire into a predetermined matrix. Deleuze and Guattari pose the question: 'what does it mean to say that Freud discovered Oedipus in his own self-analysis? Was it in his self-analysis, or rather

in his Goethian classical culture?'[19] A materialist psychiatry interprets Oedipus as an 'ideological form', a referential axis – the in-
variant 'daddy-mommy-me' – around which desire is oriented,
channelled and above all domesticated. But for schizoanalysis desire
is not reducible to a given structure, it constitutes 'the Real in itself,
beyond or beneath the Symbolic as well as the Imaginary'[20] and
remains a fundamentally transgressive force. Freud's Oedipalization
of unconscious desire served to restrict an essentially orphan unconscious to the endless repetition of a Greek tragedy, while, to the
contrary, it was not the desire that begat the prohibition but the
prohibition that begat the desire.

The radicalism of Deleuze and Guattari's project derives from their
attempt to reformulate the relationship between unconscious desire
and the social. For them, social repression not only presupposes
psychic repression but social liberation can only be achieved when it
is accompanied by psychic liberation, when we realize our own desire
rather than accepting its prohibition. The failure of previous Marxist-
Freudian syntheses, such as those of Wilhelm Reich or Herbert
Marcuse, was that they retained a separation between the rational
world of social production and the irrational domain of desire, and
that desire remained a fundamentally negative and subterranean
force. Deleuze and Guattari on the other hand argue that both forms
of repression are linked in a single process, and thus their central
concept of desiring-production encapsulates both the Freudian conception of desire and the Marxian emphasis on social production. For
Deleuze and Guattari desire is never the desire for something lacking;
the object of desire is rather desire itself. In a kind of Nietzschean
eternal return, as an endless cycle and return of the positive, desire
seeks only its own affirmation and reproduction in a continual
process of desiring-production. Desire, for Deleuze and Guattari, is a
hylé, or material flow.[21]

Brian Massumi suggests that desire for Deleuze and Guattari is
never desire for an object; it is neither a drive in the Freudian sense nor
a structure, but the production of singular states of intensity. In its
broadest sense, desire is a plane of consistency, what Massumi
describes as multiple co-causal becoming; in terms of the subject,
desire is never an individual affair but represents a tension between
subpersonal and suprapersonal tendencies that intersect in an empty
category we designate as the subject.[22] I shall argue below that such
a definition of desire essentially empties the term of any meaningful
value whatsoever, while the uncritical celebration of the liberatory
potential of unconstrained desire is at best naive and at worst results

in an endorsement of capitalism itself. Furthermore, Deleuze and Guattari's conception of desire is hardly consistent with Jameson's implicit use of Lacanian theory and it remains difficult to see how he can maintain both positions simultaneously. For the present I follow Deleuze and Guattari's usage of the term.

For Deleuze and Guattari, then, desiring-production is neither the incestuous desires of the Oedipus complex, nor the Lacanian desire as lack; desire is rather a real, productive and affirmative force. The unconscious, write Deleuze and Guattari, is not a classical theatre but a factory of production and there is only one kind of production, 'the production of the real'.[23] If desire produces, its product is the real; if desire is productive, it can be productive only in the real world and can produce only reality. Schizophrenic desire is the universe of production in the 'real' world and acts as the absolute limit of social production. In other words, there is *'only desire and the social, and nothing else'*,[24] coextensive in a single process of desiring-production, each directly investing the other without mediation. Desiring-production and social production are not the same thing, however, they are rather two poles of the same process: that is to say, at one end of the process we find the 'molecular' processes of desiring-production and at the other the 'molar' formations, or aggregates, of social production.[25] And, according to Deleuze and Guattari, to encourage the free flow of desire is to encourage it to surpass, to overflow the final limits and constraints of the capitalist order.

For Deleuze and Guattari the ultimate fallacy of the notion of individual fantasy resides in its adherence to a conception of the ego or subject as retaining an integrity or centredness, what they describe as the 'global subject'. According to Deleuze and Guattari we are first and foremost social beings, 'private persons are . . . images of the second order, images of images – that is, *simulacra* that are thus endowed with an aptitude for representing the first order images of social persons.'[26] What Massumi calls personhood is an empty state, a place where nothing happens, but which is receptive to the forces of desire, and it needs to be replaced with a conception of subjectivity as contingent, permanently displaced and decentred, that is, the residual or nomadic subject. The nomadic subject, therefore, represents a certain balance of forces, the partiality or bias of desire at any given moment in time, and as desire is constantly in flux, the partiality of the subject will be constantly changing from moment to moment. Desire is not something *in* the subject as there is no *interiority* for Deleuze and Guattari, but rather the subject is a by-product of the process itself. Nomadic subjects are the products of desiring-production, the secretions of desire as it intersects, couples and decouples with other forces of desire. The question that arises for an avowedly revolutionary and emancipatory politics is precisely what kind of subject is being liberated here and, moreover, whether we can describe it as a 'subject' in any meaningful sense of the term. Marxism is grounded on an understanding of historical agency; in what sense, therefore, can this contingent empty subject be reconciled with Jameson's historicist project? I return to this question below.

Anti-Oedipus equates the schizophrenic process of fragmentation with capitalist production, in the sense of capitalism's inexorable drive towards universalization and its accompanying appearance of fragmentation and dispersion. For Deleuze and Guattari schizophrenic desire marks the absolute limit of capitalism's capacity for expansion and reproduction, as it is the force that goes beyond all limits. A truly revolutionary theory, they insist, will not constrain this process but will rather encourage it to follow its own logic, to its own ultimate conclusion – in short, encourage capitalism to go over the edge: 'To go still further, that is, in the movement of the market, of decoding and deterritorialization? For perhaps the flows are not yet deterritorialized enough, not decoded enough, from the viewpoint of a theory and a practice of a highly schizophrenic character.'[27]

It would appear to be difficult to reconcile such voluntaristic and gesture politics with Jameson's systematic Hegelianism and rigorous understanding of the complex dialectics of advanced capitalism. Furthermore, Deleuze and Guattari's whole view of history as an essentially aleatory, contingent and heterogeneous series of intensive states experienced by partial, nomadic subjects secreted by schizophrenic desiring-production would seem to be completely incommensurable with Jameson's own conception of a single great adventure of class struggle. Indeed, in an otherwise sympathetic treatment of Deleuze and Guattari's work, Teresa Brennan observes that its central problem is that it rules out the very kind of historical thinking that both her own and Jameson's work seeks to achieve.[28] Jameson's capacity to incorporate such a Nietzschean and detotalizing text into his own Marxist discourse hinges on two principal manoeuvres: first, to reveal how the former is a second-order philosophical system, and secondly, to show how this ostensibly anti-interpretative text projects its own theory of interpretation.

Jameson describes *Anti-Oedipus* as a second-degree or critical philosophy in the sense that it rests on prior, although unstated, assumptions and presuppositions. For example, the authors reject the concept of 'totality' in favour of a theory of singularity, that is to say, the flux and pure multiplicity of desire. Deleuze and Guattari assert that they 'no longer believe in a primordial totality that once existed, or in a final totality that awaits us at a future date'.[29] The authors propose instead the notion of 'peripheral totalities' which are produced alongside the process of desiring-production and are themselves subject to flux; that is to say not totalization in the conventional and accepted sense but a totality that encompasses a set of forces at a given moment before once more dissolving into process. For Jameson, any assertion of heterogeneity or difference rests on a prior conceptualization of homogeneity and identity, as it is only against such concepts that they can be defined. Thus Deleuze and Guattari's claims of partiality and 'nomadism' rest on prior conceptions of unity or totality and a fixed structure. The *Anti-Oedipus*, then, can be read as a reaction against overly totalizing thought and the inflexibility of our social and psychic structures, but in the act of reacting against them they paradoxically ratify and legitimate these very structures. Foucault encapsulates the paradoxicality of the situation in his observation that 'if everything were absolute diversity, thought would be doomed to singularity . . . it would be doomed also to absolute dispersion and absolute monotony.'[30] In true dialectical fashion, absolute diversity and singularity pass over into their opposite to become a totalizing conformity and endless repetition of the same as real difference is erased. Deleuze and Guattari's celebration of the pure multiplicity and flux of schizophrenic desiring-production only has meaning when it is defined against a background of enduring structures and an initial totality.

Jameson consistently reiterates the need to maintain a distinction between different levels of abstraction. In the present analysis, therefore, we must distinguish between *Anti-Oedipus* as a 'theory of history' and History itself. According to Jameson, theories of history 'merely offer alternate ways to "punctuate" the rise of the middle-class world itself and the various cultural and psychic metamorphoses or "coupures épistémologiques" which accompanied it' (*MF*, 321). The strength of such theories and also their weakness is their limitation to a single cultural sphere. They provide invaluable synchronic analyses of their given sphere but lack the conceptual framework with which to give a full diachronic account of historical development. As a consequence theories of history tend to identify their own object of study as the actual motor of social and historical change. In the case of the *Anti-Oedipus*, the identification of the schizophrenic tendency of capitalism comes to be seen as an ideological absolute. Schizophrenia, the authors tell us, 'as a process is the only universal'[31] and desire is not simply seen as a force co-extensive with other forces but becomes the ultimate determining instant: 'desire is always constitutive of a social field.'[32] For Jameson the proliferation of theories of history is itself a sign of some deeper cultural malaise, as 'an attempt to outsmart the present, first of all, to think your way behind history to the point where even the present itself can be seen as a completed historical instant' (*MF*, 320). It will come as no surprise therefore to discover Deleuze and Guattari proclaiming schizoanalysis as the end of history, 'it is our very own "malady", modern man's sickness. The end of history has no other meaning.'[33] The inevitably reactionary implications of proclaiming the 'end of history' will be discussed below.

Jameson's second gesture is to reveal how Deleuze and Guattari's anti-interpretative position can be seen implicitly to conceal, and rest on, an initial act of interpretation. The authors claim to be developing an immanent and transcendent, although non-transcendental, form of criticism which is founded on a shift from the old interpretative operation – 'what does it mean?' – to an immanent analysis – 'how does it work?' Criticism, for Deleuze and Guattari, will no longer be the search for an absent signified or the imposition of pre-existing structures of meaning, but a question of 'use': at the molecular level, how does a specific sign work within the text, what function does it perform, and at a molar level, what forces come into play and for what purposes at any given moment in time. Immanent criticism therefore will be not so much an interpretation of the text as a laying bare of its complex operations and functions.

If this is not to be a purely descriptive exercise, however, there will be an implicit purpose behind the act of interrogation, in the sense of a prior interpretative decision that there is something there, in the text, to be extracted in the first place. For Deleuze and Guattari, this prior assumption is the repressed revolutionary potential of desire. The 'schizoid exercise', they write, 'extracts from the text its revolutionary force.'[34] In short, schizoanalysis uncovers the libidinal investments that are always present in social production. Thus, suggests Jameson, the *Anti-Oedipus* can be seen to project a new hermeneutic, whereby 'the object of commentary is effectively transformed into an allegory whose master narrative is the story of repressed desire itself, as it struggles against repressive reality' (*PU*, 67). The schizophrenic process of productive desire provides Deleuze and Guattari with a degree zero, their bottom line against which all other forms of social and psychic production can be judged. Desire is simply the hermeneutic key through which we can reinterpret history and judge other forms of production. Deleuze and Guattari have not so much discovered the absolute contradiction and conclusive death of capitalism but rather have described our fractured and dislocated experience of it, or as Jameson puts it: 'the realm of separation, of fragmentation, of the explosion of codes and the multiplicity of disciplines is merely the reality of the appearance' (*PU*, 40).

The *Anti-Oedipus* is nothing less than one more symptom of our fragmented sensibility in what appears to be an increasingly confusing and disorientating global reality but therein also lies its utility and value, as an attempt to articulate the existential experience of the subject within advanced capitalism. With a return of the repressed, the political unconscious of the *Anti-Oedipus* turns out to be that very englobing and totalizing force of North American capitalism that the text was supposed to be undermining. As the authors themselves suggest, 'the more [the social machine] breaks down, the more it schizophrenizes, the better it works, the American way.'[35] This barely qualified endorsement of advanced capitalism is also evident in Massumi's *A User's Guide to Capitalism and Schizophrenia*. For Massumi, capital itself must be seen as a form of social agency, in the sense that it is a form of unmediated desire or a network of virtual relations. Any society actualizing that desire, he contends, constitutes a mix of fascist-paranoid and anarcho-schizoid relations, with a strong tendency towards the latter. It is then a short step for Massumi from capitalism's actualization of schizoid desire to a whole-hearted celebration of postmodernity's lack of depth, interiority, affect, belief and its creative self-becoming. Massumi rather belatedly acknowledges that the 'culture of "postmodernism" is incapable of rising to the challenge of disarming the final constraint of capitalism', because in a strikingly mechanistic and reductive formulation the 'two strictly coincide'.[36] It hardly needs mentioning that Marxism has always acknowledged the creative as well as the destructive potential of capitalism, but contrary to schizoanalysis it recognizes the need to *organize* resistance rather than blithely celebrate the free market in the hope that one day it will exhaust itself and collapse.

It would appear, then, that Jameson is correct to assign *Anti-Oedipus* a secondary position with respect to more totalizing and holistic modes of thought. It remains difficult, however, to see exactly how the *Anti-Oedipus* is in the spirit of Jameson's text, especially with regard to its detotalizing and schizophrenic impulse. For Jameson, Marxisms retains a position of theoretical priority through its 'semantic richness', or sheer capacity to subsume other theoretical discourses, and through the legitimation of its own primary concerns as other discourses are seen as essentially reactive and descriptive. This being said, *Anti-Oedipus* still appears to be reacting in the opposite direction to Jameson's totalizing and interpretative method. Jameson can only reconcile his text with that of the *Anti-Oedipus* through a very selective reading of the latter and the degree of selectivity involved has significant implications, I contend, for his project as a whole.

In a stringent critique of *Anti-Oedipus* Manfred Frank reflects upon its claims to 'proffer a theory of liberation', noting that 'one cannot revolutionise existing relations without referring to a "value" in the name of which what exists is negated.'[37] For Deleuze and Guattari, this value is simply desire itself. But, argues Frank, an insistence on the immanent presence of desire in the social field would appear to negate its ethical value:

> Such identification robs wish [desire] of the contra-factual character that would make possible its virtualization, i.e., guarantee its displacement on the level of representation, and would make the fictions – constantly quoted by the authors – into a quasi-ethical authority as opposed to existing repression. Wishes transposed into the imaginary act against the happiness that real society has left behind. By emphatically denying the counter-real character of those phantasies, Deleuze and Guattari condemn wish production to a frenzied approval of existing power.[38]

In other words, desire acquires its disruptive force and ethical value precisely by being 'other', by not being conflated with the real and thus being able to project, at the level of representation, an alternative to the real. Without such an alternative or counterfactual character, desire will only be able to endorse, albeit in a reactive and critical fashion, existing power structures.

Moreover, Deleuze and Guattari's conception of immanent desire raises an even more intractable problem for an emancipatory politics. Their appeal to the liberation of desire from all restrictions and prescriptions of structure and code implicitly conceals a conception of the subject who is to be liberated. Their own categorical and epistemological framework, however, destroys 'the conditions under which a free subject can be considered'.[39] Deleuze and Guattari insist that the unconscious is an orphan, it has no parents, therefore the productions of the unconscious or desiring-production are autoproductive; desire produces under its own momentum and seeks its own affirmation, it is a molecular phenomenon 'devoid of any goal or intention'.[40] Clearly there is no necessity for a subject in this process, not even as a by-product of the process, Deleuze and

Guattari's residual or nomadic subject, as the process has its own logic and momentum. A subject requires a degree of consistency and continuity over time if it is to be able to resist rather than be subjugated to existing repressive structures at each discontinuous moment. With *Anti-Oedipus*'s annihilation of the conditions of possibility for a renewal of the subject, it would be appropriate to ask in whose name liberation is called for.

Jameson's doctrine of a political unconscious as the uninterrupted narrative of collective or class struggle also requires a commitment and identification over time. It requires a certain stability of the subject as well as the historical potentiality for reconstituting itself, that is to say, the ability to conceptualize oneself as not merely an isolated and fragmented identity subjugated to the autoproduction of external forces but also as a subject, determined by social and historical forces, who at the same time through filiation with other subjects can actively transform and change those material forces. Indeed, one of the great strengths of Jameson's Marxism has always been his insistence on the centrality of class struggle and class analysis for any genuinely Marxist politics and theory. Deleuze and Guattari, though, reject any notion of class affiliation. For them there is only one class, that is, the class that accepts the axiomatics of capitalist society, be that positively or negatively. They insist that the primary issue is no longer the struggle between classes but the struggle 'between the class and those who are outside the class'.[41] While Deleuze and Guattari's conception of molecular politics and group formation may bear a superficial resemblance to Jameson's endorsement of 'alliance politics', the *Anti-Oedipus* remorselessly undermines the very conditions of possibility on which such alliances could be forged or on which the retheorization of the collective subject can be commenced.

The problem here is of a dual nature: first, the use Jameson makes of other discourses, and secondly, the claim for the theoretical primacy of Marxism. To take the latter issue first, clearly one text cannot say everything or cover every aspect of its area of study. Thus to criticize Jameson for not addressing particular concerns would seem somewhat overly scrupulous. On the other hand, Jameson's claim for Marxism's priority on the grounds of 'semantic richness' and that final untranscendable horizon, as well as his eclectic method, leaves him open to accusations of selectivity. In other words Jameson leaves out those areas of other discourses that do not fit quite so comfortably with his own perspective and narrative. Kenneth Burke has made just such claims with Jameson's reading of his own work.[42] A more telling example, however, is Jameson's deployment of Nietzsche, in *The Political Unconscious*.

Throughout the 1970s and 1980s post-structuralism in general trod a path through and beyond both Marx and Freud with the guidance of Nietzsche. *Anti-Oedipus* was no exception to this trend, although Deleuze's previous emphasis on the 'will-to-power' in *Nietzsche and Philosophy* had now been replaced by the self-affirmative force of desire as the quality of the strong. *The Political Unconscious* is also sensitive to the pervasive cultural presence of Nietzsche. More than any other of Jameson's texts, it is suffused with Nietzschean overtones. As Jonathan Arac has pointed out, the presence of Nietzsche plays an important strategic role for Jameson in that it enables him to build bridges with post-structuralist theory. In particular Jameson uses Nietzsche to offer a critique of the binary opposition and to transcend ethics:

> To move from Derrida to Nietzsche is to glimpse the possibility of a rather different interpretation of the binary opposition, according to which its positive and negative terms are ultimately assimilated by the mind as a distinction between good and evil. Not metaphysics but ethics is the informing ideology of the binary opposition; and we have forgotten the thrust of Nietzsche's thought and lost everything scandalous and virulent about it if we cannot understand how it is ethics itself which is the ideological vehicle and the legitimation of concrete structures of power and domination. (*PU*, 114)

Jameson goes on to say that the concept of good and evil is itself 'positional' and, as Nietzsche taught us, evil is associated with 'Otherness' and radical difference which 'seems to constitute a real and urgent threat to my existence' (*PU*, 115). The critique of ethics, suggests Jameson, is inextricably tied up with the problem of the individual subject, in the sense that if we are to transcend the categories of the individual subject then we must go 'beyond good and evil' and

> as Nietzsche taught us, the judgmental habit of ethical thinking, of ranging everything in the antagonistic categories of good and evil (or their other binary equivalents), is not merely an error but is objectively rooted in the inevitable and inescapable centredness of every individual consciousness or individual subject: what is good is what belongs to me, what is bad is what belongs to the Other. (*PU*, 234)

For Jameson we can only resolve this ethical double bind by historicizing both the ethical categories and our categories of the individual subject, in other words, by transcoding the ethical categories of good and evil to the political and historical categories of 'regressive' and 'progressive' or, as I shall discuss below, the terms 'ideological' and 'utopian'.

This reading of Nietzsche is by no means uncontentious and Arac identifies two specific problems with it. First, for Nietzsche ethics 'even as a means of legitimating domination . . . was not imposed from above';[43] ethics are in fact a tool of the slaves and not masters. Secondly, 'the positional analysis in the original situation did not for Nietzsche depend upon a fallacious "seems" . . . the masters did unquestionably threaten the existence of the slaves.'[44] Moreover, Nietzsche did not define all binary oppositions as ethical but in the first essay of *The Genealogy of Morals* considered 'the *difference* between two binary systems, that of good/bad and that of good/evil',[45] only the second being considered ethical. Both of these oppositions were considered by Nietzsche to be 'class-positional', that is to say they were '"political" notions, deriving from the domination or subjugation of one group by another'[46] and in this sense ethics constitutes a class weapon of the slaves against the masters. As in the *Anti-Oedipus*, the place of the subject in relation to this 'ethical class warfare' is as a by-product of the process, a fiction added after the fact. Arac writes, quoting Nietzsche:

> The notion of individual responsibility allowed for blame to be accorded to the activity of the strong and praise to the impotence of the weak: 'The subject . . . has perhaps been believed in hitherto more firmly than anything else on earth because it makes possible to the majority of mortals, the weak and oppressed of every kind, the sublime self-deception that interprets weakness as freedom.'[47]

In other words, Arac's reading of Nietzsche runs counter to Jameson's and, as with Jameson's tendency to suppress the presence of history and human labour in texts, we once more, suggests Arac, find in Jameson that tendency to repress the political in order to find it somewhere else. It would appear, therefore, that taken on its own terms Jameson's strategy of appropriation works but that it can do so only through the elision of real differences. Just as Deleuze and Guattari leave no space for the reconceptualization of the subject, of class or socialism, 'Nietzsche disrupts every "totality"'[48] and cannot be reincorporated into a new form of totalizing thought. Jameson's capacity to appropriate such diverse theoretical tendencies within his own Marxist horizon would therefore appear to be seriously in doubt.

Versions of a Libidinal Apparatus

So far I have focused on two aspects of Jameson's reading of *Anti-Oedipus*: the historicization of post-structuralism and the formulation of a concept of group fantasy. There is a third way, however, in which Jameson reads *Anti-Oedipus*, that is, as an aesthetic. Deleuze and Guattari reject orthodox barriers and distinctions between academic disciplines, drawing freely on literature to substantiate their ideas and insights, particularly writers such as Antonin Artaud, Henry Miller, Malcolm Lowry and D. H. Lawrence. They see in these writers 'a violence against syntax, a concerted destruction of the signifier'[49] as they attempted to break with accepted codes and conventions, facilitating an uninhibited flow and circulation of desire. Deleuze and Guattari are concerned not with the text as expression, in terms of what it signifies, but how it works, what is motivating the text. In this sense they suggest literature is inherently schizophrenic, it is 'a process and not a goal, a production and not an expression'.[50]

Literature though is not only a process of production but also an object of consumption and as such conforms to certain conventions and established practices. Deleuze and Guattari attribute to the commodification of literature the tendency towards ossification, or Oedipalization, of the texts' libidinal investments; but this is not, they argue, 'a question here of the personal oedipalization of the author and his readers, but of the *Oedipal form* to which one attempts to enslave the work itself, to make it this minor expressive activity that secretes ideology according to dominant codes'.[51] In other words, a text's 'form' attempts to check and restrain the free flow of desire, imposing on the multiplicity of libidinal investments a structure which is inherently ideological.

In *Fables of Aggression* Jameson develops Deleuze and Guattari's distinction between the molecular and molar levels of form production, designating the molecular level as 'the here-and-now of immediate perception or of local desire, the production-time of the individual sentence, the electrifying shock of the individual word or the individual brush-stroke' (*FA*, 8). Alternatively, the molar level 'designates all those large, abstract, mediate, and perhaps even empty and imaginary forms by which we seek to recontain the molecular: the mirage of the continuity of personal identity, the organizing unity of the psyche or the personality, the concept of society itself, and, not least, the notion of the organic unity of the work of art' (*FA*, 8). Since the advent of modernism, suggests Jameson, a gap has emerged between individual styles and the narrative systems or generic structures within which the isolated words and sentences are recontained. Thus we are able to read texts and view paintings from two distinct perspectives: either focusing on sentence construction and individual brush strokes; or standing back and reading the text in terms of narrative and generic conventions, or viewing the painting as itself one element in a history of forms. For Jameson, Deleuze and Guattari's distinction allows one to respect the specificity of both levels of the text while at the same time subjecting them to different kinds of analysis, specifically psychoanalytic and ideological analysis. Indeed, psychoanalysis provides a good model for this process whereby we shift from the molecular properties of an individual style to larger, molar, formal unities:

> I would rather see its enlargement as a process that drives the personal beyond itself, in much the same way that the x-ray process of psychoanalysis blows your private thoughts and fantasies up to the point at which they become impersonal again, the algebra or syntax of the unconscious.[52]

Jameson's recourse to psychoanalysis is by no means arbitrary, the incorporation of yet one more discourse in Jameson's own will-to-style. On the contrary, the various antitheses which psychoanalysis projects between the sexual and the political, between childhood and society, archaic fantasy and ideological commitment reflect for Jameson 'an objective dissociation in contemporary experience' (*FA*, 9). This dissociation finds cultural expression through the modernist emphasis on individual style and in particular the fragmentation of the surface of the canvas or the narrative structure. We experience, suggests Jameson, 'a kind of psychic "division of labour", the advanced form of which can be observed in just this reification and autonomization of the various senses from one another'.[53] Psychoanalysis, however, has frequently been used to legitimate psychologizing and subjectivizing forms of ideology which seek to explain all political commitment and social relations as merely questions of psychic states or psychological projection. Jameson's attention to the specificity of distinct levels of experience avoids this kind of psychological reductionism and at the same time does not go down the path of the *Anti-Oedipus*, simply repudiating the findings of psychoanalysis. Therefore, and contrary to the whole thrust of the *Anti-Oedipus*, Jameson proposes to isolate from the psychoanalytic material proper an autonomous narrative moment with its own specificity and dynamism, the function of which 'in psychic life is then to win some distance from the ruses by which the unconscious can be seen to make use of it' (*FA*, 9).

What Jameson is proposing is the formulation of a 'libidinal apparatus', or 'an empty form or structural matrix in which a charge of free-floating and inchoate fantasy – both ideological and psychoanalytic – can suddenly crystallize, and find the articulated figuration essential for its social actuality and psychic effectivity' (*FA*, 95). For Jameson, this 'empty form' or 'structural matrix' is essentially a narrative structure or, more precisely, an outmoded narrative structure which allows for the articulation of desire through the reinvestment of the symbolically empty coordinates of a now redundant narrative system. Two examples of this libidinal apparatus can be found in Jameson's reading of Wyndham Lewis in *Fables of Aggression*, subtitled *Wyndham Lewis, the Modernist as Fascist*, and the chapter on Balzac and desire from *The Political Unconscious*. Jameson reads Lewis's early work as exemplary of the national allegory, in the sense that 'the use of national types projects an essentially allegorical mode of representation, in which the individual characters figure those more abstract national characteristics which are read as their inner essence' (*FA*, 90).

Such a narrative system though will have certain preconditions, or 'logic of content', in other words, conditions which are not causal in a crudely deterministic way but which must exist prior to the text and without which the emergence of the text is inconceivable. Thus Lewis's 1918 novel *Tarr* can be said to 'presuppose not merely the nation-state itself as the basic functional unit of world politics, but also the objective existence of a system of nation-states, the international diplomatic machinery of pre-World-War-I Europe' (*FA*, 94). That is, precisely the system of nation-states that the First World War brought to a close. After 1918 the subjects of history were no longer nation-states as such but the transnational forces of Communism and Fascism and the emergence of the Superstate. Therefore, suggests Jameson, the national allegory can be seen as a formal attempt to bridge the gap between existential experience and the tendency of monopoly Capitalism to develop on a global, transnational scale. With the decline of the older diplomatic and political system this particular narrative form will become redundant as a way of recounting either psychological or social events. The older narrative system now evacuated of its specific historical resonance will be freed up for new ideological and libidinal investments:

> the empty matrix of national allegory is then immediately seized on by hitherto unformulable impulses which invest its structural positions and, transforming the whole narrative system into a virtual allegory of the

fragmented psyche itself, now reach back to overdetermine the resonance of this now increasingly layered text. (*FA*, 96)

In this second-level allegory, the characters which previously stood as figures for national types will now be seen as figures for the psyche, its impulses and drives, and project a whole new sexual ideology. I will not consider Lewis's 'openly misogynistic' but, according to Jameson at least, by no means phallocentric sexual ideology here, as Lewis offers but one version of a libidinal apparatus, and for each artist and writer it would be possible to map on to their formal systems and mode of representation similar libidinal investments. Jameson's own analyses range from Flaubert to the paintings of De Kooning and Cézanne.[54] I shall restrict myself below to his reading of Balzac.

In a series of brilliant studies[55] Jameson analyses the motivating device behind Balzac's narrative production as not so much the desire for money or wealth but 'desire' itself. As I pointed out above this is not merely a psychological insight but a recognition of the formal convention that enables Balzac to construct his narratives; 'the novelistic creation of Balzac rests in general on the premise that human existence is at all times motivated by *appetency*, that is, by a clear desire that always poses a precise object before itself.'[56] In *The Political Unconscious* Jameson examines two of Balzac's texts, *The Old Maid* and *The Black Sheep*, specifically in terms of the relationship between desire and Realism, and the problematic relationship between subject and object of desire within classical realist narrative structures. Classical realism is, for better or worse, associated with the notion of an 'omniscient narrator', and for Jameson the significance and value of this particular form of narration lie in the way that it operates posthumously, after the fact. In other words, it is an after-effect of classical narration, signifying a closure of the narrative, which in turn projects 'something like an ideological mirage in the form of notions of fortune, destiny, and providence' (*PU*, 154), in the sense that there appears to be a certain inevitability about the sequence of events that take place. It is this narrative structure which Balzac inherits and at the same time invests with new forms of libidinal energy.

If desire itself is a constitutive feature of Balzac's narrative structure, the positing of an 'object of desire' within a realist narrative paradigm presents specific formal difficulties. The signifying value of objects of desire, writes Jameson, 'is determined by their narrative position: a narrative element becomes desirable whenever a character is observed to desire it' (*PU*, 156). Balzac's texts, however, predate notions of the centred subject, and thus we are not presented with a single privileged perspective but a multiplicity of perspectives. Balzac's narratives lack an identifiable hero as such and, therefore, the subject is decentred through 'a rotation of character centres which deprives each of them in turn of any privileged status' (*PU*, 161), or what Jameson calls a 'character system'.[57] Within Balzac's narratives a structural reversal takes place whereby an object becomes desirable not because it is desired by a particular character but because it is desirable in its own right. Balzac must 'validate or accredit the object as desirable, before the narrative process can function properly' (*PU*, 156). Thus the Cormon townhouse, in Balzac's novella *The Old Maid*, functions as the quintessential object of desire, not because we can attribute it to the desire of a single character but rather it is *the* central object around which the character system as a whole revolves and motivates the narrative itself. According to Jameson, the desire 'here comes before us in a peculiarly anonymous state which makes a strangely absolute claim on us' (*PU*, 156); it is not so much the desire for a particular object but a figure for desire in general and in particular for what Jameson calls the 'Utopian Impulse'.

The peculiarity of this particular desire is all too evident, suggests Jameson, when we shift from its landed manifestation to its actantial figuration in the character of Mademoiselle Cormon herself, who is 'comic, grotesque, and desirable all at once' (*PU*, 158). Therefore,

> to insist on the Utopian dimension of this particular desire is evidently to imply that this particular comic narrative is also an *allegorical* structure, in which the sexual 'letter' of the farce must itself be read as a figure for the longing for landed retreat and personal fulfilment as well as for the resolution of social and historical contradiction. (*PU*, 158)

In short, the wish-fulfilling fantasy or daydream functions at two levels simultaneously: as the imaginary resolution of the specific individual fantasy as well as the symbolic resolution of a real social and historical contradiction.

Jameson's libidinal apparatus marks a significant advance over previous psychologizing approaches to literature in that it does not reduce the cultural text to a symptom of the author's psyche or life history but rather endows a private fantasy structure with what Jameson calls 'a quasi-material inertness' (*FA*, 10) which has its own logic and dynamism. Jameson's conception of the libidinal apparatus is indebted to the work of Jean-François Lyotard, but diverges from Lyotard in one important sense. Jameson writes:

For Lyotard the 'dispositif' is what captures and immobilizes desire, rather than as in my use, what allows it investment and articulation. Lyotard's emphasis is on the ways in which 'desire' breaks through such 'dispositifs,' rather than on the social and historical conditions of possibility of the libidinal apparatus. (*FA*, 10 n8)

There is no adequate translation for *dispositif*. Geoffrey Bennington translates it as a 'set-up' in the sense of the structures and representations through which libidinal energy is channelled and regulated; however, dispositif is not a particular 'set-up' which defines a given desire, 'but a certain desire which produces a set-up'.[58] Libidinal analysis, then, is not the same as psychological or psychoanalytic analysis, in the sense that 'libidinal investments are essentially matters of shifting relationships, whose content is not fixed: the representational frame, however . . . seeks to freeze this mobility and to endow it with some more permanent, quasi-material symbolic value'.[59] The libidinal apparatus can be seen as an independent structure, and in terms of a given fantasy it is a structure for which we can write its various permutations, forms of closure and internal limits. In short, the process of libidinal analysis entails the mapping of these relationships as they find figuration in the text. This, suggests Jameson, would 'allow us to reverse the traditional priorities of psychoanalytic and psychologizing interpretation' (*FA*, 11), in that one is no longer reducing textual material to a particular psyche or psychic structure but rather analysing the way in which certain relationships, impulses and responses can achieve figuration through the text. What is meant by this will become clearer if we consider Jameson's defence of the use of biographical material in literary analysis.

Jameson distinguishes his use of biography from previous forms of biographical criticism, that is, the genetic and the existential psychobiography. The genetic version, according to Jameson, treated the author's biography as essentially an archive within which to discover 'the source, model, or original of this or that character, event, or situation', while the existential version saw the 'life' as 'yet one more text by the same author, no more, but no less privileged than his other works' (*PU*, 179). Jameson, on the other hand, uses the 'life' as 'the traces and symptoms of a fundamental family situation which is at one and the same time a fantasy master narrative' (*PU*, 180). This unconscious master narrative is not a fixed form but an unstable and contradictory structure which will be constantly re-enacted in the author's narratives as they attempt to find some form of resolution. The biographical details therefore provide the matrix or set of co-ordinates within which the narrative will be produced and positioned.

But, as Deleuze and Guattari insisted, the familial situation is not merely a private, psychoanalytic or psychological affair but also a social one and we must grasp 'the family situation as the mediation of class relationships in society at large, and . . . the parental functions as socially coded or symbolic positions as well' (*PU*, 180). The fantasy master narrative can be seen to function as a symbolic act in the same way as other cultural artefacts and enact the same kind of imaginary resolution. Again, therefore, we must respect the specific levels of analysis and not reduce questions of social relations to individual psychological determinates. On one level the isolated text acts as the wish-fulfilling fantasy of a specific subject, while on another it is the actualization of its own conditions of possibility. According to Jameson, it 'becomes a significant political "principle" [that] the production of the fantasy-text knows a peculiar "unconscious" reflexivity, as, in the process of generating itself, it must simultaneously secure its own ideological positions' (*PU*, 182). In other words, a text must produce, or presuppose, a complex ideological system in order to indulge its own specific wish-fulfilling fantasy or daydream. Just as Lewis's national allegory was predicated on the existence of a system of nation-states, the Oedipalization of given texts presupposes that the conditions of Oedipal relations exist.

The libidinal apparatus, therefore, can be seen to forestall the reductive psychologizing of applied psychoanalysis and, furthermore, to restore the counterfactual dimension of desire and the unconscious that the *Anti-Oedipus* erased by reinscribing the gap between the symbolic and real. Jameson's insistence on the realization of the conditions of possibility of a given text does not conflate the symbolic with the real but consistently holds it before us as a problematic which cannot be wished away but at the same time marks the limit of thought.

The Dialectic of Ideology and Utopia

I suggested in the previous chapter that Jameson's three horizons of interpretation shared certain affinities with Lacan's three orders: the imaginary, the symbolic and the real. This analogy was underscored through Jameson's conception of History as an absent cause as well as by the structural function of contradiction and desire in both his and Lacan's systems respectively. Lacan also plays a significant role in another area of Jameson's theory, that is, in relation to the question of ideology and the problem of the subject. In a 1983 article, 'Science

versus Ideology', Jameson defends the relevance of the old opposition within Marxism, most recently restaged by Althusser, between
science and ideology. The problem is not whether Marxism can be
defended as a science, which, for Jameson, it assuredly can, but
whether Marxism has a theory of 'ideology'. Any Marxism, he argues,
that is reduced to a method, the science of society or a theory of
history, is worthless. Marxism cannot be severed from practice, from
political struggle in the present and the need to project alternative
visions of the future. This projection of a qualitatively different image
of the future is the ideological function of Marxism. Marxism, then,
has a science but what it needs to re-invent is a properly Marxist
ideology, the prophetic discourse of the *Communist Manifesto*, or what
Jameson now defines as the Utopian Impulse.

In his earlier essay, 'Imaginary and Symbolic in Lacan: Marxism,
Psychoanalytic Criticism and the Problem of the Subject', Jameson
first sketched these ideas and suggested that there were lessons to be
learnt from the Lacanian distinction between 'science' and 'truth',
and in particular the 'Lacanian conception of science as a historically
original form of the decentring of the subject',[60] rather than as the site
of truth. Both Marxism and psychoanalysis are constituted by a body
of knowledge which Jameson and many psychoanalysts define as
'scientific knowledge', but neither position embodies 'the "truth" of
the subject'.[61] While Lacanian psychoanalysis had begun the process
of developing a properly psychoanalytic theory of language and the
subject, Marxism in the late 1970s and early 1980s had still to address
these fundamental problems. The bridge between Marxism and
Lacanian psychoanalysis was initially forged through Althusser's
well-known reformulation of ideology as the imaginary relation of
individuals to their real conditions of existence. According to Jameson:

> Ideology conceived in this sense is therefore the place of the insertion of
> the subject in those realms or orders – the Symbolic (or in other words the
> synchronic network of society itself, with its Kinship-type system of places
> and roles), and the Real (or in other words the diachronic evolution of
> History itself, the realm of time and death) both of which radically
> transcend individual experience in their very structure. But if this is how
> ideology is understood, then it is clear that it has a function to play in every
> conceivable social order, and not merely those of what Marx called 'pre-
> history' or class societies: the ideological representation must rather be
> seen as that indispensable mapping fantasy or narrative by which the
> individual subject invents a 'lived' relationship with collective systems
> which otherwise by definition exclude him insofar as he or she is born into
> a pre-existent social form and its pre-existent language.[62]

The weakness of Althusser's formulation, however, was that it focused exclusively on the individual subject and how individuals were 'interpellated' as ideological subjects through the operation of the dominant ideology. What Althusser's formulation lacks is any mediation by class and conception of 'class consciousness'. For Jameson, Althusser's notion of ideology is not the final word but simply the first steps towards developing a properly Marxist ideology. Furthermore, Althusser's rather free use of Lacan does not exhaust the possibilities for a psychoanalytically informed conception of ideology. Lacan's conception of the decentred subject, a subject that is structurally distanced, or alienated, from both language and the Real, offers a model of collective ideology, argues Jameson, that is more than 'merely' suggestive. Jameson cites Lacan's theory of 'foreclusion' and the discourse of the analyst as potential ways in which psychoanalysis can inform a Marxist theory of ideology, but unfortunately he does not develop these ideas.[63]

For Jameson, then, a renewed theory of ideology needs to transcend both the aporias of the bourgeois-centred subject and the anarchism and indeterminate flux of the schizoid-subject. What is required, he suggests, is a 'renewal of Utopian thinking, of creative speculation as to the place of the subject at the other end of historical time, in a social order which has put behind it class organization, commodity production and the market, alienated labor, and the implacable determinism of an historical logic beyond the control of humanity'.[64] Such a situation would at once avoid privileging a particular form of subjectivity while at the same time forestalling the excesses of post-structuralism. Placing the subject at the other end of historical time, however, would not appear to solve the problem as such but simply to displace it and indefinitely defer the confrontation. Jameson's conception of utopian thought also raises a number of unanswered questions.

Marxism's conception of ideology as 'false consciousness' or as 'structural limitation', argues Jameson, represents the historic originality of its negative dialectic, that is to say, its negative demystifying hermeneutic. But at the same time Marxism also has a tradition of a positive or redemptive hermeneutic and it is, suggests Jameson, within this arena that 'some noninstrumental conception of culture may be tested' (*PU*, 286). Jameson identifies in this tradition Bakhtin's notions of dialogism and the carnivalesque, and the Frankfurt School's concept of 'strong memory', but what he is particularly concerned with is Ernst Bloch's ideal of hope or 'Utopian Impulse'. Following

Bloch, Jameson argues that the ideological must be grasped at one and the same time as the utopian:

> In this sense, to project an imperative to thought in which the ideological would be grasped as somehow at one with the Utopian, and the Utopian at one with the ideological, is to formulate a question to which a collective dialectic is the only conceivable answer. (*PU*, 286–7)

At its simplest this dialectic operates as a form of 'compensatory exchange'. For example, theories of the manipulatory aspects of the media, and of 'mass' culture in general, must account for the address-ee's acquiescence if they are not to posit an entirely passive spectator. Audiences are not simply duped into consuming reactionary culture but derive pleasure from it, and therefore the addresser must be providing some form of compensatory gratification in return for the spectators' acquiescence. For Jameson, ideological manipulation and utopian gratification are inseparable aspects of *all* cultural texts. The question inevitably arises: all texts? Even the most overtly reaction-ary? The proposition that all cultural texts contain a utopian dimen-sion is for Jameson the logical extension of 'the proposition that *all* class consciousness – or in other words, all ideology in the strongest sense, including the most exclusive forms of ruling-class conscious-ness just as much as that of oppositional or oppressed classes – is in its very nature Utopian' (*PU*, 289). Class consciousness emerges from the struggle between various groups or classes, and therefore class consciousness is always defined in relation to another class. In this sense class consciousness, of whatever class, is utopian to the extent that it expresses the unity of a collectivity. Jameson, however, insists that this proposition is allegorical to the extent that 'all such collectivities are themselves *figures* for the ultimate concrete collec-tive life of an achieved Utopian or classless society' (*PU*, 291). Thus even the most reactionary forms of ruling-class culture and ideology are utopian to the extent that they affirm collective solidarity.

Terry Eagleton argues that 'Jameson's startling claim to discern a proleptic image of utopia in any human collectivity whatsoever, which would presumably encompass racist rallies'[65] is ridiculously gullible or faintly perverse. While Jameson would insist that a racist rally is indeed Utopian to the extent that it projects a (white) collectivity, this must be seen as a compensatory projection rather than an 'anticipatory' one. In other words, racism could be said to offer forms of compensation and gratification for present social problems: unem-ployment, bad housing, lack of services, etc., but in so far as it does not project a fully classless society it is not a positive anticipation of Utopia. The question of distinguishing between compensatory and anticipatory projections, though, is problematic. Bloch's notion of Utopia as 'anticipatory consciousness' rests on the definition of Utopia as a function rather than a matter of a particular form or content. The distinction between what is an anticipatory and what is a compensatory projection of Utopia, however, can only be made in practice through reference to its content. With the elision of the functional property of utopian thought, one can easily conceive of a situation whereby Jameson may interpret a racist rally as compensatory, but the racists themselves would see it as being anticipatory. In which case the heuristic value of the concept would appear to be seriously compromised.

4

Postmodernism and Late Capitalism

In the preface to *Marxism and Form* Jameson charted the changed terrain in which Marxist criticism found itself in the early 1970s. In particular he pointed to the development of the postindustrial society, the concealment of class structure through an expanded media, the fragmentation of the subject, the disjunction between our existential or quotidian experience and the global expansion of the capitalist system, the effacing of the final traces of production by an increasingly image dominated society, and finally the decline and dissolution of metaphysics. In retrospect Jameson's analysis can be seen to identify all the essential characteristics of what was to become by the mid-1980s the postmodern debate. In his introduction to *Jameson, Postmodernism, Critique*, Douglas Kellner suggests that such passages in Jameson's earlier work provide 'anticipations' of 'lacunae' in his theoretical project and of his later theoretical concerns. In other words, the preface can be seen as a description of postmodernism *avant la lettre*.

A strong case for such a reading can clearly be made. As we have already seen, *Marxism and Form* was essentially concerned with familiarizing a North American academic readership with an unfamiliar tradition of European Marxist cultural theorists. *The Prison House of Language* provided a similar critical survey of an alternative tradition of Russian Formalism and French structuralism. A decade later *The Political Unconscious* provided Jameson's most sustained intervention in contemporary theoretical debates, specifically the contemporary French theories of Althusserian Marxism, poststructuralism and deconstruction. What was missing from all these texts was an analysis of the contemporary situation itself and Jameson appeared to be calling for this in his preface to *Marxism and Form*. In particular, *The Political Unconscious* and *Fables of Aggression* could be seen, as Kellner writes, to 'knock on the door of the present but neither crosses the threshold of our own historical milieu',[1] as both texts focus on literary modernism. This is not to say that Jameson was unconcerned at this juncture with other forms of cultural practice or contemporary culture, as his continuing writings on film, painting and science fiction testify, but rather that until the early 1980s the centre of Jameson's theoretical project remained 'modernism'.

If we follow this intellectual and theoretical trajectory a little further, it would be feasible to argue that with the publication of *The Political Unconscious* Jameson's aim of establishing a strong Marxist presence in the American academy had been achieved. Therefore, no longer needing to argue the very legitimacy of his own discourse, Jameson could pursue that long deferred project of theorizing the contemporary cultural scene, as he did with characteristic bravura and style in his influential 1984 essay 'Postmodernism, or, The Cultural Logic of Late Capitalism'.[2] For Kellner, this text presents:

> the culmination of a series of historical and theoretical studies which provide part of the methodology, framework, and theoretical analyses requisite for a theory of contemporary society which Jameson conceptualizes as a product of a specific historical trajectory: the transition from a discrete national system of state/monopoly capitalism to an interlocking system multinational corporate capitalism.[3]

Thus, far from being a radical departure for Jameson, his conceptualization of postmodernism represents the culmination of 'his efforts to introduce, defend, and develop the Marxian theory in a climate and situation often ignorant of or hostile to the radical tradition of which Marxism is a key component'.[4]

Kellner's narrative is a persuasive one and I shall seek to both develop and problematize it here. As Kellner writes, 'to understand any of Jameson's texts one needs to grasp their place in the history of the Jamesonian *oeuvre*, as articulations of a relatively stable and coherent theoretical project.'[5] The implications of this statement, however, are rather different depending on whether one places the emphasis on *relatively* or *stable and coherent*. Jameson's project did not take place in isolation but represents a response to changing theoretical, political and cultural demands. An overemphasis on the 'oeuvrism' of his work can all too often ignore the extent to which his work changed to meet these demands. The 1971 preface, for example, identifies at once the specific context which *Marxism and Form* addresses and, at the same time, what differentiates this particular situation from the pre-Second World War era of class struggle and Popular Front cultural politics. Within this context, here defined as postindustrial rather than late capitalism, Jameson called for a revitalized form of Marxist criticism, a Marxism for which the great themes of Hegel's philosophy – the relationship of part to whole, the opposition between concrete and abstract, the concept of totality, the dialectic of appearance and essence, the interaction between subject and object – are once again the order of the day' (*MF*, xix).

Two decades later in his 1991 Welleck lectures, published as *The Seeds of Time*, Jameson speaks in a markedly different tone, characterizing postmodernism as a culture more amenable to the concept of antinomy than dialectical contradiction; a culture in which oppositions remain opposed rather than reconciled at some higher level of abstraction as with the classical dialectic. Therefore those 'great themes' of Hegelian philosophy that seemed so much the order of the day in 1971 no longer appear in the least appropriate for the analysis of postmodern culture. Jameson himself acknowledges this situation and the need for his own discourse to evolve to meet that challenge. Thus in *Late Marxism* he notes that to describe the dialectic in terms of self-consciousness or reflexivity, as he did in *Marxism and Form*, is but one way of rendering it and no longer necessarily the most effective:

> its effectiveness depends very much on the freshness of this rhetoric of self-consciousness, which, at a time when 'consciousness' itself has been called back into question, as a concept or a category, has apparently ceased, to convey very much. Reflexivity . . . is part of the baggage of a modernist thinking no longer very authoritative in the postmodernist era. (*LM*, 25)

Superficially, there may seem to be a certain symmetry, or continuity, to Jameson's return to Adorno and dialectical aesthetics after two decades of skirmishes with structuralism, post-structuralism and postmodernism; but for Jameson the Adorno of the 1990s is unambiguously not the Adorno of the 1960s and 1970s and those concepts which appeared so appropriate to a culture of the 1970s must now be rethought in the light of a changed situation.[6]

Moreover, it is not simply a question of language and terminology that has changed with the advent of postmodernism; the problematic itself has radically altered. In the introduction to *Postmodernism, or, The Cultural Logic of Late Capitalism* Jameson enumerates the four principal themes of his book: 'interpretation, Utopia, survivals of the modern, and returns of the repressed of historicity' (*PLC*, xv). These are all familiar Jamesonian themes; what is new is that they have now been, supposedly, invalidated by the very concept of the postmodern. Postmodernism, as it is characterized by Jean-François Lyotard, marks a scepticism towards all grand, universal narratives such as the Enlightenment view of progress, psychoanalysis and, above all, the Marxian narrative of emancipation. In a postmodern world, according to Lyotard, these narratives no longer have credibility or legitimation.[7] The postmodern condition, then, signals the end of Marxism's traditional historical narrative and throws into question not only Jameson's own theoretical project but the very status of Marxism itself. In short, the argument runs that if postmodernism marks a structural break, or systemic transformation, the path leads inexorably to post-Marxism in one form or another. On the other hand, if no such break has taken place, the Marxian critique of capitalism and its emancipatory narrative retain their political and explanatory force. Jameson, characteristically, refuses both of these options, accepting that a structural transformation has taken place, but one that does not invalidate the Marxian narrative.

In this chapter I examine Jameson's conception of postmodernism as *the cultural logic of late capitalism*, initially focusing on his characterization of postmodernism as a modification of our sense of time and space. I then consider the use of postmodernism as a *periodizing* concept, insisting that Mandel's theory of 'long waves' of capitalist development cannot be used to at once inspire and confirm Jameson's theory, since his own analysis of postmodernism appears to undermine the non-synchronicity of modes of production that this theory rests on. I will explore how this discrepancy between Jameson's theoretical and critical imperatives operates in relation to an analysis of what Jameson sees as the paradigmatic postmodern form, video. Finally, I suggest that a less dichotomous conception of the relationship between modernism and postmodernism may be more useful for an understanding of postmodern culture. Jameson's influential analysis of contemporary architecture and his developing spatial theory will be addressed in the following chapter and will be only briefly alluded to here.

The Cultural Logic of Late Capitalism

Jameson's seminal 1984 essay on postmodernism was itself a montage of two previous essays: 'The Politics of Theory: Ideological

Positions in the Postmodern Debate' and 'Postmodernism and Consumer Society'. In the first of these essays Jameson sought to map the various ideological positions that were emerging around the concept of postmodernism. For Jameson, the problem of postmodernism was seen from the outset as both an aesthetic and a political one. He argued that all positions adopted in relation to postmodernism could be shown to project particular visions of history:

> Indeed, the very enabling premise of the debate turns on an initial, strategic, presupposition about our social system: to grant some historic originality to a postmodernist culture is also implicitly to affirm some radical structural difference between what is sometimes called consumer society and earlier moments of the capitalism from which it emerged. (*PLC*, 55)

In other words, defining a position on postmodernism necessarily involves one in taking a position on the modernism that preceded it as well as a conception of the nature of the relation between these moments and the transition from one to another.

Jameson identified four principal positions as having emerged in the postmodern debate: the pro-postmodernist/antimodernist stance associated with the architects Charles Jencks and Robert Venturi, as well as writers such as Tom Wolfe; the anti-postmodernist/pro-modernist stance associated with the American critic Hilton Kramer and the journal *New Criterion* and also the work of Jürgen Habermas; the pro-modernist/pro-postmodernist position articulated by Jean-François Lyotard; and finally the rather bleak and pessimistic antimodernist/anti-postmodernist view exemplified by the work of the Venetian architectural historian Manfredo Tafuri. The first two of these positions, argues Jameson, are characterized by their acceptance, be it positively or negatively, of the new term, postmodernism, which is itself tantamount to an acceptance of a break between the moments of modernism and postmodernism. The latter two, however, call into question the category of postmodernism by repudiating any notion of a historical break and seeing the present moment as a continuation of modernism; or, in the case of Lyotard, projecting postmodernism indefinitely backwards. At this juncture Jameson eschews what he sees as these essentially moralizing positions, either stigmatizing postmodernism as corrupt and hedonistic, the latest form of cultural degeneration, or alternatively hailing it as a positive form of innovation and as culturally and aesthetically healthy. Repudiating ahistorical moralizing, Jameson calls for a genuinely historical and dialectical analysis:

The point is that we are *within* the culture of postmodernism to the point where its facile repudiation is as impossible as any equally facile celebration of it is complacent and corrupt . . . it seems more appropriate to assess the new cultural production within the working hypothesis of a general modification of culture itself within the social restructuration of late capitalism as a system. (*PLC*, 62)

Jameson defers such an analysis in the present context. His initial position, however, raises two of the recurrent themes and persistent question marks over his theorization of postmodernism. Taking into consideration that this essay was written in 1982, before the term 'postmodernism' was quite as ubiquitous and generally accepted as it is today, one could legitimately ask to what extent we are already 'within' the culture of postmodernism and how pervasive this new cultural production is. Or, to anticipate Jameson's later terminology, to what extent is postmodernism a cultural 'dominant'? The second issue is the rather more difficult question of the nature of the relationship between this new cultural production and the general modification of culture and social restructuration of the capitalist system. I shall return to these questions below, but for the present I would note that Jameson's acceptance of the term postmodernism, following his own criteria, implicitly posits a 'radical structural difference' from the preceding moment of capitalism.

Jameson's characterization of postmodernism at this stage amounts to little more than a heterogeneous list of names, styles and forms: a problem of definition, he notes, inherent within the very concept itself, of which there will be as many local variants as there were of modernism proper. His first, acknowledgedly limited, attempt at a description of key features of postmodernism is to be found in 'Postmodernism and Consumer Society'. As his title indicates, one of the strong influences on Jameson's conception of postmodernism is Baudrillard's work on 'consumer society'. In his early work Baudrillard developed a critique of the Marxian distinction between use value and exchange value, arguing that the distinction between use and exchange value rests on latent assumptions of an anthropological conception of 'need'. Such a conception of need, argued Baudrillard, is no longer appropriate for our understanding of contemporary consumer society where consumption has nothing to do with the satisfaction of needs but is rather an 'active mode of relations . . . a systematic mode of activity and a global response on which our whole cultural system is founded'.[8] In other words, the objects of consumption are not material goods but rather 'signs'. The transformation of the object into the systematic status of signs entails a correlative transformation of human relations as relations of consumption. Baudrillard suggests that the only way to move beyond a political economy which is grounded in need and to understand the commodity structure of consumer society is to see that use value no longer corresponds to human need; indeed there is no longer use value as such, just exchange value. Jameson does not fully endorse this complete eclipse of use value but does suggest that postmodernism represents a further intensification of exchange value over use value.

Jameson's characterization of postmodernism emphasizes postmodernism's new experience of space and time and in particular its key features of pastiche and schizophrenia. In the former case he contrasts modernism's use of parody and quotation with the postmodern practice of pastiche. Parody, he suggests, plays on the uniqueness of a style; it 'seizes on [its] idiosyncrasies and eccentricities to produce an imitation which mocks the original'[9] but in doing so it retains an implicit linguistic norm against which the original is being judged. Above all, parody retains a subversive 'other' voice. As an imitation of a particular unique individual or personal style, parody also rests on assumptions about the nature of the subject which, since the post-structural dissolution or decentring of the subject, are no longer held to be tenable. Pastiche, on the other hand, while sharing many of these features, is in a sense a neutral practice. It lacks parody's 'ulterior motive', its satirical impulse and any sense of a norm against which the original is to be compared. Language has now disintegrated into a proliferation of private languages and discourses. Postmodern literature, suggests Jameson, does not simply 'quote' popular texts as a modernist such as Joyce may have done, but rather it incorporates those texts within itself to the extent that the boundaries between them are effaced. This effacing of key boundaries, or 'de-differentiation' as the process has been called, between previously distinct cultural realms, specifically between 'high art' and 'mass' or 'popular' culture, is frequently cited as one of the most significant democratizing and popularizing features of postmodernism.

The full aesthetic realization of postmodern pastiche is to be found in what Jameson designates as 'nostalgia films'. Nostalgia films are in their narrowest sense films about the past – or specific generational pasts – but more broadly would seem to comprise a whole range of metageneric films, remakes, and big budget glossy productions. The notion is as much to do with form and the quality of image as it is with any ostensible content. The classical nostalgia film, writes Jameson, 'while evading its present altogether, registered its historicist deficiency by losing itself in mesmerized fascination in lavish images of specific generational pasts' (*PLC*, 296) – the privileged generational moments being the 1930s and 1950s. Postmodernism pastiche is symptomatic, contends Jameson, of a general loss of historicity, and our incapacity to achieve aesthetic representations of our own current experience' (*PLC*, 21). I return to the central issues of spatial disorientation and the inability of individual subjects to represent or map themselves in relation to the new global network of multinational capitalism in the next chapter.

In the last chapter I suggested that postmodern temporality is essentially 'schizophrenic'. Taking his definition of schizophrenia from Lacan, Jameson deploys this category in a descriptive rather than a clinical sense. Lacan saw schizophrenia as primarily a language disorder, a failure to accede fully into the symbolic order, the realm of speech and language; it, therefore, represents a break in the chain of signification. For Lacan our experience of temporality is an effect of language: as words and sentences move in time, they have a past and a future, as well as a present. The schizophrenic's failure to fully grasp language articulation will affect their experience of temporality, or, more accurately, they will experience a lack of temporal continuity. The schizophrenic, therefore, is condemned to a perpetual present, an 'experience of isolated, disconnected, discontinuous material signifiers which fail to link up into a coherent sequence'.[10] This lack of temporal continuity has the corresponding effect of making the present more intense and vivid, the signifier in isolation becoming ever more material or 'literal'. These twin features of pastiche and schizophrenia result in postmodernism's pervasive flattening of space and the displacement of diachronic time with synchronic immanence.

In 'Postmodernism, or, The Cultural Logic of Late Capitalism' Jameson extends this analysis, arguing that a fundamental mutation has taken place 'both in the object world itself – now become a set of texts or simulacra – and in the disposition of the subject' (*PLC*, 9). This mutation finds expression through the 'waning of affect', which is not to suggest that all affect, all emotion and feeling, or all subjectivity has vanished, but that the old autonomous centred subject has now been displaced and fragmented and with it a shift has taken place in the emotional ground tone. Concepts such as anxiety and 'alienation' no longer seem appropriate to describe the psychic experiences of the decentred and fragmented subject, experiences which can best be described as schizophrenic intensities. In terms of the object world, postmodernism is, following Baudrillard, a culture of the image and simulacrum, that is to say, it is essentially depthless. The theoretical correlative of this has been the discrediting of all the old depth models: the Hermeneutic of inside and outside, the Existential of authenticity and inauthenticity, and Freudian of latent and manifest, the Dialectic of essence and appearance, and more recently, that of the Semiotic signifier and signified. These older models have now been replaced by notions of textuality, which is not simply a movement from deep structure to surface but rather the play of multiple surfaces as well as the spaces that exist between surfaces or texts. According to Jameson, a fundamental restructuration of historical experience has taken place; historicity has been replaced by 'historicism', or 'the random cannibalization of all the styles of the past, the play of random stylistic allusion, and in general . . . the increasing primacy of the "neo"' (*PLC*, 18). In this sense the past has become nothing but a vast collection of images, a multitudinous photographic simulacrum. Adopting Guy Debord's famous slogan, 'the image has become the final form of commodity reification,' Jameson suggests that the past as 'referent' has been gradually bracketed until all that we are left with now are texts.

The Periodization of Late Capitalism

For Jameson, the term postmodernism does not designate a particular style but rather a periodizing concept which serves to 'correlate the emergence of new formal features in culture with the emergence of a new type of social life and a new economic order'.[11] This new economic order emerged post-Second World War, that is to say, somewhere around the late 1940s or early 1950s for the United States, and in the late 1950s for Europe. The key transitional decade, though, is seen to be the 1960s. Jameson describes this new economic order as variously 'modernization', 'postindustrial or consumer society', 'the society of the media or the spectacle', 'multinational capitalism' and finally 'late capitalism'. Postmodernism retains many of the features of high modernism – for example, its self-consciousness, the disruption of narrative forms, its cultural eclecticism and sense of parody – but to see postmodernism simply as a continuation of modernism is to fail to grasp the restructuration that these features have undergone and above all to fail to take account of the social position of the older modernism. Postmodernism and modernism, writes Jameson, 'remain utterly distinct in their meaning and social function, owing to the very different positioning of postmodernism in the economic system of late capital and, beyond that, to the transformation of the very sphere of culture in contemporary society' (*PLC*, 5). With modernism the sphere of culture was seen to have retained a degree of semi-autonomy: whether from the left or right, it retained an oppositional stance and critical distance towards capital. But postmodern culture has become fully integrated into commodity production in general, annulling its oppositional and critical stance. Postmodernism, then, is what Jameson calls a cultural dominant, a notion that allows for 'a range of very different, yet subordinate, features' (*PLC*, 4), since it presupposes the residual characteristics of modernism as well as emergent characteristics of post-postmodern culture. As a concept it allows for both continuity and difference.

Jameson's claim has been inspired and, paradoxically, confirmed by the work of Ernest Mandel, in particular *Late Capitalism*, in which Mandel identifies three distinct moments of capitalism: market capitalism, imperialism or monopoly capitalism, and our present moment, which is often misleadingly called postindustrial capitalism but which is more properly defined as multinational or late capitalism. Mandel's periodization is based on a theory of 'Kondratiev cycles' or 'long waves', each wave evolving through approximately a 50-year cycle and representing a dialectical expansion over the previous stage.[12] Each of these long waves encompasses a number of 'business cycles', that is to say, the periodic expansion and contraction of commodity production, or what is commonly known as capitalism's cycle of boom and bust.

Thus, argues Mandel, the history of capitalism on a global scale can be seen as the succession of cyclical movements every seven to ten years and at the same time the succession of longer periods of approximately 50 years duration, of which we have experienced four to date: the period from the end of the eighteenth century to 1847, from the crisis of 1847 to the early 1890s, from the 1890s to the Second World War and finally our present moment from the Second World War to the present. Each of these long waves can be characterized by the form of technology specific to it. The first wave was characterized by the gradual spread of the handicraft-made or manufacture-made steam engine to all the most important branches of industry and industrial countries. The second long wave, from 1847 to the early 1890s, was characterized by the generalization of the machine-made steam engine, which Mandel identifies with the first technological revolution. The third long wave and second technological revolution was characterized by generalized application of electric and combust-ion engines. Finally, our own moment can be characterized by the electronic apparatuses and nuclear power, and represents the third technological revolution.[13] It is these last three phases that Jameson is primarily interested in and which, as we will see in the following section, he identifies with the aesthetic moments of Realism – Modernism – Postmodernism respectively.

The significance of Mandel's proposition is that late capitalism, far from invalidating Marx's analysis of capital, rather presents our current historical moment as a purer form of capitalism. Late capitalism, writes Mandel, 'is necessarily defined by intensified competition among large concerns and between these and the non-monopolized sectors of industry. But on the whole, of course, this process is not qualitatively different from that of "classical" monopoly capitalism.'[14] According to Jameson, late capitalism also represents the final colonization of the last enclaves of resistance to commodification: the Third World, the unconscious and the aesthetic. Therefore, following the example of Lenin's identification of imperialism as a new stage in the global development of capitalism, Jameson can argue that a modification of the system has taken place, indeed even a structural transformation, but that fundamentally the system itself remains the same. Consequently, for Jameson, the Marxist critique, adapted to meet the current historical situation, remains intact and unscathed by all the Baudrillardian hyperbole of postmodernism.

Jameson's project is audacious but at the same time somewhat precarious. As one examines his periodization of postmodernism closely, certain problems begin to recur which the initial bravura of the performance served to mask. There appears to be a certain discrepancy between his own periodization and Mandel's. For Mandel, the term 'late capitalism' designates that period of economic history 'which clearly began after the Second World War'.[15] As with the shorter business cycle, the long wave is characterized by a period of accelerated capital accumulation, overaccumulation and deceleration or recession. For Mandel the increasing frequency of recessionary periods in the advanced capitalist states since the mid-1960s confirms his thesis that we are now in the second phase of the present long wave, that is, the period of decelerating growth. Indeed, the end of the postwar boom can be identified with the OPEC oil crisis of 1973 and the world-wide recession that followed thereafter. This raises the question, for Mandel, of whether or not 'a new long wave can be predicted from the second half of the 1960s onwards – the ebb after the flow'.[16] Jameson's periodization of postmodernism is somewhat equivocal: defining it both as the period post-Second World War – thus identifying it with Mandel's periodization of late capitalism –

and the moment emerging from the late 1960s and early 1970s – thus identifying it with Mandel's second phase of decelerated accumulation, or possibly a new long wave. In his introduction to *Postmodernism, or, The Cultural Logic of Late Capitalism* Jameson seeks to clarify this situation:

> Thus the economic preparation of postmodernism or late capitalism began in the 1950s, after the wartime shortages of consumer goods and spare parts had been made up, and new products and new technologies (not least those of the media) could be pioneered. On the other hand, the psychic *habitus* of the new age demands the absolute break, strengthened by a generational rupture, achieved more properly in the 1960s. (*PLC*, xx)

Jameson goes on to argue that the crystallizing moment of crisis for both the economic and the cultural spheres was the oil crisis of 1973. In other words, Jameson is proposing that we respect the 'semi-autonomy' of each distinct level – the economic, the psychic and the cultural – and the non-synchronicity between levels. But if, as Jameson insists, late capitalism marks the final colonization of our psyche and the complete erosion of aesthetic autonomy as culture becomes fully integrated into the commodity system in general, then how does this economic, psychic and cultural autonomy persist? I am not suggesting that we return to a reductive form of mechanical causality, but I am asking how, if the logic of postmodernism is as totalizing as Jameson argues, he is to achieve the non-synchronicity that his periodization requires.

This still does not, however, resolve the discrepancies between Mandel's periodization and Jameson's own. The problem may become a little clearer if we briefly look at two other accounts of the transition from modernism to postmodernism: those of David Harvey in *The Condition of Postmodernity* and Edward Soja in *Postmodern Geographies*. Both writers share Jameson's analysis that significant structural transformations have taken place in the economic sphere over the last few decades but that these changes do not constitute a final rupture with the capitalist mode of production. Moreover, both writers subscribe to the economic consensus that the long postwar boom came to its final crashing halt with the oil crisis of 1973, at the very moment that postmodernism emerged as a full-blown concept. Harvey writes: 'Somewhere between 1968 and 1972, therefore, we see postmodernism emerge as a full-blown though still incoherent movement out of the chrysalis of the anti-modern movement of the 1960s.'[17]

Harvey ascribes the condition of postmodernity not to the extension of long waves of capitalist reproduction but rather to the transition in the nature of capital accumulation, that is, in the transition from a system of 'Fordist' production with its rather rigid and fixed system of capital accumulation to a more 'flexible' system of accumulation in the 1970s and 1980s. Postmodernism, then, correlates with the ebb rather than the flow of Mandel's latest long wave. Soja also locates the 'passage to postmodernity in the late 1960s and the series of explosive events which together marked the end of the long postwar boom in the capitalist world economy'.[18] Like Harvey, Soja defines the transition in the economic realm as post-Fordist and draws on Mandel's theory of long waves to support the thesis of economic transformation. However, unlike Jameson, Soja identifies postmodernity not with the third technological revolution but with the fourth modernization and the 'most recent phase of far-reaching socio-spatial restructuring that has followed the end of the long post-war economic boom'.[19]

What divides these otherwise mutually sympathetic analysts of postmodernism is essentially which side of the economic crisis of the early to mid-1970s they see as the economic preconditions for postmodernism itself. Jameson argues that it is the pre-1970s boom. Harvey and Soja, on the other hand, locate postmodernism's economic basis as Thatcherite monetarism and Reaganomics. Postmodernism may have emerged in the 1970s but it came of age in the 1980s and is now irredeemably associated with the conspicuous consumption of that decade, in other words, with the rise of that new breed of entrepreneurs and young high-earning financial service workers, the so-called Yuppies. Thus Frank Pfeil argues that, contrary to Jameson's notion of postmodernism as the cultural expression of the global logic of late capitalism, postmodernism is much more of a local phenomenon, and more precisely the cultural practice of a specific group. Postmodernism, writes Pfeil, is 'a cultural-aesthetic set of pleasures and practices created by and for a particular social group at a determinate moment in its collective history'.[20] – that particular social group being the 'P-M-Cs' or professional-managerial-class who were the children of the postwar baby boom and who came of age in the Thatcher/Reagan era. Jameson goes some way to endorsing this analysis:

> one can also plausibly assert that 'postmodernism' in the more limited sense of an ethos and a 'life-style' . . . is the expression of the 'consciousness' of a whole new class fraction . . . This larger and more abstract category has variously been labelled as a new petit bourgeoisie, a professional-managerial-class, or more succinctly as 'the yuppies'. (*PLC*, 407)

Furthermore, Jameson acknowledges the repudiation of post-modernism's universalizing tendencies by micro groups and various 'minorities' since it 'is essentially a much narrower class-cultural operation serving white and male dominated elites in the advanced countries' (*PLC*, 318). Jameson even goes so far as to acknowledge that postmodernism is a specifically North American cultural phenomenon, but with the rider that it is the first truly 'global' North American cultural phenomenon. Postmodernism, then, may be a more limited phenomenon than Jameson suggests and its status as a 'global' cultural dominant is seriously questionable.

Jameson insists that postmodernism is the cultural expression of the deep structural dynamics of global capitalism and more precisely the cultural expression of the third machine age. This assertion is crucial for Jameson's reworking of the postmodern debate in terms of a ternary scheme of Realism – Modernism – Postmodernism. But if we reflect on Mandel's third machine age of electronic control, nuclear power and early generation computerized data processing systems, these hardly seem to characterize postmodern technology. Indeed postmodern technology is not generally thought of as electronic so much as computerized: the cumbersome and slow electronic machines associated with the sixties have given way to digital microtechnology, while the monolithic and megalomaniac visions of nuclear power have been replaced by privatized energy markets. As Baudrillard observes:

> Something has changed, and the Faustian, Promethean, (perhaps Oedipal) period of production and consumption gives way to the 'proteinic' era of networks, to the narcissistic and protean era of connections, contact, contiguity, feedback and generalized interface that goes with the universe of communication. With the television image – the television being the ultimate and perfect object for this new era – our own body and the whole surrounding universe become a control screen.[21]

What could be more Faustian or Promethean than those early utopian visions of the nuclear scientists? Baudrillard's ecstasy of communication represents the fourth technological revolution, the so-called information technology revolution, as the properly postmodern moment. Postmodernism appears to be irrevocably the cultural logic of this fourth technological revolution, characterized by the new technologies of the microchip and cyberspace, and not Jameson's third. These arguments do not in themselves discredit Jameson's analysis of postmodernism but they do serve to fuel the criticism of historical periodization, that is, that such periodization homogenizes time and conflates cultural difference. Furthermore, it seriously problematizes his dialectic of Realism – Modernism – Postmodernism.

Video Art and Postmodern Textuality

As Jameson has observed, there is something of a 'winner loses' logic to postmodernism: if one identifies one's object of study and then submits it to analysis, one runs the risk of canonizing and prioritizing texts which it is the very rationale of postmodernism to disrupt and undermine. One also risks bringing to play on those texts modernist assumptions of depth, truth, subjectivity, etc., which are no longer appropriate in the discussion of postmodern phenomena. Postmodernism is inherently disparate, heterogeneous and eclectic, its impulse is to resist fixed categorization through a perpetual dissolution of boundaries. So while the possibility of posing alternative individual readings of texts to those of Jameson's is feasible, these would not in themselves undermine his central thesis of postmodernism as a cultural logic, as it is in the nature of that logic itself to generate and sustain a multiplicity of readings. Faced with this theoretical impasse, where to pursue either option – of advancing a critique or abandoning the terrain altogether – ensnares one in the discourse of postmodernism, I shall take the former course. I shall not, however, propose alternative readings to individual texts but rather take Jameson's own readings and suggest that analysis of the texts themselves undermines the theory. In this chapter I focus on video and in the following chapter on architecture, both of which are central forms in the postmodern debate.

The television screen has come to epitomize the new technology of the fourth technological revolution, representing the perfect object for this new era. The pure immanence of its unreflecting surface has come to replace any sense of depth, reflexivity and transcendence. Today, the television, writes Baudrillard, 'is the very space of habitation that is conceived as both receiver and distributor, as the space of both reception and operations, the control screen and the terminal which as such may be endowed with telematic power – that is, with the capability of regulating everything from a distance, including work in the home and, of course, consumption, play, social relations and leisure'.[22] Television provides the perfect figure for that new world of communication networks and cyberspace in which isolated individuals are plugged into their own control panels and divorced from any contact with reality unless, and in so far as, it is simulated on the screen in front of them.

Although video and television share the same channel of communication, both usually coming to us through a small screen and in our own homes, they are not the same thing. Moreover, video itself is by no means a single unified form but designates a number of different activities and modes of reception: for example, the playing of video games, interactive television, the renting of video films and what I will be examining here as 'video art'. For Jameson, video is the hegemonic cultural form today and 'is rigorously coterminous with postmodernism itself as a historical period' (*PLC*, 73). Jameson distinguishes between commercial television and experimental video or 'video art', but unfortunately does not pursue this distinction any further. Indeed, he immediately blurs the distinction by borrowing Raymond Williams's notion of television as 'total flow' (*PLC*, 70), while discussing experimental video for the rest of his chapter.

Jameson sees video as characteristically postmodern in a number of key respects. First, the concept of total flow seems to render obsolete any possibility of 'critical distance', as the viewer is immersed in the continuous production of images. Secondly, memory plays no role in video and therefore it can be said to lack a sense of history. The former claim rests on a proposition about television rather than video itself and thus has uncertain value for a theory of video, while the latter claim appears to be demonstrably wrong. For Jameson, though, these dual features produce that fundamental paradox for any theory of postmodernism with which I began this discussion, that is, that postmodernism is untheorizable. A description of the structural exclusion of memory and critical distance, writes Jameson, 'might well lead on into the impossible, namely, a theory of video itself – how the thing blocks its own theorization becoming a theory in its own right' (*PLC*, 71). In other words, it is impossible to have a theory of video, unless, and in so far as, we can theorize this impossibility of theorization. I shall, therefore, follow Jameson's theorization of this aporia in some detail.

Jameson argues that the process of modernization marks the end of the sacred and the spiritual and the ascendance of brute materiality: 'Capitalism, and the modern age, is a period in which, with the extinction of the sacred and the "spiritual," the deep underlying materiality of all things has finally risen dripping and convulsive into the light of day' (*PLC*, 67). Culture has not suddenly become 'material' in late capitalism – it always was so, but now we can recognize it as such. Video holds a privileged position in this respect because with long and repetitive experimental videos our traditional notions of deciphering and interpretation – of intention, meaning and message – no longer seem to apply. What is foregrounded in contemporary video art and video installations is the machine and technology rather than an underlying hidden message.

Behind this insistence on the materiality of the medium lies a related but slightly different subtext. Jameson takes as axiomatic that the centred, autonomous, bourgeois subject has disappeared, that our sense of ourselves as subjects has become more fragmented and decentred. The correlative of the eclipse of the unified subject for cultural practice and production, argues Jameson, is that one can no longer see the 'signature' of the individual artist on given works. Whereas with modernism one could recognize a particular individual style, specific to the work of an individual artist, with postmodernism there is no longer a unified subject to articulate or give voice to that singular vision, to unify a particular style. Moreover the eclecticism of postmodernism seems to have led to a blurring of the boundaries not only between high and low culture but also between the cultural artefacts of distinct artists. Again, I shall argue below, this appears to be a peculiar and contradictory position for Jameson to maintain and, in terms of literature, one needs only to think of the very different styles of Thomas Pynchon and Toni Morrison to see that individual signatures are still very evident in contemporary cultural artefacts.

According to Jameson, then, with video production it is no longer possible to see the hand of the individual creative artist. Consequently, there can be no video canon since there will be no individual works which can be isolated, attributed to particular artists and prioritized. There is only an intertextual video plane in which all texts exist in coextension with one another. Thus there can be no great monuments of postmodern culture in the sense that we have the great monuments of modernism, 'there are no video masterpieces, there can *never* be a video canon, and even an auteur theory of video (where signatures are still evidently present) becomes very problematical indeed' (*PLC*, 78, emphasis added). Jameson follows these pronouncements with an analysis of a video text called *AlienNATION* and poses the question: what is the text about? Not surprisingly the question, or theme, of 'alienation' arises, but as this is a psychic experience belonging to modernism rather than postmodernism, it proves too weak a candidate to carry the meaning of the text. Indeed the postmodern video text does not mean anything at all:

If interpretation is understood, in the thematic way, as the disengagement of a fundamental theme or meaning, then it seems clear that the postmodernist text – of which we have taken the videotape in question to be a privileged exemplar – is from that perspective defined as a structure or sign flow which resists meaning, whose fundamental inner logic is the exclusion of the emergence of themes as such in that sense, and which therefore systematically sets out to short-circuit traditional interpretative temptations. (*PLC*, 91–2)

In so far as the interpretation of a postmodern text is possible, argues Jameson, that text must be considered bad or flawed.

One cannot help but feel that there is a certain self-fulfilling momentum to Jameson's analysis of postmodernist texts. Theoretically he rules out the possibility of their individuation or their possession of a latent meaning, through the contemporary fragmentation of the subject and the collapse of critical distance and depth. He then proceeds to analyse a text, the very title of which inscribes the kind of superficial interpretation that one immediately knows must be rejected and cannot provide (to use Baudrillard's term) the alibi for the text, only to discover that the text – which we have already been told cannot have a meaning – does not have a meaning and if it did it would not be a good example to take in the first place. In short, if specific cultural artefacts are to be interpreted as the expression of a universal cultural logic, this would appear, *a priori*, to rule out certain aesthetic and interpretative possibilities.

In an essay 'Jameson's Complaint: Video-Art and the Intertextual "Time-Wall"' Nicholas Zurbrugg persuasively argues against Jameson's reading of video and in particular the meaningless anonymity which Jameson insists on as such a crucial feature of its aesthetic. The crux of Zurbrugg's argument is that Jameson is trapped behind an intertextual 'time-wall', that is to say, his formative intellectual background is essentially that of a literary/print culture and, in his analysis of visual and multimedia culture, he carries those literary/print cultural assumptions over into his analysis of image-based media. Thus Jameson's insistence that there can be no auteur theory of video because the signature of the creative artist is necessarily absent from video production is nothing more than an extension of Barthes's thesis of the death of the author, reworked with a couple of metaphors from Williams and Baudrillard. As with many contemporary intellectuals, argues Zurbrugg, who are faced with the debilitating situation in which their traditional interpretative practices are not appropriate, Jameson projects his own 'conceptual confusion'[23] on to the object itself. In other words, it is not video art that is caught in a postmodern malaise of meaningless, depersonalized self-referentiality but that sense of meaninglessness is, rather, symptomatic of Jameson's inability to come to terms with a new form which he does not fully understand and cannot appreciate.

In place of Jameson's ahistorical, non-canonical and impersonal perspective of video, Zurbrugg suggests an alternative perspective in which the work of Nam June Paik (whom Jameson also cites) and Robert Wilson have now become canonical. Paik's work in particular contains a great deal more personal and biographical material than Jameson would deem permissible in video art, as well as having thematic content. Wilson's work similarly presents a much more 'meaningful' version of postmodern multimedia performance than Jameson describes. Video art, argues Zurbrugg, 'requires at least partial contemplation in its own terms, rather than those of other more familiar prior discourse'.[24] Jameson's analysis of video lacks that sense of 'renewed joy' before a significant discovery because he rules out the possibility of there being anything there beforehand.

As suggested above, there is no advantage to be gained by merely opposing one set of postmodernist readings against another. Zurbrugg's article, however, does raise two important issues with respect to Jameson's analysis of postmodern cultural artefacts: first, the textual nature of his analyses, of which I will say more in the following chapter, and secondly the issue of Jameson's ambivalence towards postmodern culture in general. In the conclusion to *Postmodernism, or, The Cultural Logic of Late Capitalism* Jameson assures his readers that he is an 'enthusiastic consumer of postmodernism' (one cannot help but think that if he were that enthusiastic about it there would be no need for such a reminder). Jameson further assures us:

> I like the architecture and a lot of the newer visual work, in particular the newer photography. The music is not bad to listen to, or the poetry to read; the novel is the weakest of the newer cultural areas and is considerably excelled by its narrative counterparts in film and video . . . My sense is that this is essentially a visual culture, wired for sound – but one where the linguistic element . . . is slack and flabby, and not to be made interesting without ingenuity, daring, and keen motivation. (*PLC*, 298–9)

Perhaps with the exception of architecture, one does not sense that enthusiasm when reading Jameson's analyses of postmodern culture, where much is derived from secondary sources, and certainly not the sheer joy of the language that one feels when reading a Jamesonian analysis of Balzac, or Flaubert, or indeed of any modernist writer. Jameson appears to be adrift between his totalizing theory of postmodernism as a global logic and his own existential experience of postmodernist phenomena. Theoretically he emphasizes the profoundly illiterate nature of late capitalism and the predominantly visual character of postmodern culture. This appears to preclude his enjoyment of postmodern fiction – with the exception of E. L. Doctorow and Michael Herr – but at the same time his interpretative practice remains literary and textbound, which precludes any genuine appreciation or analysis of other cultural forms on their own terms. It is interesting to note, however, which writers are excluded by Jameson's own definition of postmodernism: writers such as Toni Morrison and Gloria Naylor – writers whose work explicitly deals with issues of history, memory and narrative, the very thematics which are supposedly absent from contemporary culture. Otherwise, along with Jameson, and with good reason, we have to exempt these writers from postmodernism, in which case the whole notion of postmodernism as a cultural dominant becomes problematic, since these latter writers surely represent one of the main currents of contemporary North American literature.

Jameson's ambivalence towards postmodernism is succinctly expressed in a 1984 review of Don DeLillo's *The Names*. Jameson writes: 'For many of us, Don DeLillo has been the most interesting and talented of American post-modernist novelists (which is to say finally, I suppose, of current white male novelists, although the category may also include a few individuals of other gender and racial specifications).'[25] However, as the notion of a postmodern masterpiece, or great work, is ruled out *a priori*, Jameson must qualify his assessment of DeLillo: 'you will be more satisfied if you read it as a determinedly minor work.'[26] In other words, this is a great book, as long as one does not try to think of it as great literature. This confusion as to whether or not postmodern fiction can constitute great literature is only heightened when Jameson poses the question as to whether *The Names* 'was to have been the "major novel" and the great modernist statement (or the Book of the World, a la Pynchon)'; indeed, 'do post-modernists make major statements of that kind?'[27] The answer is implicitly No! Postmodernist authors do not, or can no longer, make grand statements and monumental works. If this is the case what is the status of Pynchon in the above statement? If postmodernist writers can no longer make major statements in the modernist sense, is Jameson trying to suggest that Pynchon is a modernist writer, since he has written a Book of the World? One must either draw the conclusion that Pynchon is not a postmodernist writer or that he is a postmodernist writer and that postmodernists can produce monumental works in the modernist tradition – if not in the same way.

Pynchon is assuredly a, if not 'the', postmodernist author and the Book of the World in question (presumably *Gravity's Rainbow*) the paradigmatic postmodern work of fiction. Indeed *Gravity's Rainbow* now appears to stand in relation to postmodernism in much the same way that Joyce's *Ulysses* stands to modernism. Furthermore, *Gravity's Rainbow* would appear to be just the kind of text – one which attempts to map individual existential experience on to the new spatial logic of post-Second World War global capitalism – which Jameson is calling for under the slogan of 'cognitive mapping' but which he insists does not yet exist. On the one hand, Jameson argues that postmodernism is utterly distinct from modernism with its individual styles and monumental character, but on the other, he persistently exhibits this non-monumentalism as a sign of postmodernism's political and aesthetic impoverishment. It would certainly appear from Jameson's theorization, therefore, that postmodernism is caught in a 'winner loses' logic.

Realism – Modernism – Postmodernism

There is an inherent reversibility to postmodern theory, observes Jameson, whereby its various binary oppositions tend to fold back into each other and 'the position of the observer is turned inside out and the tabulation recontinued on some larger scale' (*PLC*, 64). Consequently, to reflect upon the nature of postmodern political art in a situation which rules out its possibility beforehand may not be the best way of addressing the dilemma. A more productive approach is to reflect upon the conditions of possibility of the problem itself, that is, why it is no longer possible to conceive of political art in the older sense, of Brecht say, and the conditions in which a renewed political art would once more become possible. To stage the problem in this way is to begin to move away from the inherent circularity of postmodern theorizing, or alternatively the static presentation of its various dichotomies. Jameson suggests that this can be achieved and the whole problem can be articulated by a more genuinely historical schema if modern/postmodern dualism is lifted on to a higher level of abstraction through the addition of a third term – realism.

In fact Jameson has hinted at this dialectic of Realism – Modernism – and as yet to be theorized post-Second World War culture since his earliest writings. In 'On Politics and Literature' (1968) Jameson described the psychological fragmentation of the subject in postwar North American society, suggesting that he could 'best do this by suggesting three general stages that political literature has undergone'.[28] These three general stages are the realism of Balzac, the modernism of Brecht or Aragon and – what we would now call – the postmodern decentred subject of contemporary capitalism. Similarly, in 'On Raymond Chandler' (1970), Jameson sketches a loose version of this dialectic, and in his first discussion of 'nostalgia' in film gives an early formulation of his later periodization of genre – auteur – nostalgia films, with the final term remaining a vacant slot: 'This evolution in the movie industry parallels the movement in serious literature away from the fixed form of the nineteenth century towards the personally invented, style conscious individual forms of the twentieth.'[29] However, we should note that these reflections are situated in a particular national context rather than the later global theorizing on postmodernism, and underwritten by the sociology of C. Wright Mills rather than Mandellian economics.

The fullest exposition of Jameson's dialectic of Realism – Modernism – Postmodernism is given in the long concluding chapter, 'The Existence of Italy', to *Signatures of the Visible*. Here Jameson suggests that film history can be clarified by period theory, that is, the notion that specific formal and aesthetic tendencies can be correlated to particular historical stages. The historical periodization in question is the familiar Mandellian one of market, monopoly and late capitalism, which Jameson proposes to correlate with the aesthetic moments of realism, modernism and postmodernism respectively. Jameson, however, immediately qualifies this periodization with the warning that these stages 'are not to be grasped exclusively in terms of the stylistic descriptions from which they have been appropriated; rather, their nomenclature sets us the technical problem of constructing a mediation between a formal or aesthetic concept and a periodizing or historiographic one' (*SV*, 155). The cultural component of this historical schema is to be understood not as a set of stylistic features or practices but as a 'cultural dominant'. At the same time, the historical period designates a 'mode of production' which Jameson defines in its broadest sense as the unity of both the forces and relations of production. Furthermore, such a periodization, with the qualifications just enumerated, does not represent a simple chronology, or linear narrative, in which each moment inevitably follows on from the previous one, but rather a situation in which each moment dialectically presupposes all the others. The three stages are not symmetrical, writes Jameson, 'but dialectical in their relationship to each other: the later two now build on the accumulated cultural capital of the first and no longer "reflect" or "correspond to" a social public with the same immediacy, although clearly the various modernist and postmodernist moments in such a dialectic then reach back to create new publics in their own right' (*SV*, 157).

The initial problem that any discussion of realism and modernism now faces is our deeply embedded preconceptions of what each of these aesthetics entails. We celebrate modernism, writes Jameson, 'as an active aesthetic praxis and invention, whose excitement is demiurgic, along with its liberation from content; while realism is conventionally evoked in terms of passive reflection and copying, subordinate to some external reality' (*SV*, 162). Jameson, therefore, proposes to 'estrange' these traditional views of modernism and realism respectively in order to throw the problematic of an aesthetic moment's correlation to a specific historical period into a whole new light: in other words, to view realism as a praxis and modernism as 'scientific representation'. However, such an experiment, writes Jameson:

> at once confronts us with two fundamental methodological problems: what is the nature of the 'world' thus produced by realism (it being understood that the very concept of world or worldness is itself a modernist, or phenomenological, one); and how, once we talk ourselves into a positive or productive concept of the realist aesthetic, are we to restore its negative and ideological dimension, its essential falseness and conventionality (as we have learned such structural lessons from the contemporary critique of representation)? (*SV*, 163)

According to Jameson, the way to resolve this dilemma is to conflate the two questions by providing a single answer, that is to say, we must at once acknowledge that the world produced by realism is false but at the same time insist that it is objectively false. The model for such a theoretical resolution derives from Marx's analysis in *Capital*. To this analysis Jameson adds that 'the peculiar object of realism (and its situation of production) is . . . the historically specific capitalist mode of production' (*SV*, 163). The second stage in resolving this dilemma is to substitute the term 'narrative' for 'representation'. For Jameson, the notion of narrative 'has the initial advantage of at once dispelling forever the temptations of the copy theory of art, and of problematizing beyond recognition many of the assumptions implicit in the notion of representation itself' (*SV*, 165). Narrative, or rather the act of narration, takes place after the event so to speak; it is a retelling of events that have already taken place. In the act of retelling, the gap between *fabula* and *szujet* is foregrounded. The act of narrating transforms and restructures the materials of the story, and this, suggests Jameson, may be the ideological aspect of narrative. To speak of narrative rather than representation, then, avoids the debate over realism sliding into problems of reflection theories of art, as well as questions of verisimilitude, which seeks to identify the object in question with its representation.

What Jameson is proposing, therefore, is that we can only begin to understand the significance of cultural production when we see it in terms of (what has been described in a previous chapter as) cultural revolution. In short, 'the function of any cultural revolution . . . will be to invent the life habits of the new social world, to "de-program" subjects trained in the older one' (*SV*, 164). Jameson's thesis proposes that all great transitions from one mode of production to another have entailed at one and the same time an equally momentous aesthetic transformation. This is not to suggest that cultural artefacts merely 'reflect' changes in the economic base. As Jameson writes:

> In a more general way, the relationship between art and its social context can be freed from inert conceptions of reflection by the proposition that the social context . . . is to be grasped as the *situation* – the problem, the dilemma, the contradiction, the 'question' – to which the work of art comes as an imaginary solution, resolution, or 'answer'. (*SV*, 164)

In other words, we have the formulation familiar from *The Political Unconscious*, that the work of art functions as myth does for Lévi-Strauss as the imaginary resolution of real social contradictions.[30] Unfortunately, the nature of the relationship between the work of art and its social context does not become any more precise as Jameson, rather than moving closer to a definition, moves further into abstraction and generalization.

Each aesthetic moment, according to Jameson, will not only be seen to presuppose a particular economic stage of development but also a specific conception of the subject and the subject's relations to her or his lifeworld. We are now in a position, therefore, to identify the situation to which realism provides the imaginary resolution, that is, the materialization and corresponding desacralization of the lifeworld under the process of modernization. Realism, in other words, served to deprogram the older providential and sacred narratives and to construct new narrative paradigms of the subject's relations to 'what will now come to be thought of as reality' (*SV*, 166). Realism's particularly privileged cultural position, for Jameson, derives not from its narrative structure, nor from its accurate representation and analysis of classical capitalism, but from its particular epistemological claim: that is, that we can have access to reality and that specific representations of reality can be said to represent the 'truth' of that reality. Although, the position is not quite as simple as contemporary debates over 'representation' would suggest, realism is 'a peculiarly unstable concept owing to its simultaneous, yet incompatible, aesthetic and epistemological claims' (*SV*, 158). Whichever side of the dualism we emphasize we simultaneously undermine the claims of the other side: 'Thus, where the epistemological claim succeeds, it fails; and if realism validates its claim to be a correct or true representation of the world, it thereby ceases to be an *aesthetic* mode of representation and falls out of art altogether' (*SV*, 158).

Realism, according to Jameson, is unique in its epistemological claim. Whatever we assert as the 'truth content, or the "moment of truth", of modernism, or postmodernism . . . those versions of aesthetic truth do not, except in very indirect or supplementary or mediated ways, imply the possibility of *knowledge*, as "realism" emphatically does' (*SV*, 158). At the same time, it is the very instability of realism's epistemological claim that endows the concept with its historic significance and facilitates the understanding of the situation in which such claims are no longer feasible. To put it another way, realism is historically specific rather than an eternal formal possibility. Just as the social and historical conditions must exist in the first place for realism to emerge, once those conditions have passed realism is no longer an aesthetic possibility. That is, its narrative structures will be seen to be outmoded and redundant, as no longer capable of adequately 'representing' the world.

If realism, then, inscribes within itself its own conditions of impossibility, the conditions in which it can no longer provide the imaginary resolution to its social context, as much may be said for the concepts of modernism and postmodernism. As Jameson writes: 'most anti-realistic or anti-representational positions still do in some sense require a concept of realism, if only as an empty slot, a vacant preliminary historical "stage", or secondary (but essential) aesthetic counterposition' (*SV*, 158–9). The schema here is the now familiar one of the reification of the sign and the commodification of the aesthetic, which is at one and the same time the aestheticization of the commodity. In these terms, realism's epistemological claims can be said to presuppose a correspondence, or a logic of equivalence, between the sign and its ground or referent. In a sense, the sign could be said to be 'natural' and self-validating. As capitalism's modernizing project evolved, with its corresponding intensification of the process of reification, the sign's self-validating quality was undermined – the real is bracketed as the arbitrary nature of the sign becomes visible. Modernism, then, will be seen to inscribe within its own form the separation of the sign and its referent, the real will be bracketed and the autonomy of the sign, or the work of art itself, will be emphasized.

If the concept of realism can be estranged through the notion of praxis, then the concept of modernism can similarly be estranged through the notion of autonomy. 'Many of the now conventional descriptive features of modernism – such as style, plotlessness, irony, and subjectivity,' writes Jameson, 'can be productively rewritten or defamiliarized by rethinking them in terms of the problematic of artistic or aesthetic *autonomy*, provided this last is suitably enlarged' (*SV*, 201). The concept must be enlarged because the value of such a transcoding operation depends on what we mean by the concept of artistic autonomy in the first place: that is, the autonomy of the aesthetic experience, of the work of art or of culture in general. Indeed, just as structural linguistics presupposes a structure or system against which the isolated and arbitrary sign is differentiated, the notion of artistic or aesthetic autonomy always turns out to mean *semi*-autonomy. In other words, 'the independence and self-sufficient internal coherence of the object or field in question is generally understood dialectically to be relative to some greater totality (in relation to which alone it makes sense to assert that it is autonomous in the first place)' (*SV*, 201). Just as with realism, therefore, what is of most interest to Jameson about modernism is not so much the solutions to the problem, the individual interpretations, or meaning-effects, generated by each text, but the conditions of possibility for those meaning-effects to exist in the first place. Thus Jameson proposes a neologism, 'autonomization', for an as yet untheorized theory of modernism which would seek to identify 'the traces of "autonomy" within the structural processes' of modernist artefacts (*SV*, 205). In short, modernism can be characterized as the process of the autonomization of the sign and of culture itself.

The complete autonomy of the sign, however, will only be achieved with the advent of full-blown postmodernism, when reification enters the sign itself, asserting the arbitrary relationship not only between the sign and referent but also between the signifier and the signified. Therefore, the differential logic of the various modernisms gives way to the complete dispersion and schizophrenic logic of postmodernism proper. The punctual or episodic elements of Joyce's texts or Hitchcock's films no longer have to be coordinated by some principle of totality but exist in their own right as free-floating material signifiers. The subject of this new cultural logic is no longer the centred ego posited by realism, or the alienated subject of modernism, but the decentred fragmented subject celebrated by post-structuralism. Paradoxically, then, at the very moment when the aesthetic is finally integrated into the commodity system in general it simultaneously achieves 'genuine autonomy' in the form of the materiality of the signifier. In short, the concept of the autonomy of culture 'allows us to witness with greater precision its historical dissolution, and at the same time to register the paradox of a thing that disappears by becoming universal, rather than by extinction' (*SV*, 202).

One problem with Jameson's historicizing project, I suggested above, is the non-synchronicity of his own periodizations and Mandel's. In 'The Existence of Italy' Jameson tries to circumvent this problem through his use of the concept of a cultural dominant and insistence on the non-chronological, non-narrative nature of his historical schema. Responding to the postmodern suspicion of 'master narratives', Jameson suggests that 'the Marxian sequence of modes of production is not a narrative of that kind, nor even a narrative at all,' but rather 'some deeper unconscious narrative does subtend a great many Marxian histories and discussions, and not only Marxian ones' (*SV*, 226). That deeper unconscious narrative is none other than the transitionary moment of 'modernity' itself, the transition from feudalism to capitalism and the emergence of the modern world.

This being said, Jameson's periodization can be recapitulated at different levels and historical stages with a well-nigh Hegelian obsession for ternary schema. Thus market capitalism, imperialism and late capitalism can be correlated to the literary moments of realism, modernism and postmodernism respectively; or, in the case of film, to the genre films of the 1930s and 1940s, the 'auteurs' of the 1950s and 1960s, and the nostalgia and punk films of the 1970s or 1980s. More recently with popular music we get the distinction between the old rhythm and blues, the auteurs of 'classic' rock and the postmodern punk. Finally, there are the 'microchronological' levels of 'semi-autonomous sequences of cultural history such as American Black literature, where Richard Wright, Ralph Ellison, and Ishmael Reed can be taken as emblematic markers' (*SV*, 156). At this level Jameson's periodization is at risk of collapsing into a mechanistic formalism. Real differences and differentiation are conflated in overly abstract and generalized categories, but at the same time continuity and identity must be understated in order to differentiate the larger categories themselves. Jameson appears to be doing precisely what he proscribed in *The Political Unconscious*, that is, using the periodizing categories as slots to drop the particular cultural artefacts into. There is no sense of the 'determinate contradiction' at the heart of the work or the schema which in Jameson's previous work provided the mark of a genuine Marxist criticism and the subtlety of his periodization.

The Dialectic of Modernism and Postmodernism

In an article 'Divergences: Modernism, Postmodernism, Jameson and Lyotard' Peter Nicholls argues that Jameson's ambivalence towards postmodernism, and in particular towards postmodern literature, derives from too rigid a demarcation between modernism and postmodernism, a demarcation which is grounded in the association of modernism with temporality, narrative and above all memory, while postmodernism is associated with space, non-narrative structures and immanence. Utilizing Lyotard's distinction between 'discourse' and 'figure', Nicholls proposes a perspective on postmodernism that allows us to register continuities as well as divergences between the modern and the postmodern. Lyotard's proposal, writes Nicholls, has the 'advantage that they do not suppose any "retreat" of language in the postmodern but rather conceive of the postmodern as a disruption of the discursive systems on which modernity depends'.[31] Modernism and postmodernism should not be opposed along the lines of discursive and visual forms of signification respectively; the figural and the discursive are not polar opposites but rather the figural represents 'the resistant or irreconcilable trace of a space or time that is radically incommensurable with that of discursive meaning'.[32] Lyotard's categories, therefore, are not mutually exclusive, designating different regimes of signification, but rather operate dialectically within all regimes of signification.

It is not that the figural is absent from modernist writing, insists Nicholls; on the contrary 'it is characteristic of imagism and its derivatives (like the Hemingway style) to seek to make the reader "feel" something which eludes understanding.'[33] Through an analysis of Baudelaire, Pound, Eliot, Expressionist theatre and modernist painting, Nicholls shows how this dialectic of discourse and figure functions within modernist culture in the sense that the figural dimension constantly disrupts the order of discourse. Nicholls, therefore, proposes an alternative perspective on postmodernism:

the spatial model used by Baudrillard and Jameson is closely tied to the synchronic order of signification, to sign-*systems*. In contrast, another form of postmodernism has turned its attention very deliberately to questions of temporality and narrative, and specifically to what Lyotard has called the 'event', the singular moment which can be spoken about only after it is over, and which is composed of 'simultaneous and heterogeneous temporalities'.[34]

In short, he refers to the kind of themes to be found in those writers I have already mentioned, Toni Morrison, Gloria Naylor or indeed, E. L. Doctorow, those whom, with the exception of Doctorow, Jameson is compelled to exclude by his very definition of postmodernism. Narrative for these writers, observes Nicholls, is not simply the pastiche of older literary styles but the very medium through which a number of histories can be thought simultaneously. Postmodernism, in this sense, is not so much the loss of the historical imagination as its renewal and revitalization in the attempt to retrieve the multiplicity of temporalities that capitalism's modernizing project seeks to flatten out.

Postmodernity for Lyotard, then, is a 'mode' rather than an 'epoch' whereby, in what Nicholls describes as a stylish reversal of the postmodern problematic, the modern is that which is first postmodern. Nicholls's reading of modernism and postmodernism in relation to the discursive and the figural serves to emphasize the degree of continuity between modernism and postmodernism as well as their dialectical relation. At the same time, however, it simply side-steps a number of problematic issues. First, Jameson's conception of 'mode of production' also sees postmodernity as a restructuration of previous modes of production rather than an epochal break. Furthermore, Lyotard's formulation simply avoids the question of the historical ground of postmodernity that Jameson has attempted to address through his periodization. Lyotard's work presupposes some form of epochal break, but by projecting the problem backwards, or reversing it, he avoids the necessity of theorizing this break as we are always already in the postmodern.

Jameson's periodization of postmodernism as the cultural logic of late capitalism remains one of the most sustained attempts to eschew not only the moralizing tone of much postmodern criticism but also the exaggerated hyperbole of many postmodernists, and to historically ground this most slippery of concepts. Jameson concedes that there is a great deal of continuity between modernist and postmodernist cultural practice, but argues that these elements function differently within specific works, while the cultural artefacts themselves have an utterly distinct social position in modernity and postmodernity respectively. The proposition that modernism and postmodernism are distinct in their social position and function facilitates an acute analysis of postmodern culture but at the same time, I contend, leads to an overly homogeneous theory. The problems of periodization that Jameson seeks to banish at the level of theory, in terms of a cultural dominant and the non-synchronicity of distinct levels, invariably appear to recapitulate themselves in his analysis of specific cultural artefacts. Jameson has come to characterize modernism as dealing with themes of temporality, narrative and history, while postmodernism, despite all his professed enthusiasm for it, is defined negatively against this, as being concerned with space, the play of surfaces and immediacy. Jameson's ambivalence towards postmodern spatiality and the discrepancy between the theoretical and the phenomenological experience of postmodernity are the subject of the following chapter.

5

The Spatial Logic of
Late Capitalism

In the previous chapter I emphasized the significance of Jameson's historical periodization of postmodernism as the cultural logic of late capitalism. Following his analysis of video art I insisted that there was a marked disjuncture between the theoretical framework Jameson proposes and his specific analysis of cultural artefacts. In short, his analysis of postmodern culture tends to reproduce certain kinds of dichotomous thinking that the conception of postmodernism as a cultural dominant sought to forestall. I suggested, moreover, that this was a consequence of Jameson's overreliance on postmodern conceptions of textuality. In this chapter I will further extend this criticism through a consideration of probably the most influential aspect of Jameson's analysis of postmodernism, that is to say, his intervention in postmodern architectural and spatial debates.

Initially, I briefly situate Jameson's work in relation to what Edward Soja has identified as the reassertion of space in social theory, before tracing the increasing predominance of spatial categories in Jameson's work. Through an examination of his two principal analyses of postmodern architecture, that is, the Bonaventure Hotel in Los Angeles and Frank Gehry's own private house in Santa Monica, California, I question just how representative of postmodern spatiality Jameson's readings are. Jameson frequently cites the work of Henri Lefebvre and, in particular, Lefebvre's magnum opus, *The Production of Space*, as a major influence on his conception of postmodern spatiality. I explicate Lefebvre's notion of socially produced space in some detail and suggest that while there is a certain family resemblance between Jameson's work and that of Lefebvre, Jameson's analysis only considers one level of Lefebvre's 'unitary theory' and consequently tends towards reductionism in precisely the manner that Lefebvre's conception of spatiality challenges. Finally, I shall reconsider the spatio-temporal dialectic of modernity and postmodernity within Jameson's work, contending that he is in fact insufficiently dialectical in his conception of postmodern spatiality and as a result fails to see the possibilities for any meaningful postmodern politics.

The Reassertion of Space in Social Theory

Jameson's reassertion of the category of space can be seen in the wider context of a renewed interest in space within the social sciences, crystallizing in debates within Marxist geography in the 1970s. Historically space has been accorded a subsidiary position within social theory, generally identified as a realm of stasis and neutrality, a realm utterly opposed to time. In more sophisticated versions of this theory space has been designated the realm of closure in which meaning is fixed, as opposed to the fluidity and heterogeneity of temporality. Time, in contrast, has been seen as dynamic, disruptive and transformative; temporality is the realm of change and historical progress. Thus, time and history have been valorized as primary fields of theoretical and political interest, while space and geography have been disregarded as merely peripheral concerns. For at least the past century, writes Soja, 'time and history have occupied a privileged position in the practical and theoretical consciousness of Western Marxism and critical social science.'[1] Space has always been assumed to be a neutral objective category; in other words, space is simply given, a void in which phenomena exist and events take place. Soja observes that space still tends to be treated as fixed, dead and undialectical; whereas time is associated with richness, life and the dialectic. The appeal of the historical imagination has always been its emancipatory potential: history is dynamic, it is about change and transformation and therefore contains the seeds of a qualitatively different future, the utopian transformation of the present social conditions. Modern geography, on the other hand, was 'reduced primarily to the accumulation, classification, and theoretically innocent representation of factual material describing the areal differentiation of the earth's surface'.[2] Space, in short, is static and inert, space is simply 'given', it is a neutral category, an emptiness which is filled up with objects.

The Marxist geographers of the late 1960s and early 1970s challenged this neutral conception of space, focusing specifically on the relation between space and society and how this relationship has been conceptualized. Drawing on the work of Lefebvre, they suggested that space is not simply given but produced. Socially produced space, or spatiality, is neither inert nor static but rather constitutive of social relations. As Doreen Massey writes, all 'so-called spatial relations and spatial processes were actually social relations taking a particular geographical form.'[3] Geographical issues, therefore, 'could ... not be explained without a prior understanding of the economy and of wider social and political processes'.[4] What was required was what Lefebvre called a unitary theory of space, that is to say, a theory of space which brings together all its constituent elements: physical space, mental space and social space. I will return to Lefebvre's theory of space below; first I turn to Jameson's own steadily increasing interest in issues of postmodern spatiality.

As outlined in the preceding chapter, postmodernism for Jameson involves a transformation of our conception and experience of both time and space. He contends that postmodernism represents a significant decline in our sense of history, narrative and memory, and simultaneously an erosion of aesthetic depth and critical distance. Above all postmodernism ushers in a new sense of spatial disorientation in relation to the globalized economy of late capitalism. Initially, in 'Postmodernism and Consumer Society', space was theorized as *a* characteristic feature of contemporary experience, an experience that had undergone restructuration with the advent of postmodernism in conjunction with a corresponding change in our sense of temporality. As these notions were subsumed into the 1984 essay, a notable revision had taken place whereby it becomes 'empirically arguable' that space is a cultural dominant. By the time we reach the postmodernism book, the need for empirical verification and argument appears to have been abandoned, postmodernism being seen as unequivocally spatial. Postmodernism, writes Jameson, eschews temporality for space (*PLC*, 134), and if temporality has any place left in a postmodern world 'it would be better to speak of the writing of it than of any lived experience' (*PLC*, 154).

Throughout *Postmodernism, or, The Cultural Logic of Late Capitalism* Jameson developed this spatial theme with analyses of video, film and television, as well as sculpture and architecture, all media which particularly offer themselves to spatial analysis. At the same time, Jameson's book exhibited a marked decline of interest in literature, which he sees as the least satisfactory component of postmodern culture. Narrative is, of course, a temporal medium which has had its day. Indeed, of the ten chapters only two are concerned with what we may call linguistic or discursive regimes and only a single chapter is devoted specifically to the question of temporality. It would appear, therefore, that space has evolved from being one of the constituent elements of postmodern culture to *the* constitutive feature of it, as 'an existential and cultural dominant' (*PLC*, 365). Jameson appears, on the one hand, to fall prey to what David Harvey calls 'spatial fetishism' while paradoxically, on the other, his residual modernist assumptions preclude a sense of the full political potential of this radically new spatial configuration.

The Phenomenology of Postmodernism

Architecture occupies a particularly privileged position in Jameson's analysis of postmodern culture as a consequence of its own economic centrality to the forces of late capitalism:

> Of all the arts, architecture is the closest constitutively to the economic, with which, in the form of commissions and land values, it has a virtually unmediated relationship. It will therefore not be surprising to find the extraordinary flowering of the new postmodern architecture grounded in the patronage of multinational business, whose expansion and development is strictly contemporaneous with it. (*PLC*, 5)

As the critic Donald Preziosi has pointed out, while the other arts, painting, photography, literature, etc., may offer us 'glimpses' into the postmodern sublime, or 'evoke' that new spatiality of multinational capitalism, it is only through architecture that the full sense of postmodernism is spatially *figured* forth.[5] Architecture, writes Jameson, 'remains in this sense the privileged aesthetic language; and the distorting and fragmenting reflections of one enormous glass surface to the other can be taken as paradigmatic of the central role of process and reproduction in postmodern culture' (*PLC*, 37). Architecture, therefore, most clearly embodies that mutation in space brought about by the globalization of multinational capital, a mutation that, according to Jameson, has not yet been accompanied by a corresponding transformation in the disposition subject – in the sense that we still tend to conceive of our subjectivity as autonomous and unified and have yet to come to terms with the implications of a dispersed, transnational spatial order for our identities and sense of self.

What is particularly distinctive about postmodern space, as opposed to modernist conceptions of space, is its apparent depthlessness and lack of distance, be that critical distance, metaphysical depth, or the discreteness of political and economic levels of late capitalism. The erosion of critical distance and depth is closely associated with the post-structuralist critique of representation and the referentiality of language. The fundamental premise for referential theories of language is that there exists a relationship between a word and an object in which the former stands in some way for the latter. There is, to use Baudrillard's phrase, a logic of equivalence between the signifier and the referent. Saussure's insight into the function of language was to decouple this dualism, insisting on the arbitrary nature of the relationship and the need to bracket off the referent. Baudrillard contends that the arbitrariness of the sign does not reside in the relationship between the signifier and the referent but within the sign itself, that is, between the signifier and the signified itself. On one hand, therefore, we have the signifier as form, and on the other, the signified as the thought content and the referent as reality content. Just as Baudrillard came to see use value as merely a projection of exchange value, he now argues that the referent is no more external to the sign than is the signified: both are internal to it, the referent being a projection of the sign itself. That is to say, there is no reality, just a reality effect; the 'world' that the sign 'evokes' is nothing but the effect of the sign, its signified/referent. Thus Baudrillard avoids the metaphysical illusion of a separation between the sign and the real, as the 'real' in-itself does not exist as an independent concrete reality but merely as 'the extrapolation of the excision . . . established by the logic of the sign onto the world of things'.[6]

Baudrillard's critique of political economy and the economy of the sign provides a path for him to map a full historical periodization of the sign, and to formulate a new theory of 'symbolic exchange'. Baudrillard posits three orders of representation: the counterfeit, the productive and the simulation, each governed by its own specific law of value. The first order demarcates the period from the Renaissance to the industrial era and is governed by a natural law of value. The second order designates the industrial epoch, which is governed by the commodity law of value. The final order is the present phase of late capitalism or consumer society, which is governed by a structural law of value: 'Today, the entire system is fluctuating in indeterminacy, all of reality absorbed by the hyperreality of the code and of simulation. It is now a principle of simulation, and not reality, that regulates social life.'[7]

For Baudrillard, the logic of the sign remains essentially one of equivalence. Even when one acknowledges that a given signifier may refer to multiple signifieds, the structure remains untouched, the equivalence has simply transmuted into polyvalence. Therefore, against what he calls the determinacy of the sign Baudrillard opposes the indeterminacy of the code and symbolic exchange. Although the exact nature of the code is never clearly defined, the symbolic designates the realm of ambivalence beyond the structural determinacy of the sign. There is no symbolic value as such, just symbolic exchange. In short, the symbolic is a realm beyond all value. What Baudrillard calls the structural 'law' of value is in effect the structural 'play' of each indeterminate code in relation to all the other indeterminate codes. This realm beyond the commodity structure of value is essentially a realm in which no normative statements can be made and all value is contingent and relativized.

The concept of critique is bound up with the second order of representation – that is, the order of the sign and the commodity law of value. It emerged in the West, writes Baudrillard, 'at the same time as political economy and, as the quintessence of Enlightenment rationality'.[8] The whole notion of critique, therefore, is inextricably entwined with the hermeneutics of suspicion, that is, it presupposes that there is something latent, something hidden which can be retrieved or demystified. Thus critique depends on the separation between the sign and the real, in the discrepancy that exists between our representations of the real and the real itself, which Baudrillard has laboured to dissolve. Critique presupposes not merely a metaphor of depth but also an assumption that one can maintain a critical distance, that one can be outside or have a particular self-conscious reflective position with respect to the discourse one is analysing. Whereas today, according to Baudrillard, we live in a hyperreal world of fluctuating and aleatory codes, of simulacra and simulations, of floating signifiers which are indeterminate, non-referential and unconscious. The concept of critique, along with such other redundant notions as rationality, referentiality, functionality, historical consciousness and all their metaphysical baggage of equivalence and depth, has no place in this volatized, depthless world of hyperreality.

The persuasiveness of Baudrillard's work resides in its rhetorical quality rather than its analytic or explanatory force. At a purely descriptive level it appears to provide a good, albeit rather unsubstantiated, account of a subject's lived experience within advanced capitalist or consumer societies. Baudrillard's world of ubiquitous information technology – the technologies of reproduction and proliferation rather than production as such – approximates well to the situation of North America and, to an extent, Western Europe. It remains descriptive, however, and as Baudrillard extrapolates beyond the specific social and historical situation, his ideas tend towards the universal totalizing theories postmodernism supposedly marked the end of. Jameson does not accept the political complacency of Baudrillard's work, but his conception of postmodern spatiality is significantly influenced by it. In particular, Jameson emphasizes the disorientating and saturated quality of this new sense of space: 'the suppression of distance . . . and the relentless saturation of any remaining voids and empty places, to the point where the postmodern body . . . is now exposed to a perceptual barrage of immediacy from which all sheltering layers and intervening mediations have been removed.'[9]

Everything has now been conflated into a play of surfaces – postmodern space is what Baudrillard defines as 'hyperspace', the space of simulacra and simulation, a space of pure immediacy and surface. Hyperspace is a space for which no originary space exists, it is a simulation of a space; like its correlative 'hyperreality', it is a space that is reproduced and reduplicated. Hyperreality is, so to speak, more real than Real; it conveys the sense of the thing, its 'thinginess', without the sordid materiality of the thing itself. We can therefore have the tropical*ness* of hotel atriums in Los Angeles or Chicago without the inconvenience of the tropics, 1930*ness* without the great depression. Hyperspace, however, is not simply something, a space or an object, that can be reproduced. On the contrary, it is that which must be reproduced, that has no existence unless and in so far as it *is* reproduced. Postmodern hyperspace inaugurates a new spatial paradigm and we as subjects do not as yet have the perceptual or sensory apparatus to accommodate it. Above all, there is an 'alarming disjunction' between our sense and perception of our own bodies and their immediate situation and the surrounding built environment.

Jameson's analysis of the Bonaventure Hotel in Los Angeles initially proved to be one of the most persuasive aspects of his analysis of postmodernism but has subsequently been subjected to a great deal of critical analysis. According to Jameson:

> with a certain number of other characteristic postmodern buildings, such as the Beaubourg in Paris or the Eaton Centre in Toronto, the Bonaventure aspires to being a total space, a complete world, a kind of miniature city; to this new total space, meanwhile, corresponds a new collective practice, a new mode in which individuals move and congregate, something like the practice of a new and historically original kind of hypercrowd. (*PLC*, 40)

The Bonaventure is characteristically postmodern in the sense that it is 'populist', it is after all, Jameson informs us, a tourist attraction. However, that other characteristic of postmodern architecture, the respect for the vernacular of the American city fabric, is a little more difficult to substantiate. One actually enters the hotel around the back and three stories up, while its skin of reflective glass 'repels' rather than embraces the surrounding environment. Jameson does not feel that this reading is incompatible with assertions of integration with the vernacular though, insisting that 'ideally the minicity of Portman's Bonaventure ought not to have entrances at all, since the entryway is always the seam that links the building to the rest of the city that surrounds it' (*PLC*, 40). The Bonaventure does not so much want to be part of the city at all but prefers rather to be its replacement or substitute. Although how such a substitution constitutes a respect for the vernacular of the city remains unclear.

Once inside the hotel itself Jameson is 'at a loss' to fully encapsulate the new experience of space it affords and so falls back on description: 'the lobby or atrium, with its great central column surrounded by a miniature lake, the whole positioned between the four symmetrical residential towers with their elevators, and surrounded by rising balconies capped by a kind of greenhouse roof at the sixth level' (*PLC*, 43). What Jameson wishes to stress about the new sense of space represented in the Bonaventure is its disorientation, the confusion of inside and outside, of front and back, of height and depth, that the hotel creates. At the same time, there has been a heightening, a further intensification of modernist self-consciousness or self-reflexivity, the escalators and elevators of the Bonaventure being no longer merely functional but rather 'signs' of movement in their own right. Here, writes Jameson,

> the narrative stroll has been underscored, symbolized, reified, and re-placed by a transportation machine which becomes the allegorical signifier of that older promenade we are no longer allowed to conduct on our own: and this is a dialectical intensification of the autoreferentiality of all modern culture, which tends to turn upon itself and designate its own cultural production as its content. (*PLC*, 42)

Jameson seeks to distinguish what is specifically postmodern about this new form of spatiality from the utopianism of the modernist International style. Modernism's new utopian space, he suggests, was radically separated from the degraded and fallen city fabric which it repudiated; it was like an alien form inserted into an environment which 'would fan out and eventually transform its surroundings by the very power of its new spatial language' (*PLC*, 41). Postmodern spatiality, on the other hand, 'is content to let the fallen city fabric continue to be in its being . . . no further effects, no larger protopolitical Utopian transformation, is either expected or desired' (*PLC*, 41–2). I will return to the modernist overtones of Jameson's reading of the Bonaventure below.

This new sense of space is further developed in *Postmodernism, or, The Cultural Logic of Late Capitalism* through an analysis of the postmodern architect Frank Gehry's own house. The house is a 1920s style two-storey gambrel-roof clapboard house which Gehry has 'wrapped' in a corrugated metal surround one-and-a-half storeys high; the spaces between the surround and the original building have then been partially covered over with glass and steel meshing. This is a building, then, that explicitly plays with different kinds of space and materials; it collapses our sense of inside and outside and at the same time exudes 1920s 'Californianess'. The stark effect of the corrugated metal frame, writes Jameson, 'seems to ruthlessly cut across the older house and brutally stamp the mark and sign of "modern art" on it, yet without wholly dissolving it, as though the peremptory gesture of "art" had been interrupted and abandoned in mid-process' (*PLC*, 112). Any effect of high art is immediately undercut by the cheapness of the materials used, which connote the economic and infrastructural aspects of architectural production, further undermining the autonomy of modernist aesthetic practice. For Jameson, all these features, the collapse of inside and outside, the de-differentiation between high art and mass consumption, the emergence of the materiality of the thing itself, as well as 'the bewilderment and loss of spatial orientation in Portman's hotels, the messiness of an environment in which things and people no longer find their "place" – offer useful symptomatic approaches to the nature of postmodern hyperspace, without giving us any model of explanation of the thing itself' (*PLC*, 117–18). For an explanation we must look to another aspect of postmodern architecture, that is to say, its historicism.

The older parts of the building are, writes Jameson, 'a present reality that has been transformed into a simulacrum by the process of wrapping, or quotation, and has thereby become not historical but historicist – an allusion to a present out of real history which might just as well be a past removed from real history' (*PLC*, 118). The older and newer parts of the building are in dialogue, or dialectical relationship, whereby the traditional and modernist aspects of the building are brought into conjunction and 'the tension between the two kinds of space is maintained and exacerbated' (*PLC*, 120). Gehry's house, therefore, plays off different kinds of architectural design and space and in so doing produces a radically new kind of space, 'the result of a dialectical engagement between the two others – which can be characterized as postmodern; that is to say, as some radically new spatiality beyond the traditional and the modern alike which seems to make some historical claim for radical difference and originality' (*PLC*, 120). Jameson's proposition, in other words, is the familiar dialectic of realism, modernism, postmodernism discussed in the previous chapter. Gehry's house can be read as a figure, or allegory, for that larger and more intractable problematic of postmodern spatiality, 'the relationship between that abstract knowledge and conviction or belief about the superstate and the existential daily life of people in their traditional rooms and tract houses' (*PLC*, 128).

Gehry's house would appear to be exemplary of everything Jameson wishes to attribute to postmodern hyperspace. The dilemma is that Gehry's house is not only not exemplary of postmodern architecture generally, it is not even exemplary of Gehry's own architecture. Jameson notes that 'the more original Gehry's building turns out to be, the less generalizable its features may be for postmodernism in general' (*PLC*, 108). But he still wishes to examine this building as 'one of the few postmodern buildings which does seem to have some powerful claim on revolutionary spatiality' (*PLC*, 107). Post-modernism's inherent heterogeneity will always raise such problems of what can be said to be characteristic, but this statement does seem to resonate within Jameson's texts. The analysis of the Bonaventure Hotel commences with the statement that it is 'a work which is in many ways uncharacteristic of that postmodern architecture whose principal proponents are Robert Venturi, Charles Moore, Michael Graves, and, more recently, Frank Gehry, but which to my mind offers some very striking lessons about the originality of postmodernist space' (*PLC*, 38). If Jameson's examples of postmodern architecture are by his own acknowledgement not exactly representative of postmodernism, then what, we may ask, would be?

David Shumway has pointed out that postmodern architecture 'as defined by Jencks and Venturi does not fit any of Jameson's claims for postmodernism, except one: its historical reference, or historicism', but, he adds, the latter is fulfilled by just about every other 'suburban dwelling above the economic level of Levitt's first developments of the 50s'.[10] Even in this respect Jameson's choice of the Bonaventure would seem to be rather strange as it displays none of the historicism that is so characteristic of postmodernism. On the contrary, the Bonaventure is 'an almost perfect example of what Charles Jencks calls late modernism'.[11] As for Jameson's description of hyperspace, Shumway comments that it is simply wrong: 'What the lobby of the Bonaventure contains is enormous depth; what it lacks are precisely the surfaces which are normally significant in hotel lobbies: walls which divide eating spaces from waiting spaces, which advertise services, or which display merchandise.'[12] Even Jameson's rhetoric, the sense of 'plummeting to splashdown' on the elevators, is a classic modernist trope of the exhilaration of speed. The disorientation of space, of which Jameson makes so much, the concealed entrances and the hotel's flat reflective skin of mirror glass, has as much to do with keeping out the populace – the indigenous downtown Angelenos, the poor, the homeless, the blacks and the hispanics – as it has with evading modernist utopian aspirations.

Indeed, postmodern architecture's obsession with security and surveillance would seem to be as protopolitical as any modernist utopian vision. In *City of Quartz: Excavating the Future of Los Angeles*, Mike Davis describes Frank Gehry as the Dirty Harry of postmodern architects, whose work 'clarifies the underlying relations of repression, surveillance and exclusion that characterize the fragmented, paranoid spatiality towards which Los Angeles seems to aspire'.[13] While Davis's rhetoric tends towards the apocalyptic, there does indeed appear to be something rather paradoxical about an ostensibly populist and democratic architecture whose basic design features are often based on prisons. Indeed, Gehry's own house with its high metal fencing and steel mesh resembles nothing less than a modern privatized prison, or perhaps, in a more playfully postmodern vein, a parody of the contemporary suburban obsession with home security.

The overriding problem with postmodern hyperspace, for Jameson, is our inability to conceive (or indeed the impossibility of conceiving) our situation as individual subjects within this new global network of multinational capital. This space has become unrepresentable and we are left with the ability to grasp only our most immediate surroundings. What is required is a new form of political aesthetic which places spatial issues at the centre of its concerns. Jameson proposes the term 'cognitive mapping' for this as yet untheorized aesthetic. The notion of cognitive mapping is derived from a famous 1960s study, *The Image of the City*, by the urban planner Kevin Lynch. As Preziosi describes it:

> Lynch conducted research into the ways in which residents of particular American cities conceptualized and internally represented their native habitats; in essence he found that individuals develop 'cognitive maps' of

their urban environments which enable them to negotiate, navigate, and conceptualize their urban spaces.[14]

What interests Jameson in this notion is that 'the alienated city is above all a space in which people are unable to map (in their minds) either their own positions or the urban totality in which they find themselves' (*PLC*, 51). Jameson sees a striking analogy between Lynch's idea of the alienated city and the need for cognitive maps and Althusser's conception of ideology:

> Surely this is exactly what the cognitive map is called upon to do in the narrower framework of daily life in the physical city: to enable a situational representation on the part of the individual subject to that vaster and properly unrepresentable totality which is the ensemble of society's structures as a whole. (*PLC*, 51)

The notion of cognitive mapping, then, hinges on a dialectic of immediate perception and imaginative or imaginary conception: that is to say, our ability to extrapolate from the mental map we have of our immediate perceptible situation to a larger imaginary spatial context. In other words, how we make the shift from our immediate urban and city environment to 'that mental map of the social and global totality we all carry around in our heads in variously garbled forms'.[15] We all necessarily, writes Jameson, cognitively map our individual social relations locally and nationally but now must attempt to map them in terms of the totality of class relations on a global, multinational scale. The failure to achieve such cognitive maps, argues Jameson, will have crippling effects on political experience and any socialist project in the postmodern world. For Jameson, an aesthetic of cognitive mapping is an essential precondition for the renewal of socialist politics in a postmodern age, but this as yet untheorized 'pedagogical political culture which seeks to endow the individual subject with some new heightened sense of its place in the global system' (*PLC*, 54) will have to find new forms in order to articulate this complex representational dialectic.[16]

Jameson's notion of cognitive mapping raises a number of theoretical dilemmas, not least of which is the question of who is the 'we' being appealed to here? Jameson directs too little attention to specific cultural practices and mediations, preferring to generalize from his own experience. Thus his experience of postmodern spatiality may be exhilarating, albeit disorientating and unrepresentable, but at the same time, as Davis's *City of Quartz* has shown, it presents a radically different experience for others. In the following chapter I argue that

Jameson's work directs too little attention towards the mediations between the experience of individual subjects and the global transnational forces of late capitalism. Below I consider the nature of postmodern spatiality in greater detail.

The Social Production of Space

Jameson's spatial analysis operates on two dialectically related levels simultaneously. On the one hand, he describes the individual existential experience of postmodern spatiality, and on the other, he correlates specific types of spatiality with particular modes of production. As with the dialectic of realism, modernism and postmodernism, each historical period of capitalist production produces its own distinct form of spatiality and each form of spatiality in turn engenders its own aesthetic or specific regime of representation. Jameson writes:

> I have tried to suggest that the three historical stages of capital have each generated a type of space unique to it, even though these three stages of capitalist space are obviously far more profoundly interrelated than are the spaces of other modes of production. The three types of space I have in mind are all the result of discontinuous expansions or quantum leaps in the enlargement of capital, in the latter's penetration and colonization of hitherto uncommodified areas.[17]

The first type of space, that generated by market capitalism, approximates the logic of a grid, that is, a geometrical space of infinite equivalence and extension. The second type corresponds to monopoly capitalism, or imperialism, and can be characterized as structural disjunction, that is, the increasing discrepancy between individual experience and 'a more properly structural model of the conditions of existence of that experience'.[18] Finally, we come to the postmodern spatiality of late capitalism which has been our object of study here.

The authority and theoretical foundation for Jameson's conception of spatiality is the work of Henri Lefebvre and in particular his seminal text *The Production of Space*.[19] The central thesis of *The Production of Space* is encapsulated in its title, that is to say, that space is not given but produced. In other words, space is not a neutral category, an objective and innocent realm, but it is a social construct, constituted through social and material practices. Traditionally, argues Lefebvre, there have been two ways of perceiving space: Euclidean or geometric space and mental space. The discourse of Euclidean space and classical perspectivism prevailed from roughly the sixteenth century, or the Renaissance, through to the end of the nineteenth century. Mental space, on the other hand, is the space of philosophers and epistemologists. Mental space is produced by theoretical practice and in turn becomes the site of a theoretical discourse separated from real space, the 'quasi-logical presupposition of an identity between mental space . . . and real space creates an abyss between the mental sphere on one side and the physical and social spheres on the other'.[20] Both of these conceptions of space, however, rest on a dual fallacy, that is to say, the illusion of opacity and transparency. The illusion of opaqueness sees space only in terms of immediate surface appearances, refusing to see beyond these appearances. In this sense, Soja observes, space is 'comprehended only as objectively measurable appearances grasped through some combination of sensory-based perception'.[21] Space is reduced to physical objects and forms that then 'become susceptible to prevailing scientific explanation in the form of orderly, reproducible description and the discovery of empirical regularities'.[22] We have, in other words, a neutral and depoliticized space which submerges any sense of social conflict. The illusion of transparency, on the other hand, obfuscates space not by focusing on appearances but by ignoring physical objects and concrete space altogether, reducing space to 'a mental construct alone, a way of thinking, an ideational process in which the "image" of reality takes epistemological precedence over the tangible substance and appearance of the real world'.[23] Space is once more reduced to a depoliticized sphere in which social realities and social conflicts are erased.

Traditional conceptions of space, therefore, see space as either objectively measurable and reducible to the objects and forms in space, or as an ideal construct, but both presuppose a conception of space as innocent and neutral. The problem with traditional as well as many contemporary conceptions of space, for Lefebvre, is that they fail to conceive space in its full complexity: they reduce space either to a representation of space or to a transcendental absolute – that is, space as a text or mental representation and space as simply given. As I have indicated, however, space is not simply given, it is not objective, neutral and empty; it is produced, it is the product of social practice. In contrast to these reductive theories of space, therefore, Lefebvre proposes a 'unitary theory' of space, a theory that encompasses physical space, mental space and social space, or what Lefebvre terms the perceived, the conceived and the lived.

Lefebvre returns time and again to this triad but never as a rigid formula or schema by which space can be divided up and partitioned off. For Lefebvre the production of space is always a process, each moment in that process feeding into and off the others. As soon as the perceived – conceived – lived triad is taken as an abstract model and imposed on space it loses its explanatory force. Lefebvre transcodes this overly anthropological terminology into more properly spatial terms: as spatial practice, representations of space and representational spaces. Spatial practice refers to the production, reproduction, particular locations and spatial sets characteristic of any given social formation. Representations of space refers to 'the relations of production and to the "order" which those relations impose',[24] in other words to the regime of signification, the signs, codes and knowledge which a given formation utilizes. Representational spaces, on the other hand, refers to the deep structures, the 'complex symbolisms, sometimes coded, sometimes not, linked to the clandestine or underground side of social life'.[25]

Jameson's typology of Euclidean geometric space, the structurally disjunctive space of imperialism and finally the saturated depthless quality of postmodern spatiality resonates with Lefebvre's periodization of absolute space, abstract space and differential space. Differential spatiality would appear to designate just such space as Jameson wishes to associate with postmodernism, although he himself sees Lefebvre's notion of abstract space, with its dialectic of homogeneity and fragmentation, as analogous to his own conception of postmodern spatiality. Furthermore, Jameson's conception of postmodern spatiality fails to address the full complexity of spatial relations, limiting itself to just one level of Lefebvre's unitary theory.

The Semiotics of Space

Jameson's analysis of postmodern architecture once again raises those questions I considered in relation to video; that is to say, does his theory of postmodernism rule out, *a priori*, certain interpretative options? Jameson's interpretative and analytic practice remains textually constrained and thus unable to articulate the full complexity and contradictoriness of postmodern spatiality. For example, Jameson makes a strong distinction between modernist and postmodernist architecture. The newer buildings, he writes,

no longer attempt, as did the masterworks and monuments of high modernism, to insert a different, a distinct, an elevated, a new Utopian language into the tawdry and commercial sign system of the surrounding city, but rather they seek to speak that very language, using its lexicon and syntax as that has been emblematically 'learned from Las Vegas'. (*PLC*, 39)

In short, Jameson reads space as a text and the semiotics of space as its grammar.

Indeed, Jameson goes so far as to suggest that we read the urban cityscape as the text, rooms as its minimal units, buildings as sentences, corridors, doorways, staircases as adverbs and furniture, paintings etc. as adjectives (*PLC*, 105). Rather than analysing postmodern architecture on its own terms, Jameson sees it as a set of texts. It would appear that Jameson has forgotten his own first lesson of dialectical criticism: that the critic attempts to think herself or himself back into the process of criticism. Theories of textuality are themselves a postmodern phenomenon and as such an aspect of Jameson's object of study. For Jameson, they also provide the method of analysis, as he reads all postmodern phenomena as a text in relation to an intertextual field. There is a certain circularity to Jameson's project and the disorientation of space that he locates in his object of study may be more to do with his own sense of confusion and disorientation than an inherent feature of postmodern spatiality.

Jameson makes the familiar defence of this transcoding operation – that it throws a given problematic into a new light and opens up new perspectives on the issues involved. Such a rewriting programme, writes Jameson, 'may be useful in our present architectural context, provided it is not confused with a semiotics of architecture . . . but rather to awaken the question of the conditions of possibility of this or that spatial form' (*PLC*, 105). Lefebvre argues, to the contrary, that this kind of transcoding operation can reveal nothing about the genesis of spatial forms, 'the notions of message, code, information and so on cannot help us trace the genesis of a space; the fact remains, however, that an already produced space can be decoded, can be *read.*'[26] In other words, we can read space as a text in the way that Jameson is suggesting but we cannot derive from that reading the information he proposes for the initial justification of the operation. Linguistic and semiotic analyses of space can be made, but they can be made only on spaces that have already been produced, and they are therefore limited to just one level of Lefebvre's unitary theory, that is, conceived, or representations of, space. Space cannot be reduced to the language of texts because those signifying practices themselves exist within space. It is true to say that space signifies, but, argues Lefebvre, there is no clarity as to what it signifies. Social space 'can in no way be compared to a blank page upon which a specific message has been inscribed',[27] because it is in fact overinscribed, or overdetermined. By transcoding his spatial analyses into linguistic and textual terms, Jameson has reduced the complexity of space to its representations, a position from which he will thus propose the depthlessness of this new spatial configuration. But as Lefebvre consistently reminds us, 'a spatial code is not simply a means of reading or interpreting space: rather it is a means of living in that space, of understanding it, and of producing it.'[28]

Jameson's concern to reassert the category of space has developed into what David Harvey calls 'spatial fetishism'. In a critique of Lefebvre, Harvey dissents from Lefebvre's insistence on the 'decisive' and 'pre-eminent' role of spatial structural forces in modern capitalist society.[29] For Harvey, the problem essentially revolves around the status one accords to spatial determinants within specific social formations and more generally in the process of historical and social transformation. For Lefebvre, space has a unique status, what he called the materialization of social being. Everything exists 'within' space and yet space does not exist without a subject or a body to live, perceive and conceive that space. Lefebvre frequently alludes to a spatio-temporal dialectic, in the sense that time can only be known and actualized in space and through spatial practice while, at the same time, space can only be known in and through time. He never, however, fully works through this dialectic, and temporality is marginalized within his work in much the same way as space was ignored in earlier social theory.

Indeed, Lefebvre appears to suggest at one point what Jameson terms a new theory of history with space as the primary force behind social transformation:

> The space of capitalist accumulation thus gradually came to life, and began to be fitted out. This process of animation is admiringly referred to as history, and its motor sought in all kinds of factors: dynastic interests, ideologies, the ambitions of the mighty, the formation of nation states, demographic pressures, and so on. This is the road to a ceaseless analysing of, and searching for, dates and chains of events. Inasmuch as space is the locus of all such chronologies, might it not constitute a principle of explanation at least as acceptable as any other?[30]

For critics such as Harvey, Lefebvre goes too far in this direction and rather than seeing space as '*a separate structure* with its own laws of inner transformation and construction', it should be seen as 'the *expression* of a set of relations embedded in some broader structure (such as the social relations of production)'.[31] I shall return to the question of the spatio-temporal dialectic of modernity and postmodernity in the concluding section of this chapter. First, I examine the political implications of Jameson's reading of postmodern spatiality.

While Jameson tends towards spatial fetishism he also, paradoxically, recapitulates the old problematic of space within social theory. He sees postmodernism as marked by a general loss of temporality, or more precisely by a waning of narrative and the historical imagination. But rather than seeing this as providing new possibilities for new forms of politics, Jameson appears to see the postmodern world as a realm in which no meaningful politics can exist. This situation is exacerbated by Jameson's high level of abstraction and broad generalization, which has an inherent tendency to become overly schematic. Thus temporality, narrative and historical thought have become almost exclusively associated with modernism, while space, the play of surfaces and an ahistorical imagination signify our postmodern experience. Political resistance to postmodernism would appear, for Jameson, to reside in a space outside of late capitalism itself, a space which late capitalism, by its very nature, has abolished. Consequently, the potential for successful political action within advanced capitalist states would now appear to be rather remote.

Doreen Massey has convincingly shown how Jameson's conception of space deprives it of any meaningful politics. In particular, Jameson's dichotomy of modern and postmodern spatiality remains locked within a particular form of dualistic or dichotomous thought which, either overtly or covertly, stigmatizes one side of the debate while valorizing the other. In short, modernism, temporality, history are seen as positive terms while postmodernism, space, immanence are once more taken to be negative terms. Jameson finds postmodern space 'alarming' and 'disorientating', but more than this he sees it as essentially unrepresentable, as chaotic and depthless. Despite his ostensible intentions, space has once more become defined negatively in relation to time. Space is defined as the absence of time, as stasis or atemporality, while time once more is defined positively as the realm of change and transformation. Massey notes how in Jameson this kind of dichotomous thinking clearly relates to another of Jameson's dualisms, that between transcendence and immanence, 'with the former connotationally associated with the temporal and immanence with the spatial'.[32] Consequently, Jameson's views on postmodernism and the possibility of any new cultural politics are extremely pessimistic. Faced with the 'horror of multiplicity' of postmodern space Jameson can only call for new forms of global cognitive mapping.

What is unusual in Jameson's formulation is its rather undialectical application. The dialectical corollary of the global logic of late capitalism has been a redefinition and renewed significance of the local.

Political struggles at a local level are increasingly a response to global restructuring, for example the 'local' insurrection of the Zapatistas in Chiapas, Mexico, in relation to the North American Free Trade Agreement. At the same time, local political actions are being forced to internationalize their struggles. In the UK's longest running strike, by Liverpool dockworkers, the unions made extensive use of the new 'postmodern' information technologies to gain support and action in sympathy throughout Europe and North America.

Jameson's conception of postmodern space as depthless, chaotic and atemporal is a far cry from Lefebvre's conception of social space as differential, contradictory and conflictual, as a space not reduced to its representations but a social reality occupied by bodies in a constant state of struggle. I shall, therefore, conclude this section with one of the salutary lessons of *The Production of Space*, the need to constantly resist all forms of reductionism:

> reductionism entails the reduction of time to space, the reduction of use value to exchange value, the reduction of objects to signs, and the reduction of 'reality' to the semiosphere; it also means that the movement of the dialectic is reduced to a logic, and social space to a purely formal mental space.[33]

The Spatio-Temporal Dialectic of Modernity and Postmodernity

Following on from the critique I advanced in the final section of the previous chapter, I want to suggest that Jameson's conception of postmodern spatiality is insufficiently dialectical. Consequently it appears to be inconceivable for Jameson to imagine any form of properly postmodern politics. Jameson commences 'The Antinomies of Postmodernity',[34] the opening lecture of his 1991 Welleck lecture series (published as *The Seeds of Time*), with a consideration of the distinction between an antinomy and a contradiction. The antinomy tends to denote an opposition that is irreconcilable: 'it states two propositions that are radically, indeed absolutely, incompatible' (*ST*, 1). The contradiction, on the other hand, designates something that is susceptible to a solution or resolution. The antinomy is, following Kant, a logical and analytic category, while the contradiction, after Hegel, is dialectical. The postmodern age, observes Jameson, is one more propitious for the antinomy than the contradiction. Postmodern culture is one in which the aporia and impasse, fragmentation and schizoid flux are celebrated and for which there can be no resolution at a higher level of abstraction as in the older (modernist) language of dialectical contradiction. Jameson identifies four fundamental antinomies of postmodernism: time and space, subject and object, nature and human nature, and finally the concept of Utopia.

Postmodern temporality and spatiality are both marked by a fundamental paradox. Postmodern temporality is characterized by an accelerated rate of change: the turnover of fashions, lifestyles, beliefs even, has rapidly increased over the last twenty or thirty years. What is unusual about this is that it appears to be change without any opposite, change without real transformation. The transition from nationally based economies to a multinational economy has been accompanied by a change in both the form of production and regimes of capital accumulation. That is, Fordist production line methods entailing large factories and long production runs of exactly the same commodity have given way to post-Fordist forms of production which allow for greater flexibility of both production processes and commodities, as well as greater mobility of capital and production bases. Similarly capital accumulation has transferred from large-scale investment in infrastructural and capital projects to much more flexible forms of accumulation, share speculation, etc.

On the one hand, these transformations help to accelerate the pace of life, so that everything turns over and changes much more quickly. On the other hand, these changes are accompanied by the absolute standardization of the lifeworld, since we can now buy the same commodities the world over. We simultaneously experience an un-precedented rate of change and a complete standardization of the lifeworld which would appear to be incompatible with just such mutability. We must distinguish, therefore, between change within the system and change of the system itself. In terms of individual experience one can change one's life almost daily, but at a deeper structural level we appear to be unable to imagine change at all. Contrary to postmodernism's celebration of difference, heterogene-ity and radical otherness, argues Jameson, social life has never been so standardized and 'the stream of human, social, and historical temporality has never flowed quite so homogeneously' (*ST*, 17). As Jameson puts it, we are now in a situation in which the sheer momentum of change slides into its opposite, into stasis. The deeper logic of postmodernism is that while everything is submitted to the change of fashion, the image and the media, nothing fundamentally can any longer change. Temporality, in other words, has become essentially spatial.

As with his earlier theorization, Jameson continues to insist that postmodernism can be characterized as a spatial experience. Furthermore, it is a spatial experience that negates or represses temporality. Space, writes Jameson, 'does not seem to require a temporal expression; if it is not what absolutely does without such temporal figurality, then at the very least it might be said that space is what represses temporality and temporal figurality absolutely, to the benefit of other figures and codes' (*ST*, 21). There is an all-or-nothing rhetoric to Jameson's notion of postmodern space; the initial qualification that space cannot completely annihilate temporality is immediately undercut by the assertion that, on a representational level, it is precisely space's ability to absolutely repress temporality that is the issue.

The paradox of postmodern or late capitalist spatiality has been encapsulated in the neologism 'glocalization',[35] in other words, the global is now located in the local. While multinational corporations spread themselves across the globe, they package and market themselves through specific national identities within individual countries. As a strategy to combat multinationalism, more properly national companies are also increasingly emphasizing their local and regional identities – in short, globalization masquerading as regionalism. The complete standardization of space in a single world market is accompanied by the celebration of local diversity. Ethnic identity and lifestyles are now packaged and sold on the world market as so many options for an affluent West. The ideology of a single standardized global market has sold us back a global space and postmodern city as, to quote Jameson, 'a well-nigh Bakhtinian carnival of heterogeneities, of differences, libidinal excitement, and a hyperindividuality that effectively decenters the old individual subject by way of individual hyper-consumption' (*ST*, 31). As with temporality, therefore, postmodern spatiality appears to fold into its opposite; heterogeneity passes over into homogeneity. What is probably the most standardized and uniform social reality that we have ever known is celebrated in all its diversity and otherness.

This rather bleak and pessimistic scenario seems, as I indicated at the outset, to have paralysed Jameson's political imagination. Faced with the enormity of a fully global capitalism, Jameson can only resort to a politically rather vague notion of cognitive mapping which places the individual subject in the unenviable position of trying to map, or represent, an unrepresentable global system, the totality itself. As this, by definition, is impossible, an individual subject's last resort appears to be the hope for some as yet to be theorized form of political response. Much of the energy of Jameson's recent writing has revolved around this need to retain a utopian impulse, to restore a properly utopian dimension to current cultural and critical practice, to keep alive the sense of a qualitatively different form of society. Ironically, while we are all too ready to conceive of a complete world ecological crisis we seem to be utterly unable to conceive of a different form of social organization. For Jameson, then, we must try to detect and retrieve from within the fragmented, schizoid and heterogeneous elements of postmodern culture the smallest remnants of a repressed collective experience, a collective experience that will allow us to once more think the alternative to a global capitalist system.

In the following chapter I suggest that what is missing from Jameson's analysis is any form of institutional mediation between the individual and the social totality. Here I shall concentrate on the dialectic of time and space. In an astute analysis of an exchange between Perry Anderson and Marshal Berman, Peter Osborne has reassessed the debate over modernity's spatio-temporal dialectic. According to Berman, modernity was essentially a mode of experience, a particular historical experience of space and time that mediated between modernization as a socioeconomic process and modernism as a cultural and aesthetic vision. Anderson criticized Berman's account of modernity because it rested on an essential 'planar' conception of historical time, that is to say, as a continuous flow process in which each epoch succeeds the next without any real differentiation between them, except chronologically. Anderson argued, following Althusser, for a differential conception of historical time and conjunctural analysis. Osborne suggests that both positions are inadequate to the extent that they take modernity to designate an essentially chronological category: 'The key to the matter will be seen to lie in the relation between the meaning of "modernity" as a category of historical periodization and its meaning as a distinctive form or quality of social experience – that is to say, in the dialectics of a certain *temporalization of history.*'[36]

According to Osborne what is unique about modernity as a category of historical periodization is that it is defined solely in terms of temporal determinants. For Osborne postmodernism is not a new historical epoch but only the most recent transformation in a continuing process of modernity (a position Jameson would certainly endorse). What is peculiarly unique to the temporality of modernity is its contemporaneity: modernity designates what is new. Furthermore, what is new must be distinguished from even the most recent past, which would appear to contrast with postmodernism's historicism, or eclecticism and pastiche, which takes the form of a raiding of previous aesthetic styles but lacks any real sense of history or future transformation. As a periodizing category, modernity serves a dual function; 'it designates the contemporaneity of an epoch to the time of its classification, but it registers this contemporaneity in terms of a qualitatively new, self-transcending temporality, which has the simultaneous effect of distancing the present from even that most recent past with which it is thus identified.'[37] In other words, 'modernity is a qualitative and not a chronological category.'

Modernity cannot be reduced to a simple opposition between homogeneous (Berman) and differential (Anderson) historical time but must be grasped as a dialectic of homogenization (its contemporaneity) and differentiation (its distancing of itself from other historical epochs). This dialectic is not only constitutive of the temporality of modernity but is inextricably tied to its *spatial* relations: that is to say, the geopolitics of modernity or the history of colonialism. As Osborne writes, 'the concept of modernity was first universalized through the spatialization of its founding temporal difference, under colonialism; thereafter, the differential between itself and other "times" was reduced to a difference within a single temporal scale of "progress", "modernization" and "development".'[38] Without pursuing this further, if modernity is a particular form of spatio-temporal experience then we can begin to understand postmodernity as a further development or modification of this form of experience, what Harvey describes as an acceleration of 'time-space compression'.[39]

What is absent from Jameson's conception of postmodern spatiality is any real sense of this spatio-temporal dialectic. For Jameson, postmodern spatiality is that which abolishes alternative forms of spatiality and represses temporality absolutely. Harvey's conception of 'time-space compression' provides an alternative way to theorize the transition from modernism to postmodernism and the changing relationship between time and space. For Harvey, 'the history of capitalism has been characterized by the speed-up in the pace of life,' while simultaneously in 'overcoming spatial barriers the world sometimes seems to collapse inwards upon us'.[40] What has taken place over the last two decades, argues Harvey, is that the pace of speed-up has once more accelerated, that is, production times have accelerated and in turn brought about an acceleration in exchange and consumption. The throw-away society has increased to the extent that now not only are our commodities disposable but so too are our values. Whether we think in terms of art, music, fashion or lifestyles in

general, the turnover and built-in obsolescence of particular commodities and styles seem to have increased considerably. In other
words, we have 'witnessed another fierce round in that process of
annihilation of space through time that has always lain at the centre
of capitalism's dynamic'.[41]

But does this not contradict the assertion that space is the new
cultural dominant? On the contrary, the collapse of spatial barriers
does not imply that the significance of space is decreasing but that its
significance will increase. As the spatial barriers diminish we become
increasingly sensitized to those spaces that remain and to what
happens 'to' and 'within' those spaces. Therefore, writes Harvey,
the struggle over and within space will become an increasingly
important issue in future political struggles: 'Superior command
over space becomes an even more important weapon in class-
struggle. It becomes one of the means to enforce speed-up and the
redefinition of skills on recalcitrant work forces.'[42]

Indeed space, far from being a depoliticized zone of stasis, is
rapidly becoming *the* single most important terrain of political
struggle for the twenty-first century, as advanced capitalist states
attempt to stem the tide of immigration. To return to the example of
NAFTA, the aims of the agreement are to facilitate the free movement
of trade and goods but not the free movement of labour. North
America is now free to export grain to Mexico, potentially destroying
the local economies, yet the citizens of California can erect barriers to
keep Mexican migrants out. At the same time, the attempts of the
Zapatista to defend their own locality are suppressed. Throughout
Western Europe there has been a widespread deregulation of the
financial and trading markets during the 1980s and 1990s, but this has
not been accompanied by a corresponding relaxation of the regul-
ation of the movement of people between states. There is, in a sense,
no need to speculate on what new form a postmodern, or spatial,
politics will take when it is already being fought out across the globe.

6

Marxism, Totality and the Politics of Difference

In the preceding chapters I have analysed Jameson's oeuvre through five key areas: form, history, desire, postmodernism and spatial theory. I have suggested that his ability to subsume a multiplicity of contradictory discourses within his own Marxian framework frequently results in a tendency to erase fundamental differences and conflate distinct and specific theoretical positions, in short, to enforce identity and homogeneity over non-identity and hetero-geneity. What has been absent from the analysis so far is a direct engagement with probably the most contentious aspect of Jameson's work, that is, its holistic or totalizing character. Indeed, perhaps Jameson's most audacious gesture has been his attempt to simultane-ously accommodate the detotalizing critiques of post-structuralism while retaining the concept of totality itself. In this chapter I will examine Jameson's concept of totality and his claims for the necessity of totalizing thought. In light of this analysis I shall then reconsider the related concept of mediation. I examine Jameson's key mediatory category of reification, arguing that Jameson has privileged this category at the expense of other forms of mediation, specifically group and institutional mediations, to which I will turn in the concluding chapter. Finally, I consider the ambiguous status the 'Third World' plays in Jameson's theory of postmodernity as a consequence of an overly totalizing approach to postmodern theory.

The Postmodern Critique of Totality

In the conclusion to *Postmodernism, or, The Cultural Logic of Late Capitalism* Jameson endorses Douglas Kellner's observation that it is the concept of totality that provides continuity between his earlier work on dialectical criticism and the later analysis of postmodernism (*PLC*, 399). Martin Jay also points out in his exhaustive study of the concept, *Marxism and Totality*, that Jameson is one of the few major theorists writing today who wishes to retain the concept.[1] Jameson's commitment to the concept of totality and the necessity of totalizing thought is as strong in the mid-1990s as it was in the early 1970s. Indeed *The Geopolitical Aesthetic: Cinema and Space in the World System* presents a breathtaking attempt to map the totality, or, to put it another way, the global system of multinational capitalism, through a discrete collection of films from world cinema. The conception of totality Jameson deploys, however, or more accurately the emphasis he places on the concept, has been significantly modified over the years. There are four principal strands of totalizing thought evident in Jameson's work: first, that of Lukács and through Lukács that of Hegel; secondly, Sartre's notion of 'totalization'; thirdly, Althusser's Spinozist formulation of history as an 'absent cause'; and finally, Adorno's negative critique of identity theory and totality. Before examining each of these strands and tracing the nuances of Jameson's usage, I will briefly consider the post-structuralist and postmodernist critique of totalizing thought.

In the concluding chapter of *Marxism and Totality*, entitled 'The Challenge of Post-Structuralism', Jay observes that even on the left there has been 'a general move away from the totalistic emphasis that marked the earlier Anglo-American reception of continental Marxism' as many of the old New Left seek to accommodate the criticisms of post-structuralism.[2] For Jay, the rejection of all forms of holism, or totalizing thought, is the one issue that appears to unite the otherwise disparate group of figures that are generally designated as post-structuralist. 'If one had to find one common denominator among the major figures normally included in the post-structuralist category,' he writes, 'it would have to be their unremitting hostility towards totality.'[3] Following Foucault, Jay notes that in so far 'as Marxism of whatever variety still insisted on the category of totality it was complicitous with the very system it claimed to oppose'.[4] Indeed, for Foucault, the very idea of the ' "whole of society" is precisely that which should not be considered except as something to be destroyed'.[5] For post-structuralists such as Foucault the concept of totality is irredeemably tainted with the concept of totalitarianism, a term first used to describe the Fascist regime of Italy and then later extended to include the Nazi regime in Germany and the Stalinist regime in the USSR. All totalizing thought has now tended to become characterized, or rather caricatured, as a surreptitious form of will to power. Linda Hutcheon summarizes the suspicion of totalizing thought well in *The Politics of Postmodernism*:

> The function of the term totalizing, as I understand it, is to point to the *process* (hence the awkward 'ing' form) by which writers of history, fiction, or even theory render their materials coherent, continuous, unified – but always with an eye to the control and mastery of those materials, even at the risk of doing violence to them. It is this link to power, as well as process, that the adjective 'totalizing' is meant to suggest, and it is as such that the term has been used to characterize everything from liberal humanist ideals to the aims of historiography.[6]

What Jameson calls the 'war on totality', however, seems to be more specifically directed against Marxism than against liberal humanist views in general, as exemplified in Hutcheon's own text wherein Jameson and Marxism are portrayed as exemplary of the very kind of totalizing thought postmodernism is contesting.[7] In short, totalizing thought was seen to eradicate difference and heterogeneity, if necessary through force and violence, and as Jameson writes 'in the memorable words of the *nouveaux philosophes* . . . a direct line runs from Hegel's Absolute Spirit to Stalin's Gulag' (*PU*, 51). Marxism and postmodernism, therefore, start from radically opposing premises. As Steven Best puts it,

> dialectical, totalizing Marxism begins with the assumption that reality, despite its dynamic, contradictory nature, is ultimately an intelligible whole comprehensible through a scientific or theoretical discourse, [whereas] post-structuralism proceeds on the belief that all 'texts' are constituted of incommensurable fragments and particulars which cannot, without a reductive violence, be assimilated to some larger whole.[8]

It is within this theoretical context, as well as the specific political conjuncture of the North American left (to which I will return in the concluding chapter), that the polemical and the political aspects of Jameson's insistence on the need for totalizing thought must be situated. Jameson's attempt to co-opt certain aspects of post-structuralism, however, have necessitated a change in his use of the term and a precarious balancing act of contradictory theoretical positions. It is to this development that I now turn.

Marxism and Totality

In *Marxism and Form* Jameson works with an essentially Lu\
conception of totality, that is to say, the totality is seen as the 'co_____
whereas isolated phenomena and experience are defined as the
abstract. Lukács was indebted to Hegel for this particular conception
of the concrete as the totality:

> What from a positivist point of view would seem oxymoronic, linking
> concreteness with totality, was accepted by Lukács because of his Hegelian
> notion of the concrete. Instead of equating it with discrete entities or
> individual facts, he followed Marx's Hegelian usage: 'The concrete is
> concrete because it is a synthesis of many particular determinants, i.e. a
> unity of elements.' The totality could be concrete precisely because it
> included all of the mediations that linked the seemingly isolated facts.[9]

Thus, in his discussion of Lukács's conception of the concrete in art,
Jameson writes, 'such work permits life and experience to be felt as a
totality: all its events, all its partial facts and elements are immediately
grasped as part of a total process' (*MF*, 169). The totality is the social
whole in which 'everything depends on everything else' (*MF*, 188). At
the same time, the concept of totality also functions as a term limit, in
the sense of the inherent conceptual limits of other philosophies. The
limits of middle-class philosophy, for example, 'are signalled by its
incapacity or unwillingness to come to terms with the category of
"totality" itself' (*MF*, 184).

Without once more rehearsing Lukács's views on the antinomies of
bourgeois thought, I will briefly restate here what is necessary for the
discussion of totality below. Jameson observes that the 'privileged
nature of the worker's situation lies, paradoxically, in its narrow,
inhuman limits':

> the worker is unable to know the outside world in a static, contemplative
> manner in one sense because he cannot know it at all, because his situation
> does not give the leisure to intuit it in the middle-class sense; because, even
> before he posits elements of the outside world as *objects* of his thought, he
> feels *himself* to be an object, and this initial alienation within himself takes
> precedence over everything else. (*MF*, 186–7)

It is this privileged position, according to Lukács, that enables proletarian thought to overcome the limits of bourgeois thought. The
proletariat is both subject and object, and therefore permitted 'access
to the totality or reality, to that totalizing knowledge which was the

stumbling block of classical bourgeois philosophy' (*MF*, 186). Lukács's conception of the proletariat as the first universal subject of history rests on Vico's *verum-factum* principle, that is, that 'the true and the made are interchangeable.'[10] For Lukács, however, 'the *verum-factum* principle applied only when a universal totalizer made history in a deliberate and rational manner. To know the whole was thus dependent on the existence of a collective historical subject who could recognize itself in its objectifications,'[11] that is to say, the proletariat. Thus Lukács's conception of totality can be said to be 'expressive' in the sense that 'the whole expresses the intentionality and praxis of a creator-subject, who recognizes itself in the objective world around it.'[12]

As I argued in chapter 2, Jameson deflects the Althusserian critique of expressive totality through an insistence on the fundamental organizational role of narrative. Narratives provide an essential framework for ordering the social world, they make connections and contextualize discrete events within a unified whole. As Best observes, Jameson follows Lukács, therefore, in seeing narrative as 'a fundamental expression and realization of the "aspiration to totality" (Lukács), a yearning that Jameson's later work reconfigures as "cognitive mapping"'.[13]

Further support for the Lukácsian paradigm and the crucial role narrative plays in Jameson's conception of totality can be discerned from his consideration of Sartre. Jameson identifies Sartre's concept of totalization with Lukács's 'progressive longitudinal totality', that is, a conception of history as 'a coherent and meaningful unity'.[14] As Jameson puts it, 'the concept of totalization enables Sartre to do away with the relativism inherent in the notion of the project . . . It is only on this condition that history as a whole can have a meaning, or a single direction' (*MF*, 231). A variation of the progressive longitudinal totality re-emerges in *The Political Unconscious* in the form of Jameson's capitalized History as the single great adventure of class struggle to wrest the realm of freedom from the realm of necessity. The concept of totality invoked in this text, however, is rather different from the 'positive dialectics of Lukács' subject-object unity'[15] that Jameson worked with in *Marxism and Form*.

The second aspect of totality that I indicated above, that is, as a term limit, a methodological standard against which other forms of thought can be measured, is now brought to the fore. It has not been sufficiently grasped, writes Jameson, 'that Lukács' method of ideological critique – like the Hegelian dialectic itself and its Sartrean variant, in the methodological imperative of totalization proposed in

the *Critique* – is an essentially critical and negative, d
operation' (*PU*, 52). Certainly Jameson's own stress on
aspect of the adequation of subject to object in *Marxism a*
been abandoned, as has any appeal to a Hegelian conce
concrete. Jameson now suggests that:

> Lukács' central analysis of the ideological character of classical German
> philosophy may from this perspective be seen as a creative and original
> variant on Marx's theory of ideology, which is not, as is widely thought,
> one of false consciousness, but rather one of structural limitation and
> ideological closure. (*PU*, 52)

Quoting Marx's analysis of petty bourgeois ideology in *The Eighteenth
Brumaire*, Jameson argues for a formulation of ideology as 'strategies
of containment', that is to say, the limitation imposed on our modes
of thought by the specific historical situation from which such thinking emerges. It was Lukács's unique achievement to reveal how such
strategies of containment can 'be unmasked only by confrontation
with the ideal of totality which they at once imply and repress' (*PU*,
53).

What Jameson means by this can be seen in his exposition of the
ideological nature of post-structuralist thought. Citing the example
of Deleuze and Guattari's molecular politics and Derridean deconstruction, Jameson argues that if such repudiations of totalization
'are to be celebrated in their intensity, they must be accompanied by
some initial appearance of continuity, some ideology of unification
already in place, which it is their mission to rebuke and shatter. The
value of the molecular in Deleuze, for instance, depends structurally
on the pre-existing molar or unifying impulse against which its truth
is read' (*PU*, 53). The ideological aspect of post-structuralism is
revealed in its inability to think beyond the immediate, disparate
moments of intensity and flux and to attempt to understand the
historical conditions which produce such fragmented and isolated
experience. In so far as they assume the existence of the totality which
it is their aim to deconstruct ,the post-structural ideologies of *différance*,
schizoid intensity and heterogeneity are, argues Jameson, second
degree critical philosophies 'which reconfirm the status of the concept of totality by their very reaction against it' (*PU*, 53). The problem
with this kind of dialectical thinking, however, is that it could equally
operate in the opposite direction. Thus, as Terry Eagleton observes,
Jameson 'stubbornly refuses to contemplate the converse possibility,
one flamboyantly entertained by Jacques Derrida, that our conceptions of totality may have been all along more parasitic upon

some primordial movement of difference than we care to admit'.[16]

Jameson equates the notion of totality with the Althusserian conception of History as an absent cause. In this sense, the totality 'is not available for representation, any more than it is accessible in the form of some ultimate truth (or moment of Absolute Spirit)' (*PU*, 55): the totality can only be represented through its absence. This allows Jameson 'without any great inconsistency' to respect both the 'methodological imperative implicit in the concept of totality or totalization' (*PU*, 57) and the various kinds of 'symptomal' analysis demanded by post-structuralism. I suggested in chapters 2 and 3 that these two positions can be held simultaneously only at the expense of the specificity of each opposing conception of totality. Althusserian antihistoricism, for example, can only be folded back into Hegelian historicism once its terms have been rewritten, or transcoded, into another discourse which serves to neutralize the critique of the initial position.

On the one hand, then, Jameson has attempted to accommodate the post-structuralist critique of totality by playing down the positive aspects of the concept, with its Hegelian emphasis on the concrete, and stressing the concept's negative function as an unrealizable ideal against which our partial representations of the world can be judged. On the other hand, he has retained the concept, rewriting it at a higher level of abstraction, as an absent cause, beyond representation, whereby the various critiques of totality can only be said to make sense in terms of a prior concept of totality. Thus the concept can never be empirically verified, but at the same time it is confirmed in its absence. Individual subjects can never realize or represent the totality, but it is only against the background of the concept that our partial understanding and representations of the world make sense.

Jameson further develops this understanding of totality in *Postmodernism, or, The Cultural Logic of Late Capitalism*. Distinguishing between notions of totality and totalization, Jameson writes,

> if the word *totality* sometimes seems to suggest that some priviieged bird's-eye view of the whole is available, which is the Truth, then the project of totalization implies exactly the opposite and takes as its premise the impossibility for individual and biological human subjects to conceive of such a position, let alone to adopt or achieve it. (*PLC*, 332)

Moreover, we need to distinguish both of these concepts from any connection with totalitarianism. The term 'totalization' derives from Sartre's *Critique of Dialectical Reason* and, suggests Jameson, marks that process of partial summing up that subjects must make in order to construct a meaningful narrative of their lives. In Sartre's usage the term tended to 'envelope and find a least common denominator for the twin human activities of perception and action' (*PLC*, 332). The term therefore became synonymous with the more Marxian term of 'praxis' and designated the 'unification inherent in human action' (*PLC*, 333). Thus, argues Jameson, it seems difficult to see how the subject in a postmodern era could avoid the experience of totalization:

> Totalizing, in Sartre, is, strictly speaking, that process whereby, actively impelled by the project, an agent negates the specific object or item and reincorporates it into the larger project-in-course. Philosophically, and barring some genuine mutation of the species, it is hard to see how human activity under the third, or postmodern, stage of capitalism could elude or evade this very general formula, although some of postmodernism's ideal images – schizophrenia above all – are clearly calculated to rebuke it and to stand as unassimilable and unsubsumable under it. (*PLC*, 333)

This continual process of partial summing up is distinct from the concept of totality itself, which for Jameson is linked to the notion of 'mode of production'. In the book on postmodernism Jameson reiterates the notion of mode of production he formulated in *The Political Unconscious*, insisting that if the concept of totality is to have any meaning then we must accept that, like the Althusserian notion of structure, there is only one totality, that is, the mode of production. Jameson further distinguishes his conception of totality from the Weberian notion of a 'total system'. A 'mode of production is not a "total system" in that forbidding sense; it includes a variety of counterforces and new tendencies within itself, of "residual" as well as "emergent" forces, which it must attempt to manage or control' (*PLC*, 406). In other words, this is Jameson's formulation of non-synchronicity and uneven development. There can only be one totality, insists Jameson, the mode of production itself. The logical implication of non-synchronicity, or the coexistence of differing modes of production, however, is that there will be coexistence of differing totalities, as Balibar eventually came to recognize. Jameson fails to acknowledge this apparent inconsistency in his theory.

As one follows Jameson's argument, one becomes increasingly alert to the problems of totalizing thought. In the above discussion I have slipped from a Hegelian concept of totality as the concrete, through Lukács's negative and demystifying function of totality, to Sartre's totalization or partial summing up, and finally to Althusser's notion of structure and mode of production. Each of these categories has become synonymous in Jameson's discourse and this facilitates a slippage of register, specifically from the philosophical implications of the concept to the political. This procedure tends to elide the specificity of each differing conception of totality and enact precisely that denial of difference highlighted by post-structuralist and postmodernist critiques of totality. This overly homogenizing tendency of totalizing thought is most starkly revealed in Jameson's reading of Adorno.

Late Marxism: Adorno, or, The Persistence of the Dialectic, as Peter Osborne points out, continues Jameson's search for a Marxism fit for a postmodern age by reading Adorno 'against post-structuralism and the postmodern attack on the concept of totality in particular, but also against Habermas and the restoration of an Enlightenment concept of reason'.[17] According to Osborne, Jameson's reading 'offers us a case study of the character of Jameson's, as much as of Adorno's, Marxism – a test of the compatibility of some kind of Marxism with some kind of "postmodern" analysis of the present'.[18] A case study, I would suggest, that enacts the very slippage of register and conflation of distinct discourses I alluded to above. Adorno's special contribution to Marxist theory, maintains Jameson, 'lies in his unique emphasis on the presence of late capitalism as a totality within the very forms of our concepts or of the works of art themselves' (*LM*, 9). As discussed in chapter 4, Jameson's reading of Adorno in the 1990s is very different from his reading of Adorno in the early 1970s. In particular the emphasis Jameson placed on the reflexivity of dialectical thought in his own early work must now be rejected as 'part of the baggage of a modernist thinking no longer very authoritative in the postmodernist era' (*LM*, 25). Therefore, Jameson proposes an alternative view of the dialectical process as the attempt 'to think another side, an outside, an external face of the concept which, like that of the moon, can never be directly visible or accessible to us: but we must vigilantly remember and reckon that other face into our sense of the concept while remaining within it in the old way and continuing to use and think it' (*LM*, 25). Jameson defines this as a process of thinking both with and against the concept simultaneously and it is here, he argues, that the concept of totality in Adorno comes into its own. The 'concept can be retained and dereified all at once', maintains Jameson, through 'its reinsertion into totality or system'. Thus totality 'plays a strategic role in freeing us from the "spell" of the concept' (*LM*, 26).

In other words, there is a drive from the individual and isolated concept towards totality or unity. There is also in Adorno's work, however, a sense in which totality has 'something illicit about it, expressing the idealism and the imperialism of the concept' (*LM*, 26).

But to read this as a rejection of totality itself, or to stress its totalitarian aspect is a fundamental misunderstanding which 'lies in drawing the conclusion that philosophical emphasis on the indispensability of this category amounts either to a celebration of it or, in a stronger form of the anti-utopian argument, to its implicit perpetuation as a reality or a referent outside the philosophical realm' (*LM*, 27). In short, we should not confuse the use of abstract categories, such as mode of production or totality, with an actual belief in their substantive and empirically verifiable existence, that is a confusion between the 'concept and the thing itself' (*PLC*, 401). The totality or system is precisely that outer face of the concept that is outside and 'forever inaccessible to us' (*LM*, 28). The concept of totality, therefore, to quote Osborne, functions as 'a corrective or antidote to "identity-thinking" (a form of thought for which concepts are understood to gain their meanings from one-to-one correspondences with objects) insofar as it draws attention to the open multiplicity of suppressed or forgotten *relations* through which individual concepts are constituted'.[19]

Jameson's reading of Adorno emphasizes the critical and negative aspect of totality; it is neither immediately knowable nor representable but remains an absent presence against which our fragmented and isolated concepts stand judged. Furthermore, the notion of totality proposed in *Late Marxism* is also synonymous or interchangeable with the categories of system, universal, concept, exchange system and history itself.[20] This reading of the notion of totality would appear to be very much in line with the negative conception developed in *The Political Unconscious*. Best, on the other hand, insists that 'totality is not simply a concept but points to concretely existing structures.'[21] 'The general argument for totality', writes Best, 'is plausible to the extent that (1) things are relational and systemic in character, and (2) a method exists whereby these relational entities can be theorized and grasped.'[22] Jameson wishes to play down this sense in which the totality concretely exists and is graspable as it would sit rather uncomfortably with the more post-structuralist and postmodernist aspects of his theory.

What appears to be elided in Jameson's totalizing approach is the specificity of the concepts themselves as they are folded back into the tradition of Marxist thought which Jameson adheres to. In *Marxism and Totality* Jay stresses an alternative reading of Adorno's conception of totality and identity theory. Like Jameson, Jay focuses on Adorno's negative conception of totality, but unlike Jameson he emphasizes that Adorno's negative dialectics are strongly opposed to Lukács's positive dialectics and in particular the *verum-factum* principle which posited a subject-object unity, or 'a symmetry between making and knowing'. For Jay, Adorno's 'reluctance to link epistemological validity with social genesis'[23] rules out the expressive concept of totality advocated by Lukács. Indeed, the very notion of a metasubject capable of totalizing reality was an illegitimate hypostatization taken over from idealism's notion of a transcendental subject. Adorno's particular animus against the concept of totality, according to Jay, was 'especially directed against its longitudinal form, the belief in universal history as a coherent whole',[24] that is to say, exactly the conception of history and totality that Jameson proposes in *The Political Unconscious*.

Adorno's use of totality, Jay insists, is an example of his general anti-realist use of concepts, or the non-adequation of a concept to its real object or counterpart. For Adorno, there can be no identity as in the Hegelian-Lukácsian tradition between subject and object, concept and referent. In short, contends Jay, the concept of totality in Adorno's work is not simply a negative but is a 'pejorative' term shorn of all positive connotations and almost a synonym for totalitarianism. After Adorno, writes Jay:

> No longer could a Western Marxist defend an expressive view of the whole in which a meta-subject was both the subject and object of history. No longer could history itself be seen as a coherent whole with a positive conclusion as its telos. No longer could totality ignore the non-identity of the historical and the natural and subordinate the latter to human domination. And no longer could the totalizing epistemology of the Hegelian tradition be invoked with confidence against the antinomies of bourgeois thought.[25]

The question, then, is how Jameson can apparently do just such a thing.

Firstly, it would be erroneous to suggest that Jameson uncritically endorses any of the above positions. To speak of Jameson, as Eagleton does, as a 'shamelessly unreconstructed Hegelian Marxist'[26] overshoots the mark to the extent that Jameson has explicitly reconstructed his Hegelianism. Jameson's practice of transcoding and working through other philosophical systems enables him to adopt a position that appears at once to endorse the views enumerated and at the same time problematize them. So, for example, Jameson may not endorse the notion of a Lukácsian totalizing metasubject or the view that history has a positive telos, but he would still maintain that history remains a single great adventure and that, although the outcome remains to be decided, there is a positive aspect in the form of the utopian impulse. Similarly, the totalizing epistemology of the Hegelian tradition can still be invoked against the fragmentation and dispersion of late capitalism, but only if we grasp that the problem of totalizing thought is first and foremost a problem of representation – as Jameson formulates the problem in *The Geopolitical Aesthetic*, 'the very problem of representability now becomes in some sense its own solution – the thing being done, as it were, by showing it cannot be done in the first place' (*GPA*, 56). Jameson, then, wishes to retain both the positive and negative, or critical, aspects of the Western Marxist tradition, a position he finds tenable as long as all concepts and problems are historicized. For instance, in a footnote to *The Political Unconscious* Jameson challenges Jay's reading of the Frankfurt School:

> by overstressing the leitmotif of non-identity theory, [Jay] ends up conveying the misleading impression that the fundamental target of 'critical theory' was Marxism rather than capitalism. The non-identity between subject and object often means little more than a materialist and 'decentering' approach to Knowledge. (*PU*, 52)

Jameson substantiates this view at much greater length in *Late Marxism*: reflecting on the claims of Adorno's post-Marxism, Jameson insists that this misreading rests on a misunderstanding of one of Adorno's basic leitmotifs, that of 'non-identity'. Adorno is not so much a philosopher of non-identity, argues Jameson, as a 'philosopher of Identity in a very special case' (*LM*, 15). By folding Adorno's non-identity theory back into identity, however, in whatever special sense, Jameson has diminished the polemical and critical force of Adorno's work. Adorno simply becomes one more figure in a long tradition of Marxist philosophy rather than a powerful and remorseless critic of both capitalism and the aporias of that very tradition of Marxist thought. I am not advocating a gradual slippage into post-Marxism here, but I am suggesting that it may be politically more astute to retain a separation between certain ideas and concepts, even if they are philosophically reconcilable.

According to Jay the 'disdain for traditional logic manifested in the Hegelian tradition allowed Adorno to hold opposing, even incompatible positions simultaneously without worrying about their coherence.'[27] As much I believe can be said for Jameson's own discourse. Jameson's work frequently reveals how what we once thought were diametrically opposing views, as with the Althusserian/ Hegelian dispute in *The Political Unconscious*, can be reconciled once theory is resituated in history, that is, at a higher level of abstraction. This practice is also evident in the Adorno book whereby Jameson identifies Benjamin's and Adorno's conception of 'constellations with Althusserian structural causality' (*LM*, 60).

What is problematic with this procedure, paradoxically for Jameson, is its lack of historicity. Osborne points out that Jameson 'simply ignores that Althusser's thought is located not only in a quite different philosophical tradition, but also in a quite different political and intellectual context'.[28] As Osborne puts it, a quick fix comparative reference is used to replace an apparent contradiction. Particularly in *Late Marxism* Jameson uses the rhetorical strategy of avoiding points of dispute through a 'tendency to break off the internal investigation of Adorno's thought at precisely those points at which it approaches the fundamental philosophical issues at stake and displace it with "translations" into other, generally more recent, critical idioms deriving from quite different philosophical traditions'.[29] In particular, there is a problematic slippage throughout the text from 'philosophical' to 'literary' discourse. Jameson systematically displaces philosophical with rhetorical analysis in order to deflect 'discussion of the non-Marxian elements in Adorno's thought'.[30] We cannot, however, conflate different philosophical traditions and registers of discourse in this way. Jameson's reading of Adorno is at once too selective and too generalized. Within Adorno's thought there is an inherent resistance 'to the easy appropriations of contemporary theory [which] extends beyond its antipathy to post-structuralism to question the terms of the project Jameson uses it to recommend'.[31] If the price of Adorno's relevance to contemporary theory, writes Osborne, lies in this generalized application and transcoding into alternative discourses, 'irrelevance begins to seem the more critical option.'[32]

In a postmodern era of micro-politics, *différance* and schizophrenic flux, Jameson's reassertion of the concept of totality is timely and to be welcomed. Although the language may change, one has only to think of some of the more holistic approaches to green politics, as well as certain strains of globalization theory, to be acutely aware that totalizing thought has not disappeared. But at the same time, neither can we ignore the critique of totalizing thought. As Jay suggests, 'there has been a growing fear in certain quarters on the left that the old argument linking the Marxist aspiration for normative totality and totalitarian politics made by earlier critics like Camus may have a certain legitimacy after all.'[33] According to Best, 'by absorbing positive elements of Althusser and post-structuralism and employing a model of totality which is decentered and overdetermined', Jameson has gone 'a long way toward constructing a "plausible version" of totality which deflects the main thrust of post-structuralist attacks'.[34] The question for Marxism, then, is not so much whether society and history constitute a totality or not but rather what type of totality they constitute. In other words, is it a 'closed' totality that is teleological, predetermined and imposes identity on phenomena, or an 'open' totality that is always contingent, in process and acknowledges difference. The post-structuralist critique aims at the former, while Jameson's project stakes its claims on the adequate theorization of the latter, and central to this project is the concept of mediation.

Mediation and Reification

In chapter 2 I considered Jameson's defence of mediation against the Althusserian critique of expressive causality. The target of Althusser's critique, contends Jameson, is not mediation as such but rather the reductive application of 'homologies' between distinct and different levels of society. Jameson endorses this critique as far as it goes, while also insisting that any theory of the social totality which aspires to a systematic account of the whole, and which can accommodate difference and diversity, must first account for the interconnectedness of discrete phenomena and specific spheres of society in a non-reductive, non-mechanistic way. Althusser's own notion of relative-autonomy points not only to the separation of specific levels of society, however, but also to a relationship between the relatively-autonomous parts. First and foremost, therefore, the practice of mediation does not impose an *identity* between distinct phenomena but rather points to the existence of a *relationship* between different phenomena and social levels. In order to articulate this non-reductive, non-mechanistic theory of mediation Jameson deploys a number of key concepts. They include Althusserian notions of overdetermination and relative-autonomy, Raymond Williams's distinction between dominant, emergent and residual aspects of culture, Bloch's notion of non-synchronicity and Mandel's theory of combined and uneven development, as well as his own notions of transcoding and cognitive mapping. Jameson, as Best puts it, has all the right tools and – as in the essay 'Periodizing the 60s' – can present 'a complex dialectic of unity and diversity within a decentered totality',[35] but unfortunately he does not always use them to such effect.[36] Here I focus on Jameson's central mediatory category, reification, and suggest that he privileges this category to the detriment of an analysis of other forms of mediation. It is criticism I shall return to in greater detail in the concluding chapter.

Reification, 'that special bugbear of Hegelian Marxism', as Jay describes it,[37] remains for Jameson one of the most pressing theoretical, philosophical and political concerns today. It is a position re-affirmed in the concluding pages of *The Geopolitical Aesthetic*, where he states that 'those doctrines of reification and commodification which played a secondary role in traditional or classical Marxian heritage, are now likely to come into their own and become the dominant instruments of analysis and struggle' (*GPA*, 212). For Jameson, the logic of commodification and reification is relentless and unremitting. I have discussed in the preceding chapters how Jameson utilizes the concept to account for the waning of historicity; the effacement of traces of labour from commodity production; the aesthetization of the commodity process; the fragmentation of our psyches and the fracturing of our subjective identities; the colonization of those last enclaves of resistance to global capitalism, the aesthetic, the unconscious and the Third World; and finally the splitting of the signifier and signified couple. As Eagleton observes, the 'power and versatility of insight that Jameson can generate from these twin notions [commodification and reification] is little short of staggering'.[38]

The concept of reification has elicited a great deal of debate within Marxism itself. For Lukács the term was synonymous with 'alienation, rationalization, atomization and deactivization',[39] a position that Jameson, initially at least, appeared to endorse. Others have insisted on the need to distinguish between these distinct categories; for instance, the entry in *A Dictionary of Marxist Thought* reads:

> While some have regarded alienation as an 'idealist' concept to be replaced by the 'materialist' concept of 'reification', others have regarded 'alienation' as a philosophical concept whose sociological counterpart is 'reification'. According to the prevailing view alienation's a broader phenomenon, and reification one of its forms or aspects.[40]

Eagleton has described Jameson's equating of reification and rationalization as 'spurious',[41] whilst Philip Wood argues for the separation of the concepts, with rationalization 'designating the reorganization of the work process' and reification defining 'a definite social relation between human beings'.[42] Clearly Jameson does not accept the 'prevailing' view of reification as a specific form of alienation; on the contrary, for Jameson, alienation appears to designate a specific form of reification. In many of Jameson's texts the categories of reification, rationalization, alienation, commodification, specialization and frag-mentation frequently appear to be synonymous and interchangeable. We should not, however, be too hasty in assimilating these categories to each other since, for Jameson, Lukács's theory of reification pro-vides a synthesis of Marx and Weber rather than an identity between them. In other words, reification is not identical to rationalization but 'includes' it, providing the first systemic account of the logic of capitalism: 'it insists on extreme fragmentation as a social norm. It attempts to project a process which separates, compartmentalizes, specializes, and disperses: a force which at one and the same time operates uniformly over everything and makes heterogeneity a homogeneous and standardizing power.'[43]

Andrew Arato's incisive critique of Lukács's theory of reification, however, highlights certain inconsistencies in the formulation. 'The analysis of reification', writes Arato, 'moves through the moments of "alienated labour", of the reification of capitalist society as a whole, and of the reification of consciousness in bourgeois science and philosophy.'[44] Following Lukács's trajectory, Arato argues that it is misleading to identify the concept of reification with alienation and objectification as Lukács sought to do. Starting from the initial premise that the 'theory of reification is an indispensable part of the dialectical theory of society',[45] Arato can only conclude that without serious reformulation Lukács's theory proves to be inappropriate in an era of advanced capitalism. Although Lukács's theory of reification, he writes, 'was intended as a dialectical theory of capitalist society, it is *for us* "only" a fundamental work in the history of the philosophy of praxis'.[46]

Unfortunately, Jameson has not undertaken the task of such a reformulation. While Jameson's analysis of late capitalism is by no means limited to the theory of reification, the pre-eminence accorded to this category in Jameson's work and his tendency to conflate what I have suggested are distinct concepts result in significant and detrimental consequences. Eagleton summarizes the problem well:

> the 'question' to which the concept of reification is an 'answer' is not in the first place one of class struggle, but a dual query about the nature of capitalist economic production and the quality of lived experience within it. If reification returns a vital economic answer to the question of how we have come to experience as meagrely as we do, it promises to put cultural formation and mode of production back together only at the risk of displacing the political. If everything is mediated through the commodity, class struggle becomes an *answer* to this unhappy condition, rather than the first *question* of historical materialism.[47]

In short, the valorization of reification at the expense of questions of class struggle tends to displace the more properly political concerns of historical materialism.

If we follow the logic of Arato's critique of Lukács, we can locate a similar aporia in Jameson's work through his uncritical endorsement and adoption of Lukács's original theory. As we have seen, Lukács identified the proletariat as the universal subject of history through the principle of *verum-factum*. Arato highlights two problems with Lukács's position. First, Marx reached the position of the proletariat as a universal subject through an understanding of human 'needs', whereas Lukács bases his thesis of the proletariat as identical subject-object of history on a proposition about 'class consciousness'. Arato maintains that 'the question of class consciousness can be related to the individual consciousness of members of the class only through the dialectics of human needs and constraints'[48] and not simply through a consideration of consciousness. Lukács does not consider the question of needs and constraints. Secondly, Lukács's attempt to find the identical subject-object of history proceeds entirely from 'the side of the potential subjectivity'[49] and does not take into account the objective conditions of possibility. Lukács's claim that the proletariat is the identical subject-object of history presupposes that 'the historical process has become transparent to theory.'[50]

According to Arato, there are two dialectics at work here: the dialectic of the identical subject-object on which the philosophy of praxis is founded; and the dialectic of immediacy and mediation on which all dialectical social theory is based. These, insists Arato, derive from different conceptual presuppositions which are not reconciled in Lukács's theory:

> the subject-object dialectic (in whatever modified form) and the dialectic of immediacy and mediation remain two sides of a subject–object split within *History and Class Consciousness*, a split that appears most fundamentally as a methodological duality between philosophy of praxis and the dialectical social theory this philosophy of praxis is aiming at.[51]

Arato points out that the consideration of the identical subject-object at the expense of the dialectic of immediacy and mediation tends 'to exclude mediations between the collective subject and all individuals'.[52] As with Lukács, Jameson focuses on our subjective experience of capitalism which tends to supplant questions of politics with questions of consciousness and the need to overcome reification. Furthermore, Jameson tends to evade, or diminish the significance of, essential mediations, such as group identities, institutional practices and nation-states, as he slides from individual fragmented psyches to the global totality.

A secondary problem with the theory of reification is its tendency towards overly totalizing forms of thought. For instance, Jay identifies a specific dilemma with Adorno's usage of the concept of reification that, I believe, can be extended to Jameson. The totality for Adorno was either 'completely watertight in its reifying power and resistance could only be co-opted, or the totality still contained negations and Adorno's descriptions of its Satanic "falseness" were exaggerations'.[53] For Jameson, the reifying power of late capitalism has become all encompassing; all attempts at resistance, it appears, will 'inevitably' be co-opted and thus by implication will be hopeless. If Jameson is not exaggerating the totalizing logic of late capitalism and its reifying power, a whole series of questions arises. How can one resist such a ubiquitous force? If it has now penetrated every aspect of our lives and experience how can one achieve a position from which to provide a critique of reification? Is not the highly abstract and complex discourse of the Hegelian Marxist as much a product of reification as that of any other? If it is so all-pervasive, then where is resistance to come from? For Jameson, reification appears as unremittingly bad but, as Habermas argues in *The Philosophical Discourse of Modernity*, reification and rationalization are ambiguous processes: while on the one hand they increase specialization and separation, on the other they are also inextricably linked with the process of modernization itself. What is absent from Jameson's analysis of reification and rationalization is any sense of the positive aspects of reification and rationalization to set off their destructive and impoverishing features.[54]

The 'Third World': Identity and Difference

According to Jameson, the unremitting logic of reification and commodification has finally colonized the last areas of resistance: the unconscious, the aesthetic and the Third World. I will consider only the last of these areas in order to highlight the problems with Jameson's theory. The Third World and in particular Third World culture, argues Jameson, has been co-opted by the global economic system:

> Third-World cinema itself is rarely today defended as a space in which models for alternate cinema are to be sought. Indeed the very term Third World seems to have become an embarrassment in a period in which the realities of the economic have seemed to supplant the possibilities of

collective struggle, in which human agency and politics seem to have been
dissolved by the global corporate institutions we call late capitalism. (*GPA*,
186)

As so often with Jameson there is the problem of the 'we' to whom he
appeals here and whose experience he subsequently generalizes. For
example, the term 'Third World' is not so much an 'embarrassment'
as a strategy to reduce a diversity of cultures to the single historical
perspective of the West and in particular North American capital.
Secondly, the term 'late capitalism' is by no means as broadly acceptable as Jameson statement implies; indeed the term has some un-
welcome and unhelpful teleological implications, that capitalism
is reaching the end of its course, a proposition which is by no means
self-evident.

Jameson suggests that within postmodernism Third World culture
'has been gratefully absorbed by the international entertainment
industry, and has seemed to furnish vibrant but politically acceptable
images of social pluralism for the late capitalist big city' (*GPA*, 187).
This view of the fate of Third World culture is an extension of his
general view of postmodernism as the first global (North American)
cultural dominant, which as we know is underwritten by Ernest
Mandel's thesis of late capitalism as a new stage in capitalist expansion and development. The problem with this is that, for Mandel, the
expansion of late capitalism is dependent on those very areas of Third
World economic and technological underdevelopment that Jameson
wishes to abolish. Mandel's theory of global capitalism is predicated
on a thesis of unequal and combined development, that is to say, that
the different phases of capital accumulation – primitive accumulation
and accumulation through the production of surplus value – are not
successive or chronological phases of economic history but are also
'*concurrent* economic processes'.[55]

Mandel identifies a dialectical relation between three distinct moments: first, capital accumulation in the sphere of capitalist production proper; secondly, the continuing primitive accumulation of
capital outside this sphere of capitalist production; and finally, the
constraint and limitation of the second moment by the first through
competition and struggle. Each dialectical expansion or 'long wave'
of capitalist development marks a further penetration of capitalist
modes of production into areas of underdevelopment and primitive
accumulation. The capitalist world economy, writes Mandel, 'is an
*articulated system of capitalist, semi-capitalist and pre-capitalist relations of
production, linked to each other by capitalist relations of exchange and
dominated by the capitalist world market*'.[56]

On one level this argument would appear to support Jameson's view that late capitalism represents the final colonization of the last enclaves of under- or alternative development. Indeed, Mandel rhetorically poses this very question: does the continuing penetration of the capitalist mode of production into areas of underdevelopment indicate a 'tendency towards a thorough industrialization of the Third World, a universalization of the capitalist mode of production and the eventual homogenisation of the world economy?'[57] Mandel responds that it emphatically does not! He writes:

> It simply means a change in the forms of juxtaposition of development and underdevelopment, or more correctly: new differential levels of capital accumulation, productivity, and surplus extraction are emerging, which although not of the same nature are still more pronounced than those of the 'classical' imperialist epoch.[58]

Capitalism, according to Mandel's theory, could not exist without this interrelation of development and underdevelopment and it requires for its continuing existence the survival of these semi- and pre-capitalist enclaves. Moreover, Jameson's own emphasis on the non-synchronicity of modes of production – that no mode of production exists in a pure state – would appear to allow for just such a coexistence of differing modes of accumulation. On the other hand, Jameson's insistence on the unremitting logic of reification would seem at best to contradict the non-synchronicity of different modes of production, and at worst to rule it out all together. In terms of cultural production, the different social relations of so-called underdeveloped or pre-capitalist modes of accumulation might equally facilitate the production of alternative representations of the system and alternative forms of cultural politics that Jameson's overtotalizing view of postmodernism has ruled out.

Santiago Colás has pointed out that the 'Third World' plays a central, if somewhat paradoxical, role in Jameson's spatial logic of late capitalism. Colás writes:

> It is *both* the space whose final elimination by the inexorable logic of capitalist development consolidates the social moment – late capitalism – whose cultural dominant is postmodernism, *and* the space that remains somehow untainted by and oppositional to those repressive social processes which have homogenized the real and imaginative terrain of the 'First World' subject.[59]

What distinguishes late capitalism is nothing less than a change in the status of the 'Third World' itself, since late capitalism emerges full-blown only with its final disappearance. Yet, as Colás insightfully points out, late capitalism and postmodernism are marked by a general weakening of historicity which in turn is associated with the disappearance of the 'Third World'. The loss of historicity, writes Colás, 'posits as its precondition the emergence of late capitalism and, as we have already seen, the latter's constitutive abolition of the Nature of the "Third World"'.[60] On the one hand, therefore, the absorption of the 'Third World' into the globalized economy is the precondition for late capitalism, but at the same time, it is the previously uncommodified regions of the 'Third World' that enabled those of the 'First World' to think our present situation historically. In short, it is the 'Third World' that provided sites of resistance to the inexorable domination of capitalism. The 'Third World' is, therefore, a utopian space within Jameson's theory in the full sense that it no longer exists, it has been abolished, it is no-place, and at the same time provides us with a site of resistance in the sense of a representation of a qualitatively different form of social organization. This paradox, notes Colás, 'is visible in Jameson's account only because the logic of late capitalism is at one and the same time *totalizing and differential*'.[61]

In contrast to Mandel's theory of combined and uneven development, Colás proposes a theory of mobile and flexible accumulation, whereby 'capital is like a plague of locusts. It settles on one place, devours it, then moves on to plague another place.'[62] For Colás, this conceptualization of capitalism as a mobile process breaks with the dichotomous binary thinking of first and third worlds, of centre and periphery, of developed and underdeveloped. It also starkly brings to the fore the problems of global capitalism as not so much the result of the uniform colonization of those final enclaves of the Third World as of a further intensification of the most crude forms of exploitation and abandonment of large areas of the globe by the advanced capitalist states. This differential conception of late capitalism has the further advantage of facilitating a conception of postmodern politics that does not rest on the debilitating prospect of representing an unrepresentable totality, but rather on the articulation of a formal tension between local difference and global totality. Indeed, one response to Jameson's work, writes Colás, 'is to confront his projected concept of global totality with the details of the various local forms of cultural politics, to which he may fail to attend, but whose existence and various specific characters he does not exclude'.[63] I consider the question of postmodern politics and Jameson's elision of fundamental mediations in the concluding chapter.

Conclusion

During this Marxist conference I have frequently had the feeling that I am one of the few Marxists left. I take it I have a certain responsibility to restate what seem to me to be a few self-evident truths, but which you may see as quaint survivals of a religious form of belief.[1]

The observation above was delivered by Jameson at the beginning of his address to the 1983 Marxist Literary Group, Institute on Culture and Society, and in a sense encapsulates both the strengths and the weaknesses of his theoretical and political project. In an ostensibly post-Marxist, post-ideological age Jameson's unremitting commitment to restate the 'self-evident truths' of Marxist theory has provided a welcome antidote to some of the more excessive claims of post-structuralist and postmodernist theory. As the radicalism of many European and North American theorists throughout the late 1970s and 1980s drifted into quietism, or, as with some of the writers grouped around the journal *Tel Quel*, into outright reaction, Jameson's sustained attempt to formulate a radical cultural politics fully adequate to the contemporary moment has remained both an inspiration and a provocation. On the other hand, it is the very self-evident nature of Marxism's 'truths' that so much of post-structuralist and postmodernist theory has thrown into doubt; as Steven Best has argued, 'no theorist today can rightfully assume key Marxist concepts as axiomatic.'[2]

The acceptance of Marxism's analysis of history and society as fundamentally correct, as given, presents both the challenge of Jameson's work and its problematic nature. From *Marxism and Form* through to *The Geopolitical Aesthetic* and *The Seeds of Time*, Jameson has persuasively argued not just the continuing relevance of Marxian theory, but for the centrality of such 'traditional' categories as commodification, reification, class struggle, social totality and mode of production in an analysis of contemporary culture and society. At the same time his strategy of working through other philosophical and theoretical positions has facilitated the emergence of an open and undogmatic Marxist discourse that is anything but quaint and antiquarian. Jameson's eclecticism, that is, his method of subsuming other theoretical perspectives within an overarching Marxian framework, allows him at once to appropriate the insights of post-structuralist and postmodernist theory and at the same time to neutralize their critique of Marxism through historicizing their specific discourses. In short, Jameson appears to present the best of both worlds: traditional Marxist with the certainties of history on his side, and radical contemporary theorist sensitive to the critique of orthodoxy.

The desire to retain and reinvigorate Marxism's traditional political project through a critical engagement with, rather than outright rejection of, alternative views has always been one of the strong attractions of Jameson's Marxism. Although this procedure is not without its problems, Terry Eagleton recounts this brief anecdote concerning Jameson: 'I once heard it said of him, in a familiar piece of liberal patronage, that he "wasn't just a Marxist critic".'[3] It is, however, all a matter of where one places the emphasis in this statement, reading Jameson as not just a *Marxist* critic is certainly more amenable to the liberal academy, but the proper emphasis, argues Eagleton, is surely on not just a Marxist *critic*. The question I should like to address in this concluding chapter is just how satisfactory Jameson has been in walking this tightrope. Can Jameson subsume such a range of diverse theoretical positions within the horizon of Marxism and retain a coherent theoretical and political position himself?

Marxism and/or Postmodernism?

I have suggested that one of virtues of Jameson's work is that he refutes and systematically demonstrates how the opposition between Marxism and other philosophical or theoretical positions presents a false dichotomy. For Jameson it is not a question of Marxism and/or postmodernism, for example, but rather the analysis and critique of contemporary culture and theory through a Marxian understanding of history and society. The dilemma that has consistently arisen throughout this study is just how coherent this project remains. In chapter 2, I suggested that Jameson's attempt to reconcile post-structuralist antihistoricism with his own systematic historicism appears to reinstate a conception of history as a single seamless narrative which his endorsement of the Althusserian critique explicitly rules out. Jameson's subtle gesture of transcoding and resituating Althusser, therefore, appears to leave open as many questions as it seeks to resolve. In chapter 3, I further argued that the attempt to incorporate post-structuralist theories of difference, immanence and particularism as second degree philosophies within an interpretative and totalizing framework, while persuasive at one level, also raises questions of theoretical consistency. Jameson's eclecticism, in other words, appears coherent only through a very selective reading of alternative theories. This in itself is not a problem as no theorist can conceivably address every issue but it does raise difficult questions in the light of Jameson's claims for Marxism as the final, untranscendable horizon of all interpretation.

In chapter 4, I suggested that Jameson's conception of postmodernity as a cultural dominant marks a significant advance over the more inflated and unsubstantiated claims of theorists such as Baudrillard. Jameson's periodization seeks to articulate what differentiates postmodern culture from modernism while acknowledging its continuities, and at the same time to reinscribe the question of the economic in these hitherto purely cultural and aesthetic debates. His conception of postmodernity, however, also tends towards too monolithic and totalizing a view. Consequently the analyses often fail to exhibit those very aspects of non-synchronicity and relative-autonomy it was the virtue of his periodization to introduce into the problematic in the first place.

Finally, I considered Jameson's influential studies on contemporary spatiality. While he is right, I argued, to reassert the significance of spatiality in social and cultural theory, some of his most recent work on geopolitical aesthetics tends to exaggerate the claims of this new spatiality, exhibiting a form of 'spatial fetishism'. Moreover, too great an acceptance of postmodernist claims for a radically new configuration of spatiality appears to have robbed Jameson's theory of any potential for meaningful politics. Postmodern spatiality is perceived by Jameson to be saturated, meaningless and disorientating. Jameson, in a sense, absorbs at once too much of other theoretical positions and too little. Below I shall explore how both aspects of this paradoxical situation can apparently coexist within Jameson's work.

I suggested above that one of the strengths of Jameson's conception of postmodernism as the cultural logic of late capitalism was to reinstate the question of the economic preconditions of postmodernity. His work never fully lives up to this promise, however, and in the postmodernism book the single chapter devoted to economics is concerned with general questions of ideology and the market rather than the specific relations between the culture of postmodernism and late capitalism. Beyond his initial discussion of Mandel in the 1984 essay 'Postmodernism, or, The Cultural Logic of Late Capitalism' Jameson has never sufficiently addressed the economic issues of postmodernity. For some critics of Jameson this is just one example of where he is too postmodern and not Marxist enough. The culturalist tendencies of postmodern theory come to predominate over the Marxian emphasis on political economy and, to cite Best and Kellner, this 'thereby obscures the economic and class determination of culture he otherwise wants to foreground'.[4]

For Mike Davis, Jameson is simply too complacent in his analysis of postmodern architecture and especially of the urban redevelopment of downtown Los Angeles. What is missing from Jameson's analysis of the Bonaventure Hotel, for example, is any sense of the savagery of its insertion into the surrounding district and its manifestly political project. Davis locates postmodern architecture in relation to two coordinates: first, 'the rise of new international rentier circuits in the current phase of capitalism'; and secondly, 'the definitive abandonment of the ideal of urban reform as part of the new class polarization taking place in the United States'.[5] Postmodern architecture, for Davis, is not so much playful and populist as brutal and coercive, yet one more aspect of a continuing class war, 'its ambition, not to homogenize the city in the fashion of the great modernist buildings, but rather to polarize it into radically antagonistic spaces'.[6] Davis's analysis of postmodernism tends to view it as unequivocally reactionary and lacks the kind of dialectical understanding with which Jameson approaches the problem. Indeed, from the early essays on architecture and consumer society onwards, the value of Jameson's analysis of the new cultural forms and dynamics of postmodernity has always been his refusal of essentially moralizing responses in favour of historically situating these developments. A fully dialectical understanding of postmodernity must not only focus on what is 'wrong' with contemporary society and culture, but also draw out its positive, progressive aspects.

The difficulty with such an approach is that the critical and political dimension can become obfuscated. Davis's critique, therefore, does serve to raise the question of whether or not what we might see as a more 'traditional' form of Marxist analysis and criticism is at certain times more politically appropriate.[7] Jameson's sympathetic working through of alternative theoretical perspectives and his desire to retain the insights of opposing positions, however antithetical to Marxism their politics maybe, can serve to deflect and undermine his own critique. The endorsement of schizoanalysis, for example, or Baudrillard's notions of simulacra and hyperreality would appear to dissolve the very subjects it is Jameson's political objective to radicalize. In short, he is left in the paradoxical position of trying to radicalize non-existent subjects. Jameson would insist that this is to misconstrue his methodology and enact a conflation of his own views with the positions he is explicating. Although, as Eagleton has observed, it can often be difficult with Jameson's work to distinguish where exposition ends and critique begins. Jameson's appropriation of other theories, in short, 'too often leaves the texts in question relatively untransformed, intact in their "relative autonomy", so that the strenuously *mastering* Jameson appears too eirenic, easygoing and all-encompassing for his own political good'.[8] In this sense, Jameson is not enough of a *Marxist* critic.

I have also suggested, however, that Jameson appropriates too little of the contemporary critique of Marxism, in the sense that he simply reasserts a Hegelian-Marxian master narrative over and above all other theories, enacting precisely the kind of totalizing gesture that the post-structuralist critique has sought to forestall. Thus Davis, while arguing that Jameson is insufficiently Marxist in his appreciation of the economic and political factors of postmodern culture, also contends that, like all imposing totalizations, 'Jameson's postmodernism tends to homogenize the details of the contemporary landscape, to subsume under a master concept too many contradictory phenomena which, though undoubtedly visible in the same chronological moment, are nonetheless separated in their true temporalities.'[9] The sociologist Mike Featherstone has also criticized Jameson for too totalizing a conception of postmodernity and for directing too little attention to the changing experiences of specific groups, preferring, like many intellectuals, to generalize from his own experience. Featherstone points to the need to analyse the institutions which mediate our experience of this new form of production as well as the practices involved in contemporary culture.[10] Jameson's response is that these are indeed very interesting and necessary tasks but are not enough in themselves. It is difficult to see, he writes, 'how sociological inquiry at that level would become *explanatory*: rather, the phenomena [Featherstone] is concerned with tend at once to reform into their own semi-autonomous sociological level, one which then at once requires a diachronic narrative.'[11] If we are not to fall back into the reified specializations of academic disciplines, in other words, we need a more totalizing framework within which to situate these semi-autonomous spheres.

Jameson's insistence on the need for totalizing thought acts as a corrective to the reifying tendencies of academic discourse but at the same time, I argue below, a lack of attention to institutional mediations and distinct cultural practices elides cultural difference and, to cite Best and Kellner again, 'inflates the insights that apply to limited sectors of contemporary social life into overly general concepts representing all social spheres, thereby failing to analyse each sector in its specificity'.[12] As I argued in chapter 4, it is surely questionable just how pervasive postmodern culture is, not only as the global culture of late capitalism but also within the advanced capitalist states themselves. Jameson's periodization, for all its theoretical sophistication, ultimately serves to elide these distinct social and cultural differences.

Best and Kellner convincingly argue that Jameson's attempt to blend postmodern and Marxian theory creates certain tensions within his work which cannot be resolved within his own conceptual framework. These tensions are particularly evident when we consider the political implications Jameson draws from his totalizing theory. In the previous chapter, I considered the significance Jameson placed on the concept of social totality for any future socialist politics: 'without a conception of the social totality' (and the possibility of transforming a whole social system),' he contends, 'no properly socialist politics is possible.'[13] For Jameson, what is really at stake in the 'wars on totality' is the concept of Utopia, for which we can read 'the systematic transformation of contemporary society' (*PLC*, 334). Consequently, in rejecting the concept of totality, postmodernism is turning its back on the possibility of transforming capitalism itself, in other words, Marxism's emancipatory narrative. I discussed in chapter 3 some of the debilitating effects of post-structuralist micro-politics, whereby the radicalism of schizoanalysis is reduced to a sorry endorsement of the status quo and a rather weak form of gesture politics. At a time of micro, group and identity politics, when the whole notion of systemic transformation is being jettisoned, Jameson's reassertion of the need to retain some notion, albeit utopian, of complete social transformation is singularly important. Indeed, what 'is sometimes characterised as a nostalgia for class politics of some older type', writes Jameson, 'is generally more likely to be simply a "nostalgia" for politics *tout court*' (*PLC*, 331).

While Jameson insists on the need to retain a conception of transformative and class politics, however, he also acknowledges the emergence of new historical agents in the various 'new social movements' and forms of identity politics. Marxism's traditional privileging of class politics over all other forms of political struggle can no longer simply be taken for granted. Equally, arguments for a politics of difference and pluralism are not necessarily progressive and can serve the needs of capital rather than those of the oppressed groups themselves. Advancing a strategy of local and 'molecular' politics in a highly centralized state such as France is one thing, but in the United States the situation is very different:

> it is precisely the intensity of social fragmentation . . . that has made it historically difficult to unify Left or 'antisystemic' forces in any durable and effective organizational way. Ethnic groups, neighborhood movements, feminism, various 'countercultural' and alternate life-style groups, rank and file labor dissidence, student movements, single-issue movements – all have in the United States seemed to project demands and strategies which were theoretically incompatible with each other and impossible to coordinate on any practical political basis. (*PU*, 54)

Liberal pluralism is already the order of the day in North America and it is the very plurality of groups that mitigates against any effective political action taking place at a systemic level. The political corollary of Jameson's totalizing theory, therefore, is a specific form of alliance politics:

> The privileged form in which the American Left can develop today must therefore necessarily be that of an *alliance politics*; and such a politics is the strict practical equivalent of the concept of totalization on the theoretical level. In practice, then, the attack on the concept of 'totality' in the American framework means the undermining and repudiation of the only realistic perspective in which a genuine Left could come into being in this country. (*PU*, 54)

What distinguishes Jameson's view of alliance politics from liberal pluralism or political relativism is his insistence on the situated nature of these various movements and groups and their common experience of oppression under late capitalism. Jameson proposes a 'standpoint' theory whereby the specificity of the experiences of oppression of differing groups is accounted for, while what is common to the experience of oppression of all these groups is prioritized.

Again Jameson's manoeuvre is compelling to the extent that he

attempts to bridge the gap between Marxism's traditional critique of
the systemic, universalizing logic of capital and the particularity of
the differing experiences of groups within that system. What remains
unclear, however, is precisely how this gap is being bridged: in short,
as Best and Kellner state, how 'this alliance is to be produced and
what the nature of this engagement is remains unspecified'.[14] Jameson's
conception of alliance politics offers no detailed exposition of the
relations between these discrete semi-autonomous groups or on what
'practical political basis' they may be forged. Furthermore, the tension in Jameson's work between this 'standpoint' theory and, at other
times, his espousal of traditional Marxian politics – with issues of
race, gender, sexuality, etc., tending to be subsumed under the
primacy of class – is never fully resolved. According to Jameson, the
opposition between class and identity politics rests on the misconception of 'class' as some kind of 'empirical property', like a birth
certificate, rather than seeing it as a conceptual category:

> What needs to be argued is the difference in conceptual status between the
> idea of social class and that of race and gender: and this means something
> more than the evident fact – often triumphantly produced in evidence
> against it – that the category of class is a universalizing one and a form of
> abstraction capable of transcending individuality and particularity in a
> more successful and also a more productive way.[15]

The concept of class, therefore, must be seen to be contingent and
embodied, and necessarily having to realize itself in such categories
as race and gender, but at the same time underlying these categories.
   Two objections can be raised against Jameson's reconceptualization
of class in this manner. First, the notion of class is not simply a
conceptual category but designates a determinate relation and in this
sense can indeed be argued for as an 'empirical property'. Secondly,
Jameson's manoeuvre would appear to merely repeat the traditional
Marxist response to identity politics whereby class is displaced at one
level and then reinscribed as primary at another 'subterranean' one.
The notion of class retains its analytic priority on the basis that it alone
allows one to grasp the nature of 'the social as a systematic entity
which can only be changed in a radical and systematic way'.[16]
According to Best and Kellner, only through adopting a neo-Marxian
stance which at once recognizes the multiplicity of radical politics and
retains a notion of class struggle as of ultimate importance but not as
primary is the tension between identity and class politics resolvable.
Jameson would not accept such a neo-Marxian stance but neither has
he established that the fragmentation experienced by the traditional

working class since the Second World War has not inalterably changed the composition of class relations and politics. Thus his position needs clarification in order to define 'how the "proletariat" can be expected to become a unified subject again (if indeed it ever was) and why it should remain the epicentre of political struggle'.[17] Jameson's pluralism, in other words, may not be as pluralistic as it at first seems. Moreover, what is missing from Jameson's analysis of late capitalism, paradoxically when one considers the central role it plays within his theory, is any systematic analysis of the mediations between these discrete groups and the social totality.

The attempt to formulate a social theory that combines both micro and macro analysis has been made by a number of theorists recently and I shall briefly indicate two such attempts here. Best and Kellner argue for what they call a multidimensional and multiperspectival social theory. Multidimensional in the sense that it is dialectical and non-reductive, thus accounting for the systemic and structural nature of capitalism. Multiperspectival in the sense that it is open and pluralistic and respects the specificity of group identities, locality and particularity. Such an approach would not focus exclusively on the systemic or the particular but rather on the mediations between the local and the global and the intersections of distinct and semi-autonomous levels of society. What is required, they argue, is not so much generalizations about postmodern society and high degrees of abstraction but rather concrete analysis of the social and political changes that have taken place since the end of the Second World War and a detailed account of the transition between modernity and postmodernity. Jameson's theory goes a long way in this direction but remains insufficiently mediated to provide a fully adequate account of our present historical moment.

Nancy Fraser has also attempted to formulate a theoretical frame-work which can at once accommodate a micro and a macro critique. Fraser notes that the politics of recognition is now the paradigmatic form of political conflict in the twentieth century: group and identity politics has come to supplant class-based politics as the primary focus of political mobilization. There is a price to pay for this, however, in the sense that the cultural domination of specific groups has come to replace economic exploitation as the fundamental source of political injustice. Cultural recognition, therefore, has come to displace 'socio-economic redistribution as the remedy for injustice and the goal of political struggle'.[18] At a time when material inequality is on the increase, both on a global scale (the so-called North–South divide) and with the rise in poverty within the advanced capitalist countries themselves, the shift towards a culturally based politics of recognition would appear to be deeply problematic. As with Best and Kellner, Fraser argues that the new task facing us is 'that of developing a *critical* theory of recognition, one which identifies and defends only those versions of the cultural politics of difference that can be coherently combined with a social politics of equality'.[19] Fraser's own solution to this dilemma is to combine socialist economics with a deconstructive cultural politics, in other words, the transformative and redistributive politics of socialism with the recognition of identity and difference foregrounded by deconstruction. Fraser admits that this solution does not neatly resolve all the difficulties faced by either redistributive or recognition politics today but, to use her phrase, it allows us to *finesse* the dilemma:

> After all, gender and 'race' are not neatly cordoned off from one another. Nor are they neatly cordoned off from sexuality and class. Rather, all these axes of injustice intersect one another in ways that affect everyone's interests and identities. No one is a member of only one such collectivity. And people who are subordinated along one axis of social division may well be dominant along another.[20]

Fraser's articulation, therefore, would once again point us towards the need for close detailed analysis of the points of intersection, or mediation, between these various groups and the axes of social division.

Mediation and Cultural Politics

In a review of *The Political Unconscious*, Dominick LaCapra maintains that the major difficulties of Jameson's theoretical strategy 'cluster around the axial "dialectical" problem of mediation itself'.[21] On the one hand, LaCapra argues, there is a marked lack of attention to institutional mediations within Jameson's oeuvre, and on the other, there is the question of Jameson's own dialectical style. LaCapra suggests that the very complexity and density of Jameson's style and vocabulary is itself a symptom rather than a solution to the problem of reification:

> [Jameson's] own comments on the problem of mediation reinforce the impression of an addiction to a highly hermetic approach that remains on a narrowly hermeneutic level in attempting to 'break out of specialized compartments of (bourgeois) disciplines'. A model-centred semiotics with its own proliferating lexicon of code words becomes Jameson's all-too-modern 'political' answer to the problem.[22]

According to LaCapra, Jameson's highly restricted view of mediation is accompanied by 'an abstract and exaggerated conception of the role of codes in relation to actual usage',[23] a conception moreover that is not specifically Marxist. The problem of mediation is not simply a question of the relations between various reified and specialized disciplines but also between these disciplines, with their esoteric languages, and other social spheres, what could be termed 'ordinary language'. The mutual questioning, writes LaCapra, 'between the ordinary and the "esoteric" might help to create the "space" for an effective transformation of both'.[24] Jameson's 'oeuvrism' evades the essential issue of working out the various mediations between different social spheres, and specifically at institutional levels. At the very least, suggests LaCapra, Jameson's oeuvrism 'functions to divert attention from the problem of institutions. For it is the institution in the broad sense that mediates between individuals and society as well as between various uses of language.'[25] The theoretical and political consequences of Jameson's lack of attention to institutional mediations can be drawn out if we consider more closely the relationship between his own discourse and its institutional frame, the academy.

In a 1979 article Jameson notes that it is the 'first business of a Marxist teacher . . . to teach Marxism itself'.[26] Indeed, it goes without saying, he had written a few years earlier, 'that to teach Marxism and tirelessly to demonstrate the nature of capitalism and of its consequences is a political act which needs no apologies'.[27] With James Kavanagh, he has also elaborated on the relationship of Marxism to the more esoteric concerns of literary studies. While the universities and literary studies in particular may seem an unusual site for the resurgence of Marxism, being somewhat detached from the fray of political and economic strife, Jameson and Kavanagh suggest that to the contrary 'it is perhaps in the "weakest links" of bourgeois ideological domination – those areas where political and economic structures are less directly at stake – that Marxism can find the opportunity for its most daring advances.'[28] The politics of culture are not simply a superstructural epiphenomenon but are a crucial component for the development of a socialist politics in general:

> The analysis of literary and cultural texts and the tasks of 'cultural revolution' in general, then, increasingly appear as central, not secondary, to socialist political strategies – necessary conditions for transforming the patterns of ideological closure and political passivity that are enforced in societies like ours less by fear of the police than by fascination with the page or screen.[29]

In short, Jameson's interventions can be seen as part of a continuing process of 'cultural revolution' or ideological struggle. The university is important as it remains (not the only one to be sure but still) a central institution for propagating contemporary ideologies. The question one may well pose to the Marxist critic, therefore, is to what extent their discourse presents a challenge to that institution, or rather, however inadvertently, serves to legitimate its presence? And here the question of Jameson's style once again resurfaces. It is the primary task of the Marxist teacher, Jameson tells us, to teach Marxism itself, but his own texts can prove remarkably difficult to teach. Jameson himself can deploy such notions as the political unconscious, libidinal apparatus, national allegory, cognitive mapping and spatial systems to generate the most extraordinary and rich readings of cultural texts, but these ideas are not easily transposable. I am not suggesting that Jameson should simplify his work to the lowest common denominator; on the contrary, it is one of his strengths to have produced a philosophically sophisticated and non-reductive Marxist cultural theory. Neither do I think that a reconciliation of Marxism and a position within the academy is easily accomplished, and Jameson has certainly done more than probably any other figure over the last thirty years to establish a strong Marxist intellectual presence. But it remains legitimate I think to ask the question: if Jameson's work is to be read as essential interventions in the long process of cultural revolution, then where is their *political* cutting edge. Jameson is neither a polemical nor a satirical writer, modes which Eagleton sees as 'essential . . . for a political revolutionary'.[30] Moreover, is not what LaCapra refers to as Jameson's 'hermetic' approach, or what we might see as his oeuvrism, caught within the very reifying logic of academic discourse that he so strenuously tries to break out of? Does not, in other words, the very difficulty and complexity of his style legitimate the specialization and separation of the academy rather than present a challenge to it. The intractable nature of this dilemma perhaps goes some way to explaining Jameson's increasingly pessimistic view concerning the role of cultural politics.

In chapter 1, I discussed Jameson's earlier assessment of the significance of cultural politics for the re-emergence of socialist politics in general. In the 1970s and early 1980s Jameson argued that a strong Marxist cultural presence was one of the preconditions for development of a properly Marxist political culture. Moreover, the social position and specialization of academic discourse were not to be seen as a brake on the development of a more broad-based political movement; on the contrary, it would facilitate some of its most daring advances. Jameson's view in the 1990s is rather more sanguine. 'I don't particularly care', he states, reflecting on the status of emerging Cultural Studies programmes, 'what ultimate form the program ends up taking, or even whether an official academic discipline of this kind comes into being in the first place. That is probably because I don't much believe in the reform of academic programs to begin with.'[31] This more pessimistic strain is also evident in a 1990 interview with Stuart Hall:

> My feeling about politics, which may be an old-fashioned one, is that nothing really happens without the reconstruction of a certain basic unity among groups. My own sense of this may be too pessimistic, but from the perspective of a politics of solidarity, culture would not be a substitute for politics. . . . I am more pessimistic about a purely cultural politics than I would obviously like to be.[32]

The transition from his early optimism to these rather pessimistic conclusions is certainly understandable in the light of the changed political circumstances from the 1970s to the 1990s. But at the same time there is also what perhaps we could identify as an internal logic to this progression. One finds in Jameson's work an increasingly insistent call for renewed utopian thinking as his pessimism over political transformation in the present intensifies. It has frequently been observed that in the divergent tradition of Western Marxism a profound sense of pessimism has been accompanied by an equally strong sense of optimism.[33] In his short survey of Western Marxism, Perry Anderson has charted the shift in Western Marxism away from the political and economic concerns of classical Marxism, to questions of aesthetics and philosophy. Unlike the first generation of Marxist theorists, including Kautsky, Lenin, Luxemburg, Trotsky and Bukharin, the tradition of Western Marxism, from Lukács onwards, has been marked by the absence of strong links with the broader working-class movement. Western Marxism, in short, has remained by and large an academic phenomenon. Consequently, the canon of Western Marxism is conspicuous by the excessive stylistic difficulty of many of its greatest thinkers. The 'extreme difficulty of language characteristic of much of Western Marxism in the twentieth century', writes Anderson, 'was never controlled by the tension of a direct or active relationship to a proletarian audience. On the contrary, its very surplus above the necessary minimum quotient of verbal complexity was the sign of its divorce from any popular practice.'[34] Jameson's work is not immune from this tendency towards excessive verbal complexity. For Jameson himself, the density and complexity of his style is proportionate to the difficulty of the problem he is addressing, that is, the attempt to grasp the complex relations between culture, society and history. But, excessive abstraction and difficulty is also a sign of the political price one pays for the separation between theory and practice, a situation that has affected North American intellectuals of the left rather more starkly than their counterparts elsewhere.[35]

The advantage of dialectical criticism over and above other critical methodologies, Jameson used to remind us, was that it has the capacity to resituate the critic back into history. At his best Jameson's work presents a remarkable example of what form such criticism may take. Jameson does not always attend to his own strictures, however, and this is particularly evident in his work on postmodernism, as well as in his insistence on the theoretical priority of totalizing thought. Jameson's recent work on postmodernism, spatiality and cinema forces one to think the unthinkable, to attempt to map the global totality of late capitalism, but one could ask: is this really the most pressing political, theoretical and cultural dilemma for the left today? Or does it not rather tell us something about Jameson's own social and historical position as a global theorist with a specifically North American perspective on the world? As Martin Jay writes:

> 'totality' had a special place in the lexicon of all Western Marxists. In privileging it as they did, they betrayed their unmistakable status as intellectuals: throughout modern history, only 'men of ideas' have combined the time (and economic support) to reflect on matters beyond their immediate material concerns with the hubris to believe they might know the whole of reality.[36]

There is a marked tendency within Jameson's argument towards an 'all or nothing' logic; without a conception of social totality, we are told, there is no possibility for future socialist politics, because without totalizing theory the alliance politics without which 'no genuine' left politics can emerge today would be purely opportunistic and reformist. While Jameson is right to argue against the more debilitating effects of micro-politics, is it any less debilitating, one may well ask, to be faced with the task of conceiving of a completely new form of global politics?

In an extraordinary, and in many senses uncharacteristic, footnote in *The Geopolitical Aesthetic* one can see the dangers in this level of generalization and abstraction. For Jameson, it is 'axiomatic that what is now called fundamentalism is also a postmodern phenomenon' and that belief is rather 'a casualty of a period in which otherness' and depth still prevailed (*PLC*, 388), that is to say, modernism. So it is with some exasperation that Jameson finds he must once again return to the subject of resurgent fundamentalism and nationalism in Eastern Europe:

> May one in passing express exasperation with the various religious revivals in the East? The Roman Catholic wedding in *Man of Steel* (complete with Lech Walesa!) was already disgraceful; we have now seen the consequences. . . . Surely an anti-foundational era is able to satisfy its aesthetic, philosophical and political needs without the trappings of superstition, and is at least in a position to jettison the baggage of the great monotheisms (the animisms and polytheisms might still be acceptable on other grounds; while Buddhism is in our sense atheistic). (*GPA*, 111)

The superior tone of this footnote is breathtaking as one senses Jameson's irritation that so many have not caught on to the schizophrenic logic of late capitalism to be beyond these regressive experiences. There is more than a hint of the old intellectual Mandarin present here, the kind of universal intellectual stigmatized by Foucault, and which postmodernism apparently consigned to history. One senses the exasperation of the theoretician who after painstakingly elaborating a global theory finds a world that refuses to conform to it.

While one may share Jameson's exasperation that Eastern Europe, and indeed many other parts of the globe, have turned to religious fundamentalism and rampant nationalism rather than some socialist third way, one cannot help but feel that Jameson's diatribe, to use his own term, represents a profoundly undialectical and unhistorical appreciation of the situation. Jameson, to be sure, is not suggesting that belief and nationalism have disappeared. He does maintain that they have been 'threatened by postmodernity' (*GPA*, 117) and no longer have meaning in the old modernist sense. This may be so, but on the other hand, one of the many reasons why people are turning to fundamentalism and nationalism is that these social forces have provided a focus for collective opposition to the break-up of their social systems – in a different context, Jameson may well have read this as a positive utopian impulse. Resurgent nationalism and religious fundamentalism represent political responses to the process of globalization and the universalization of North American hegemony.[37] As such, they call for a political response in return, in other words, postmodernism must be contested on a political terrain which is at once local, institutional and national as well as multinational and global. We are once again, therefore, confronted with the central problem of the lack of mediation in Jameson's work, firstly in relation to his own discourse and the specific institutional frame within which it exists, and secondly in relation to postmodernist theory as a more specific and less global historical perspective. A closer analysis of the intermediary levels of mediation could, therefore, provide a much more positive conception of cultural politics than that which Jameson can presently envisage.

In these concluding remarks I have paradoxically slipped between criticizing Jameson, on the one hand, for being too sympathetic and uncritical in his use of non-Marxist theory, and on the other, for being too much of an unreconstructed Marxist. Thus I have argued that Jameson endorses too much of the postmodernist view of contemporary society and culture and that this tends to undercut the political force of Marxism's traditional economic and class analysis. At the same time, I have suggested that his assertion as 'axiomatic that capitalism has not fundamentally changed today'[38] is problematic to the extent that class relations and economic dynamics certainly appear to have changed radically in the last forty years. On a more philosophical level, the certainty with which Marxists can invoke history, agency and Marx's social critique has also seriously been brought into question. That Jameson can be criticized for being at once too much and not enough of a Marxist is not simply indicative of theoretical inconsistency or weakness, on his part and indeed my own, but is also a mark of the extreme complexity of the problematic and the extent of his achievement. Jameson has forged a body of work that is remarkable for its breadth, insight and intellectual integrity; and at the same time, and taking into account the more 'militant' or 'activist' criticisms I have made above, the political commitment of his work is unquestionable. More than any other figure in contemporary cultural theory, Jameson has developed an open, non-doctrinaire Marxism that can meet the challenge of the philosophically sophisticated and esoteric languages of formalism, structuralism, post-structuralism and postmodernism. He has steered a difficult path through the contemporary critique of Marxism while seeking to retain its central tenets of political emancipation. This may, as I have suggested throughout this study, eventually prove to be an impossible task, but if we wish to retain any conception of socialism within our cultural politics, it is an engagement we will be condemned to repeat.

Notes

Introduction

1 Colin MacCabe, Preface to Fredric Jameson, *The Geopolitical Aesthetic: Cinema and Space in the World System* (1992), p. ix.

2 After the publication of *The Political Unconscious* (1981) a number of journals devoted special issues to Jameson's work, see *Diacritics*, vol. 12, no. 3 (1982), *Critical Exchange*, no. 14 (1983), *New Orleans Review*, vol. 11, no. 1 (1984); a short introduction to this text also appeared, William C. Dowling, *Jameson, Althusser, Marx: An Introduction to 'The Political Unconscious'*. Douglas Kellner's 1989 Reader, *Postmodernism, Jameson, Critique*, was specifically concerned with Jameson's work on postmodernism and it was not until 1995 that the first major study devoted to Jameson's work as a whole appeared with Clint Burnham's *The Jamesonian Unconscious: The Aesthetics of Marxist Theory*.

3 See Slavoj Žižek, 'Taking Sides: A Self-Interview', in Žižek, *The Metastases of Enjoyment: Six Essays on Women and Causality*.

4 See Ernesto Laclau and Chantal Mouffe, *Hegemony and Socialist Strategy: Toward a Radical Democratic Politics*, and 'Post-Marxism without Apologies'. Also Michèle Barrett, *The Politics of Truth: From Marx to Foucault*.

5 Perry Anderson, *In the Tracks of Historical Materialism*, p. 56.

6 Ibid.

7 See Frank Lentricchia, *After the New Criticism*, in particular part I, 'A Critical Thematics, 1957–77'.

8 Lentricchia writes: 'Sartre's major early work has not made much of a difference in the general practice of literary criticism in the United States' (ibid., p. 44).

9 Philip Wood, 'Sartre, Anglo-American Marxism, and the Place of the Subject in History', p. 23.

10 In *Search for a Method*, Sartre argued that Marxism represented 'the one philosophy of our time which we cannot go beyond', while history formed both the matrix and horizon of theory. Quoted in Mark Poster, *Sartre's Marxism*, p. 17.

11 Fredric Jameson, Introduction to 'Sartre after Sartre' (1985), p. v.
12 Ibid.
13 Fredric Jameson, 'On Aronson's Sartre' (1982), p. 122.
14 Douglas Kellner, 'Jameson, Marxism, and Postmodernism', introduction to Kellner (ed.), *Postmodernism, Jameson, Critique*, p. 8.
15 See Jameson's review 'Sartre in Search of Flaubert' (1981), pp. 5, 16, 18.
16 In his analysis of *No Exit* Jameson writes, 'the theatre is a kind of mixture of language on the one hand and the *merely* seen sets and gestures, on the other.' *Sartre: The Origins of a Style* (1961), p. 17, emphasis added.
17 'However sublime, thoughts can never be much more than one of the materials of art. Sartre's plays are vehicles for the author's ideas, which have been left behind in the race of aesthetic forms.' Theodor W. Adorno, 'Commitment', in Ronald Taylor (ed.), *Aesthetics and Politics*, p. 182. Jameson responds to Adorno's criticism of Sartre in the Afterword to this volume.
18 Kellner, 'Jameson, Marxism, and Postmodernism', pp. 8–9.
19 Ibid., p. 9.
20 Ibid.
21 Ibid.

Chapter 1 The Dialectics of Form

1 Three of the chapters of *Marxism and Form* (1971) were published previously in *Salmagundi*: 'T. W. Adorno; or, Historical Tropes' (1967), 'Walter Benjamin; or, Nostalgia' (1969–70), and 'The Case for Georg Lukács' (1970). The long concluding chapter 'Towards Dialectical Criticism' also developed some of the ideas initially sketched in 'Metacommentary' (1971).
2 Terry Eagleton, 'Fredric Jameson: The Politics of Style'.
3 Fredric Jameson, 'Interview' with L. Green, Jonathan Culler and Richard Klein (1982), p. 88.
4 Fredric Jameson, 'Introduction to T. W. Adorno' (1969), p. 141.
5 Eagleton, 'Fredric Jameson', p. 66.
6 Ibid., p. 65.
7 Burnham, *The Jamesonian Unconscious*, pp. 39–48.
8 Ibid., p. 216.
9 Jameson significantly revised his view of Adorno as essayist, see for example *Marxism and Form*, p. 51, and *Late Marxism* (1990), p. 247.
10 Theodor W. Adorno, 'The Essay as Form', p. 152.
11 Ibid., p. 159.
12 Fredric Jameson, 'Reification and Utopia in Mass Culture' (1979), repr. in *Signatures of the Visible* (1990), p. 14.
13 Ibid., pp. 25–6.
14 Adorno, 'The Essay as Form', p. 160.
15 Burnham, *The Jamesonian Unconscious*, pp. 164–5.
16 Robert Scholes, 'Interpretation and Narrative: Kermode and Jameson', pp. 271–2.
17 Robert Scholes, *Textual Power: Literary Theory and the Teaching of English*, p. 85.
18 Ibid., p. 84.
19 Ibid.
20 Eagleton, 'Fredric Jameson', p. 66.
21 Ibid., p. 68.

22 Green, Culler and Klein, 'Interview', p. 73.
23 An account of this turbulent conference and the subsequent election of Louis Kampf as second vice-president of the MLA can be found in Richard Ohmann, 'MLA: Professors of Literature in a Group', in *English in America: A Radical View of the Profession*.
24 Dan Latimer, 'Jameson and Postmodernism', p. 117.
25 For a slightly longer account of the MLG see Sean Homer, 'A Short History of the Marxist Literary Group' (1995).
26 Neil Larsen, 'Fredric Jameson and the Fate of Dialectical Criticism', p. ix.
27 Jameson, 'Metacommentary', repr. in *The Ideologies of Theory, Essays 1971–1986*, vol 1: *Situations of Theory* (1988), p. 5.
28 Ibid., p. 6.
29 Ibid., p. 7.
30 Ibid.
31 Ibid.
32 Ibid., p. 11.
33 Claude Lévi-Strauss, 'The Structural Study of Myth', in *Structural Anthropology*. After breaking down the Theban myth into its constituent 'mythemes' and relations Lévi-Strauss proceeds to interpret his data, concluding that 'the purpose of myth is to provide a logical model capable of overcoming a contradiction (an impossible achievement if, as it happens, the contradiction is real)' (p. 229).
34 Jameson, 'Metacommentary', in *The Ideologies of Theory*, vol. 1, p. 5.
35 Ibid., p. 13.
36 Ibid., p. 14.
37 Ibid., p. 15.

Chapter 2 History: The Political Unconscious

1 Terry Eagleton, 'The Idealism of American Criticism', p. 57.
2 *Critical Exchange*, no. 14 (1983), *Diacritics*, vol. 12, no. 3 (1982), *New Orleans Review*, vol. 11, no. 1 (1984).
3 James H. Kavanagh, 'The Jameson-Effect', p. 20.
4 Eagleton, 'The Idealism of American Criticism', p. 64. The fate of the Marxist critic in a liberal academy has been forcefully and persuasively argued by Michael Sprinker, see 'Reinventing Historicism: An Introduction to the Work of Fredric Jameson'.
5 Robert Young, *White Mythologies: Writing History and the West*, p. 91.
6 Ibid.
7 Terry Eagleton, *Criticism and Ideology*; Pierre Macherey, *A Theory of Literary Production*. See also Eagleton's own assessment of his Althusserian moment in the introduction to *Against the Grain*.
8 See Edward P. Thompson, 'The Poverty of Theory or An Orrery of Errors', in Thompson, *The Poverty of Theory and Other Essays*, and Simon Clarke et al., *One-Dimensional Marxism: Althusser and the Politics of Culture*, for the critique of Althusserianism from within British Marxism; also Perry Anderson, *Arguments within English Marxism*, for a thoughtful assessment of the Althusser/Thompson debate. For the fortunes of Althusserianism in Europe in general see Gregory Elliott, *Althusser: The Detour of Theory*, esp. ch. 6.
9 Fredric Jameson, 'Marxism and Historicism' (1979), in *The Ideologies of Theory*,

Essays 1971-1985, vol. 2: *The Syntax of History*, p. 150.

10 Ibid., p. 156.
11 Ibid., p. 157.
12 Ibid., p. 159.
13 Ibid., p. 157.
14 Ibid., p. 153.
15 Ibid., p. 155.
16 Ibid., p. 165.
17 Ibid., p. 150.
18 Ibid., p. 172.
19 See Raymond Williams, *Marxism and Literature*, pp. 121–7.
20 Jameson, 'Marxism and Historicism', in *The Ideologies of Theory*, vol. 2, p. 175.
21 Ibid.
22 Ibid., p. 177
23 Edward, P. Thompson, *The Making of the English Working Class*, p. 8.
24 Ibid., p. 9.
25 Fredric Jameson, 'The Ideological Analysis of Space' (1983), pp. 3–4.
26 Ibid., p. 5.
27 Ibid.
28 Walter Benjamin, 'Theses on the Philosophy of History', in Benjamin, *Illuminations*, p. 248. The quotation here is Jameson's translation in *The Political Unconscious*, p. 281.
29 Michael Clark, 'Imagining the Real: Jameson's use of Lacan', p. 67.
30 Ibid.
31 For an accessible introduction to Lacanian theory see Bice Benvenuto and Roger Kennedy, *The Works of Jacques Lacan: An Introduction*.
32 Fredric Jameson, 'Imaginary and Symbolic in Lacan' (1977), in *The Ideologies of Theory*, vol. 1, p. 82.
33 François Roustang, *The Lacanian Delusion*, p. 130.
34 Slavoj Žižek, *Looking Awry: An Introduction to Jacques Lacan through Popular Culture*, p. 39.
35 Jameson, 'Imaginary and Symbolic in Lacan', in *The Ideologies of Theory*, vol. 1, p. 104.
36 Clark, 'Imagining the Real', p. 68.
37 Ibid., p. 69.
38 Michael Clark, 'Putting Humpty Together Again: Essays toward Integrative Analysis'.
39 Jameson, 'Imaginary and Symbolic in Lacan', in *The Ideologies of Theory*, vol. 1, p. 106.
40 Ted Benton, *The Rise and Fall of Structural Marxism: Althusser and his Influence*, pp. 105–7.
41 Louis Althusser, 'Marxism and Humanism', in Althusser, *For Marx*, pp. 233–4.
42 Louis Althusser, 'Ideology and the Ideological State Apparatus', in Althusser, *Essays on Ideology*, p. 55.
43 Louis Althusser, 'Freud and Lacan', in *Essays on Ideology*, pp. 170–1.
44 Michèle Barrett, 'Althusser's Marx, Althusser's Lacan', p. 175.
45 Ibid.
46 Ibid., p. 176.
47 Ibid.
48 Ibid., p. 177.

49 James Iffland, 'The Political Unconscious of Jameson's *The Political Unconscious*', p. 39.
50 Jonathan Arac, 'Fredric Jameson and Marxism', in Arac, *Critical Genealogies: Historical Situations for Postmodern Literary Studies*. A number of other critics have questioned the extent to which history is repressed in cultural artefacts, including Carol P. James, 'Does Jameson Have Any Use for Allegory', and J. Fisher-Solomon, 'Marxism and the Categories of Historical Presentation', in Fisher-Solomon, *Discourse and Reference in the Nuclear Age*.
51 Arac, *Critical Genealogies*, p. 276.
52 Ibid., p. 277.
53 Jameson, 'Marxism and Historicism', in *The Ideologies of Theory*, vol. 2, p. 164.
54 Louis Althusser and Étienne Balibar, *Reading Capital*, p. 133.
55 G. W. F. Hegel, *Hegel: The Essential Writings*, ed. Frederick G. Weiss.
56 G. A. Cohen, *Karl Marx's Theory of History: A Defence*, p. 9.
57 Ibid., p. 12.
58 Jameson, 'Marxism and Historicism', in *The Ideologies of Theory*, vol. 2, p. 157.
59 Althusser and Balibar, *Reading Capital*, p. 94.
60 Ibid.
61 Ibid., p. 96.
62 Ibid., p. 186.
63 Ibid. All emphasis shown in quotations matches the original unless stated otherwise.
64 Elliott, *Althusser*, p. 145.
65 Althusser and Balibar, *Reading Capital*, p. 188.
66 Ibid., p. 189.
67 Étienne Balibar makes interesting comparisons between *For Marx* and *History and Class Consciousness*, but far from conflating the ideas in the two he suggests that 'these two great books can indeed be viewed as the extremities of communist theory in twentieth century Marxism'; see 'The Non-Contemporaneity of Althusser', pp. 5–6 n7.
68 Young, *White Mythologies*, p. 92.
69 Ibid., p. 96. For an alternative reading to Jameson of the relationship between Althusserian theory and Sartre's philosophy see Michael Sprinker, 'Politics and Theory: Althusser and Sartre'.
70 Young, *White Mythologies*, p. 93.
71 Fredric Jameson, 'Third World Literature in an Era of Multinational Capitalism' (1986), p. 69. See also Jameson, 'Literary Innovation and Modes of Production: A Commentary' (1984) and 'World Literature in an Age of Multinational Capitalism' (1987).
72 Aijaz Ahmad, 'Jameson's Rhetoric of Otherness and the "National Allegory"', pp. 3–4.
73 Young, *White Mythologies*, p. 113.
74 Ibid.
75 Althusser and Balibar, *Reading Capital*, p. 99.
76 Young, *White Mythologies*, p. 2.
77 John Frow, 'Marxism after Structuralism', p. 39.
78 Roy Bhaskar, *Reclaiming Reality: A Critical Introduction to Contemporary Philosophy*, see ch. 1.
79 Michael Sprinker, *Imaginary Relations: Aesthetics and Ideology in the Theory of Historical Materialism*, p. 159.
80 Paul Ricoeur, *Time and Narrative*, vol. 1, p. 91.

81 Paul Ricoeur, 'On Interpretation', p. 179. The situation with Jameson is not quite as clear-cut as I have implied, though, as the emphasis he places on 'narrative' and the act of 'narration' has significantly changed over the last decade. The privileging of narrative in *The Political Unconscious* retains strong resonances of the Lukácsian position outlined in *Marxism and Form*: 'where indeed narration is valorized in that it presupposes neither the transcendence of the object (as in science) nor that of the subject (as in ethics), but rather a neutralization of the two, their mutual reconciliation, which thus anticipates the life experience of a Utopian world in its very structure' (*MF*, 190). Whereas in 'The Existence of Italy' the value of narrative is not its utopian potential of a subject-object unity but precisely the gap that it inscribes between subject (through the act of narration) and object (history itself); see *Signatures of the Visible*, pp. 165–7.

82 Louis O. Mink, 'Narrative Form as a Cognitive Instrument', p. 131.

83 Elliott, *Althusser*, p. 106.

84 Ibid., p. 167.

85 Ibid., p. 169.

86 Ibid.

87 Ibid., p. 158.

88 Cohen, *Karl Marx's Theory of History*, p. 79.

89 Ibid.

90 Ibid., p. 86.

Chapter 3 The Politics of Desire

1 Anderson, *Arguments within English Marxism*, p. 161.

2 Fredric Jameson, 'Pleasure: A Political Issue' (1983), in *The Ideologies of Theory*, vol. 2, p. 66.

3 Ibid., p. 68.

4 Ibid., p. 62.

5 Ibid.

6 Michel Foucault, 'On the Genealogy of Ethics: An Overview of Work in Progress', p. 347.

7 Roland Barthes, *The Pleasure of the Text*, p. 57.

8 Ibid., p. 53.

9 Ibid., p. 22.

10 Jameson, 'Pleasure: A Political Issue', in *The Ideologies of Theory*, vol. 2, p. 73.

11 Gilles Deleuze and Félix Guattari, *Anti-Oedipus: Capitalism and Schizophrenia*, vol. 1, p. 180.

12 Terry Eagleton, *Literary Theory: An Introduction*, p. 142.

13 Louis Althusser, 'Marxism Today', p. 270.

14 Ibid., p. 278.

15 Peter Dews, 'The "New Philosophers" and the End of Leftism', p. 4. A comprehensive overview of the complex relationship between French Marxism, anti-psychiatry and psychoanalysis can be found in Sherry Turkle, *Psychoanalytic Politics: Jacques Lacan and Freud's French Revolution*.

16 Peter Dews, *Logics of Disintegration: Post-Structuralist Thought and the Claims of Critical Theory*, pp. 110–11.

17 Michel Foucault, Introduction to Deleuze and Guattari, *Anti-Oedipus*, p. xiii.

18 Eagleton, *Literary Theory*, p. 142.

19 Deleuze and Guattari, *Anti-Oedipus*, p. 55.
20 Ibid., p. 53.
21 'The term *hylé*, in fact designates the pure continuity that any one sort of matter ideally possesses' (ibid., p. 36).
22 Brian Massumi, *A User's Guide to Capitalism and Schizophrenia: Deviations from Deleuze and Guattari*, p. 82.
23 Deleuze and Guattari, *Anti-Oedipus*, p. 32.
24 Ibid., p. 29.
25 Massumi rejects this interpretation of the molecular/molar distinction, suggesting that the 'distinction is not one of scale, but of mode of composition: it is qualitative, not quantitative'. *A User's Guide to Capitalism and Schizophrenia*, p. 54.
26 Deleuze and Guattari, *Anti-Oedipus*, p. 264.
27 Ibid., p. 239.
28 See Teresa Brennan, *History after Lacan*, pp. 86–90.
29 Deleuze and Guattari, *Anti-Oedipus*, p. 42.
30 Michel Foucault, *The Order of Things: An Archaeology of the Human Sciences*, p. 119. Massumi contends that such arguments rest on binary systems of logic that Deleuze and Guattari radically undermine; the real distinction, he writes, is not between 'identity versus undifferentiation' but 'identity-undifferentiation versus hyperdifferentiation'. *A User's Guide to Capitalism and Schizophrenia*, p. 91.
31 Deleuze and Guattari, *Anti-Oedipus*, p. 136.
32 Ibid., p. 348.
33 Ibid., p. 130.
34 Ibid., p. 106.
35 Ibid., p. 151.
36 Massumi, *A User's Guide to Capitalism and Schizophrenia*, p. 138.
37 Manfred Frank, 'The World as Will and Representation: Deleuze and Guattari's Critique of Capitalism as Schizo-Analysis and Schizo-Discourse', p. 173. See also Kate Soper, 'Postmodernism, Subjectivity and the Question of Value', for a forceful defence of normative values against postmodern relativism.
38 Frank, 'The World as Will and Representation', p. 174.
39 Ibid., p. 173.
40 Deleuze and Guattari, *Anti-Oedipus*, p. 342.
41 Ibid., p. 255.
42 See, for example, the exchange between Jameson and Kenneth Burke: Fredric Jameson, 'The Symbolic Inference; or Kenneth Burke and Ideological Analysis' (1978); Kenneth Burke, 'Methodological Repression and/or Strategies of Containment'; and Fredric Jameson, 'Ideology and Symbolic Action: Reply to Kenneth Burke' (1978).
43 Jonathan Arac, 'Fredric Jameson and Marxism', in Arac, *Critical Genealogies*, p. 266.
44 Ibid.
45 Ibid., p. 267.
46 Ibid.
47 Ibid. The quotation from Nietzsche is from *The Genealogy of Morals*.
48 Ibid., p. 271.
49 Deleuze and Guattari, *Anti-Oedipus*, p. 133.
50 Ibid.
51 Ibid.

52 Fredric Jameson, 'Towards a Libidinal Economy of Three Modern Painters' (1979), p. 190.
53 Ibid., p. 189.
54 See Fredric Jameson, 'Flaubert's Libidinal Historicism: *Trois Contes*' (1984) and 'Towards a Libidinal Economy of Three Modern Painters'.
55 See Fredric Jameson, ' *La Cousine Bette* and Allegorical Realism' (1971) and 'Imaginary and Symbolic in *La Rabouilleuse*' (1977).
56 Jameson, *'La Cousine Bette* and Allegorical Realism', p. 244.
57 For a discussion of character systems see Fredric Jameson, 'After Armageddon: Character Systems in P. K. Dick's *Dr Bloodmoney*' (1975).
58 Geoff Bennington, *Lyotard: Writing the Event*, p. 27.
59 Jameson, 'Flaubert's Libidinal Historicism', p. 77.
60 Fredric Jameson, 'Imaginary and Symbolic in Lacan: Marxism, Psychoanalytic Criticism and the Problem of the Subject', in Shoshana Felman (ed.), *Literature and Psychoanalysis, the Question of Reading: Otherwise*, p. 390.
61 Ibid., p. 389.
62 Ibid., p. 394.
63 Jameson, 'Science versus Ideology' (1983), p. 299. See Slovaj Žižek, *The Sublime Object of Ideology* and 'Between Symbolic Fiction and Fantasmatic Spectre: Toward a Lacanian Theory of Ideology' for more recent attempts to develop a Lacanian theory of ideology.
64 Jameson, 'Imaginary and Symbolic in Lacan', in Felman, *Literature and Psychoanalysis*, p. 393.
65 Terry Eagleton, *The Ideology of the Aesthetic*, p. 404.

Chapter 4 Postmodernism and Late Capitalism

1 Kellner, 'Jameson, Marxism and Postmodernism', in *Postmodernism, Jameson, Critique*, p. 19.
2 Fredric Jameson, 'Postmodernism, or, The Cultural Logic of Late Capitalism' (1984), repr. as the first chapter to *Postmodernism, or, The Cultural Logic of Late Capitalism* (1991). All quotations in this chapter are from the 1991 edition.
3 Kellner, 'Jameson, Marxism and Postmodernism', pp. 2-3.
4 Ibid., p. 3.
5 Ibid., p. 5.
6 While *Marxism and Form* focused on the shorter essays contained in Adorno's *Notes to Literature* alongside *The Philosophy of New Music*, it had very little to say about *Negative Dialectics* or *Aesthetic Theory*, except to describe them as ambitious failures; *Late Marxism* on the other hand is devoted precisely to a rereading of these later works in relation to the current problematics of postmodernism.
7 See Jean-François Lyotard, *The Condition of Postmodernity: A Report on Knowledge*.
8 Jean Baudrillard, 'The System of Objects', p. 21.
9 Fredric Jameson, 'Postmodernism and Consumer Society' (1985), p. 113.
10 Ibid., p. 119.
11 Ibid., p. 113.
12 See Ernest Mandel, *Late Capitalism*, ch. 4.
13 Ibid., pp. 120–1.
14 Ibid., p. 199.

15 Ibid., p. 23.
16 Ibid., p. 146.
17 David Harvey, *The Condition of Postmodernity*, p. 38.
18 Edward Soja, *Postmodern Geographies: The Reassertion of Space in Critical Theory*, pp. 60–1.
19 Ibid., p. 61.
20 Frank Pfeil, *Another Tale to Tell: Politics and Narrative in Postmodern Culture*, p. 98.
21 Jean Baudrillard, 'The Ecstasy of Communication', p. 127.
22 Ibid., p. 128.
23 Nicholas Zurbrugg, 'Jameson's Complaint: Video-Art and the Intertextual "Time-Wall"', p. 17.
24 Ibid., pp. 25–6.
25 Fredric Jameson, 'Review Article of Don DeLillo's *The Names*' (1984), p. 119.
26 Ibid.
27 Ibid.
28 Fredric Jameson, 'On Politics and Literature' (1968), p. 23.
29 Fredric Jameson, 'On Raymond Chandler' (1970), p. 642.
30 Jameson notes that the concept of 'situation' is clearly Sartrean while the Lukácsian model 'is one of distinct, semi-autonomous loops in which the subject and object develop without "representing" each other in any way, and yet continue to be related ... by their participation in the social totality'. Lévi-Strauss's conception of an imaginary resolution to a social contradiction is not referenced at all. Jameson compares his own procedure to 'something like' the Lukácsian model. The problem is that Jameson once again simply conflates three distinct models for situating the cultural artefact in its social context but it is by no means self-evident that these three models are compatible with each other or doing the same thing. Furthermore, simply to line up a series of potential solutions to a given problem is not the same as doing the work itself – it does not provide the solution to the problem. *SV*, 240 n1.
31 Peter Nicholls, 'Divergences: Modernism, Postmodernism, Jameson and Lyotard', p. 4.
32 Ibid., p. 10.
33 Ibid.
34 Ibid., p. 14.

Chapter 5 The Spatial Logic of Late Capitalism

1 Soja, *Postmodern Geographies*, p. 1.
2 Ibid., pp. 36–7.
3 Doreen Massey, 'Politics and Space/Time', p. 70.
4 Ibid.
5 Donald Preziosi, 'La Vi(ll)e en Rose: Reading Jameson Mapping Space', p. 84.
6 Jean Baudrillard, 'For a Critique of the Political Economy of the Sign', p. 87.
7 Jean Baudrillard, 'Symbolic Exchange and Death', p. 120.
8 Jean Baudrillard, 'The Mirror of Production', p. 116.
9 Fredric Jameson, 'Cognitive Mapping' (1988), p. 351.
10 David Shumway, 'Jameson/Hermeneutics/Postmodernism', p. 195.
11 Ibid., p. 192.
12 Ibid., p. 193.

13 Mike Davis, *City of Quartz: Excavating the Future in Los Angeles*, p. 238.
14 Preziosi, 'La Vi(ll)e en Rose', p. 88.
15 Jameson, 'Cognitive Mapping', p. 353.
16 One of the few examples of the political implications of cognitive mapping given by Jameson is the experience of the League of Black Revolutionary Workers in Detroit in the late 1960s, see 'Cognitive Mapping', pp. 351–3. In retrospect Jameson also sees his 1977 essay 'Class and Allegory in Contemporary Mass Culture: *Dog Day Afternoon* as a Political Film' as an early attempt at cognitive mapping. The fullest exposition of what form this new aesthetic may take is to be found in Jameson essays on world cinema in *The Geopolitical Aesthetic: Cinema and Space in the World System*.
17 Jameson, 'Cognitive Mapping', p. 348.
18 Ibid., p. 349.
19 Henri Lefebvre, *The Production of Space*.
20 Ibid., p. 6.
21 Soja, *Postmodern Geographies*, p. 122.
22 Ibid., p. 123.
23 Ibid., p. 125.
24 Lefebvre, *The Production of Space*, p. 33.
25 Ibid.
26 Ibid., p. 17.
27 Ibid., p. 142.
28 Ibid., pp. 47–8.
29 David Harvey quoted in Soja, *Postmodern Geographies*, p. 76.
30 Lefebvre, *The Production of Space*, p. 275.
31 David Harvey quoted in Soja, *Postmodern Geographies*, p. 77.
32 See Massey, 'Politics and Space/Time', p. 73.
33 Lefebvre, *The Production of Space*, p. 296.
34 See Fredric Jameson, *The Seeds of Time* (1994), pp. 1–71. Jameson's title echoes Lukács's seminal text 'The Antinomies of Bourgeois Thought', and at the same time starkly dramatizes the political paralysis of the postmodern imagination. Whereas for Lukács at an earlier, modernist, historical moment it was still possible for the proletariat to dialectically transcend the subject–object split of bourgeois thought, for Jameson, in a period of full-blown postmodernism we are simply locked into a theoretical and political impasse.
35 See Roland Robertson, 'Glocalization: Time-Space and Homogeneity-Heterogeneity'. The term appropriately derives from Japanese business jargon of the 1980s: 'The idea of glocalization in its business sense is closely related to what in some contexts is called, in more straightforwardly economic terms, micro-marketing: the tailoring and advertising of goods and services on a global or near global basis to increasingly differentiated local and particular markets' (p. 28).
36 Peter Osborne, 'Modernity is a Qualitative, not a Chronological Category', p. 66.
37 Ibid., p. 73.
38 Ibid., p. 78.
39 Harvey, *The Condition of Postmodernity*, p. 240
40 Ibid.
41 Ibid., p. 293.
42 Ibid., p. 294.

Chapter 6 Marxism, Totality and the Politics of Difference

1 Martin Jay, *Marxism and Totality: The Adventures of a Concept from Lukács to Habermas*, p. 51 n4.
2 Ibid., p. 513.
3 Ibid., pp. 514–15.
4 Ibid., p. 520.
5 Michel Foucault quoted in Jay, *Marxism and Totality*, p. 521.
6 Linda Hutcheon, *The Politics of Postmodernism*, p. 62.
7 See Linda Hutcheon, 'Total History De-totalized', in *The Politics of Postmodernism*, pp. 62–70.
8 Steven Best, 'Jameson, Totality, and the Poststructuralist Critique', p. 336.
9 Jay, *Marxism and Totality*, pp. 104-5.
10 Ibid., p. 35.
11 Ibid., p. 108.
12 Ibid., pp. 108–9.
13 Best, 'Jameson, Totality, and the Poststructuralist Critique', p. 343.
14 Jay, *Marxism and Totality*, p. 105.
15 Ibid., p. 251.
16 Eagleton, 'The Idealism of American Criticism', p. 62.
17 Peter Osborne, 'A Marxism for the Postmodern? Jameson's Adorno', p. 171.
18 Ibid., p. 172.
19 Ibid., pp. 173-4.
20 See Jameson, *Late Marxism*, p. 46 and p. 91.
21 Best, 'Jameson, Totality, and the Poststructuralist Critique', p. 343.
22 Ibid., p. 344.
23 Jay, *Marxism and Totality*, p. 259.
24 Ibid., p. 262.
25 Ibid., p. 274.
26 Eagleton, 'The Idealism of American Criticism', p. 58.
27 Jay, '*Marxism and Totality*', p. 266.
28 Osborne, 'A Marxism for the Postmodern?', p. 175.
29 Ibid.
30 Ibid., p. 187.
31 Ibid., p. 192.
32 Ibid., p. 177.
33 Jay, *Marxism and Totality*, p. 533.
34 Best, 'Jameson, Totality, and the Poststructuralist Critique', p. 351.
35 Ibid., p. 355.
36 See, for example, my discussion of Jameson's ternary schema of realism, modern, postmodernism in chapter 4 and the case of the Third World below.
37 Jay, *Marxism and Totality*, p. 267.
38 Eagleton, 'The Idealism of American Criticism', p. 63.
39 See Andrew Arato, 'Lukács' Theory of Reification', p. 25.
40 Tom Bottomore et al. (eds), *A Dictionary of Marxist Thought*, p. 465.
41 Eagleton, 'The Idealism of American Criticism', p. 63.
42 Wood, 'Sartre, Anglo-American Marxism, and the Place of the Subject in History'.
43 Fredric Jameson, '*History and Class Consciousness* as an "Unfinished Project" '

(1988), p. 52. This view is also expressed in a footnote in *The Political Unconscious*, p. 220.

44 Arato, 'Lukács' Theory of Reification', p. 33.
45 Ibid., p. 25.
46 Ibid., p. 66.
47 Eagleton, 'The Idealism of American Criticism', p. 63.
48 Arato, 'Lukács' Theory of Reification', p. 52.
49 Ibid.
50 Ibid.
51 Ibid., pp. 54–5.
52 Ibid., p. 54.
53 Jay, *Marxism and Totality*, p. 265.
54 Jürgen Habermas, *The Philosophical Discourse of Modernity*. I am grateful to Ken Hirschkop for pointing this out to me.
55 Mandel, *Late Capitalism*, p. 46.
56 Ibid., pp. 48–9.
57 Ibid., p. 65.
58 Ibid.
59 Santiago Colás, 'The Third World in Jameson's *Postmodernism or the Cultural Logic of Late Capitalism*', p. 258.
60 Ibid., p. 262.
61 Ibid., p. 265.
62 Ibid. This is a quotation from Neil Smith, *Uneven Development: Nature, Capital and the Production of Space*, p. 152.
63 Colás, 'The Third World', p. 268.

Conclusion

1 Jameson, 'Cognitive Mapping', p. 347.
2 Best, 'Jameson, Totality, and the Poststructuralist Critique', p. 364.
3 Eagleton, 'Fredric Jameson', p. 78.
4 Steven Best and Douglas Kellner, *Postmodern Theory: Critical Interrogations*, p. 192.
5 Mike Davis, 'Urban Renaissance and the Spirit of Postmodernism', p. 108.
6 Ibid, p. 113. For Jameson's response to Davis's 'militant' critique see *Postmodernism, or, The Cultural Logic of Late Capitalism*, p. 421 n19.
7 For a more traditional Marxist analysis of the new information technologies see Herbert I. Schiller, *Information Inequality: The Deepening Social Crisis in America*.
8 Eagleton, 'Fredric Jameson', p. 71.
9 Davis, 'Urban Renaissance and the Spirit of Postmodernism', p. 107.
10 Mike Featherstone, 'Postmodernism, Cultural Change, and Social Practice'.
11 Fredric Jameson, 'Afterword – Marxism and Postmodernism' (1989).
12 Best and Kellner, *Postmodern Theory*, p. 188.
13 Jameson, 'Cognitive Mapping', p. 355.
14 Best and Kellner, *Postmodern Theory*, p. 191.
15 Fredric Jameson, 'Actually Existing Marxism', pp. 187–8.
16 Ibid., p. 188.
17 Best and Kellner, *Postmodern Theory*, p. 191.
18 Nancy Fraser, 'From Redistribution to Recognition? Dilemmas of Justice in a

"Post-Socialist" Age', p. 68.
19 Ibid., p. 69.
20 Ibid., p. 92.
21 Dominick LaCapra, 'Review of *The Political Unconscious*', p. 103.
22 Ibid., p. 104.
23 Ibid.
24 Ibid.
25 Ibid.
26 Fredric Jameson, 'Marxism and Teaching', p. 31.
27 Fredric Jameson, 'Notes towards a Marxist Cultural Politics' (1975), p. 37.
28 James H. Kavanagh and Fredric Jameson, 'The Weakest Link: Marxism in Literary Studies', p. 1.
29 Ibid., p. 3.
30 Eagleton, 'Fredric Jameson', p. 71.
31 Fredric Jameson, 'On "Cultural Studies"' (1993), p. 18.
32 Fredric Jameson, 'Interview' with Stuart Hall (1990), p. 30.
33 See Perry Anderson, *Considerations on Western Marxism*; Jay, *Marxism and Totality*, esp. the chapter on Adorno; and Elliott, *Althusser*, ch. 6.
34 Anderson, *Considerations on Western Marxism*, p. 54.
35 Jameson, 'Actually Existing Marxism', p. 172.
36 Jay, *Marxism and Totality*, p. 12.
37 For interesting discussions of the rise of nationalism in the former Yugoslavia see Slavoj Žižek, 'Eastern Europe's Republics of Gilead' and 'Eastern European Liberalism and its Discontents'.
38 Jameson, 'Actually Existing Marxism', p. 178.

Bibliography

Works by Fredric Jameson

Sartre: The Origins of a Style (1961), 2nd edn, New York: Columbia University Press, 1984.
'T. W. Adorno; or, Historical Tropes', *Salmagundi*, no. 5 (1967), pp. 2–43.
'On Politics and Literature', *Salmagundi*, nos 2–3 (1968), pp. 17–26.
'Walter Benjamin; or, Nostalgia', *Salmagundi*, nos 10–11 (1969), pp. 52–68.
'Introduction to T. W. Adorno', *Salmagundi*, nos 10–11 (1969), pp. 240–3.
'The Case for Georg Lukács', *Salmagundi*, no. 13 (1970), pp. 3–35.
'On Raymond Chandler', *Southern Review*, no. 6 (1970), pp. 624–50.
'Metacommentary', *Publications of the Modern Language Association*, vol. 86, no. 1 (1971), repr in Jameson, *The Ideologies of Theory* (1988), vol. 2, pp. 9–18.
'*La Cousine Bette* and Allegorical Realism', *Publications of the Modern Language Association*, vol. 86 (1971), pp. 241–54.
Marxism and Form: Twentieth-Century Dialectical Theories of Literature, Princeton: Princeton University Press, 1971.
The Prison House of Language: A Critical Account of Structuralism and Russian Formalism, Princeton: Princeton University Press, 1972.
'After Armageddon: Character Systems in P. K. Dick's *Dr Bloodmoney*', *Science Fiction Studies*, vol. 2, no. 1 (1975), pp. 31–55.
'Notes towards a Marxist Cultural Politics', *Minnesota Review*, vol. 5 (1975), pp. 35–9.
Afterword to Ronald Taylor (ed.), *Aesthetics and Politics*, London: Verso, 1977.
'Class Allegory in Contemporary Mass Culture: *Dog Day Afternoon* as a Political Film', *College English*, vol. 38, no. 8 (1977), pp. 843–59.
'Imaginary and Symbolic in Lacan: Marxism, Psychoanalytic Criticism, and the Problem of the Subject', *Yale French Studies*, nos 55–6 (1977), pp. 338–95. Repr. in Shoshana Felman (ed.), *Literature and Psychoanalysis, the Question of Reading: Otherwise*, Baltimore: Johns Hopkins University Press, 1982.
'Imaginary and Symbolic in *La Rabouilleuse*', *Social Science Information*, vol. 16, no. 1 (1977), pp. 59–81.
'The Symbolic Inference; or Kenneth Burke and Ideological Analysis', *Critical*

Inquiry, vol. 4, no. 3 (1978), pp. 507–23.

'Ideology and Symbolic Action: Reply to Kenneth Burke', *Critical Inquiry*, vol. 5, no. 2 (1978), pp. 417–22.

Fables of Aggression: Wyndham Lewis, the Modernist as Fascist, Berkeley: University of California Press, 1979.

'Marxism and Historicism', *New Literary History*, vol. 11 (1979), pp. 41–73.

'Marxism and Teaching', *New Political Science*, vols 2–3 (1979), pp. 31–6.

'Reification and Utopia in Mass Culture', *Social Text*, vol. 1 (1979), pp. 130–48.

'Towards a Libidinal Economy of Three Modern Painters', *Social Text*, vol. 1 (1979), pp. 189–99.

The Political Unconscious: Narrative as a Socially Symbolic Act, London: Methuen, 1981.

'Sartre in Search of Flaubert', *New York Review of Books*, vol. 27 (Dec. 1981), pp. 5, 16, 18.

'Interview' with L. Green, Jonathan Culler and Richard Klein, *Diacritics*, vol. 12, no. 3 (1982), pp. 72–91.

'On Aronson's Sartre', *Minnesota Review*, vol. 18 (1982), pp. 116–27.

'The Ideological Analysis of Space', *Critical Exchange*, no. 14 (1983), pp. 1–15.

'Pleasure: A Political Issue' (1983), repr. in Jameson, *The Ideologies of Theory* (1988), vol. 2.

'Science versus Ideology', in *Humanities in Society*, vol. 6 (1983), pp. 283–302.

'Flaubert's Libidinal Historicism: *Trois Contes*', in N. Schor (ed.), *Flaubert and Postmodernism*, Lincoln: University of Nebraska Press, 1984.

'Literary Innovation and Modes of Production: A Commentary', *Modern Chinese Literature*, vol. 1, no. 1 (1984), pp. 67–77.

'Periodizing the Sixties', in Sohnya Sayres et al. (eds), *The Sixties without Apology*, Minneapolis: University of Minnesota Press, 1984; repr. in Jameson, *The Ideologies of Theory* (1988), vol. 2.

'The Politics of Theory: Ideological Positions in the Postmodern Debate', *New German Critique*, no. 33 (1984), pp. 53–65.

'Postmodernism, or, The Cultural Logic of Late Capitalism', *New Left Review*, no. 146 (1984), pp. 53–92.

'Review Article of Don DeLillo's *The Names*', *Minnesota Review*, vol. 22 (1984), pp. 116–22.

'Postmodernism and Consumer Society', in Hal Foster (ed.), *Postmodern Culture*, London: Pluto Press, 1985.

Introduction to 'Sartre after Sartre', an issue ed. Jameson of *Yale French Studies*, vol. 65 (1985), pp. iii–xi.

'Third World Literature in an Era of Multinational Capitalism', *Social Text*, vol. 15 (1986), pp. 65–88.

'World Literature in an Age of Multinational Capitalism', in C. Koeld (ed.), *The Current in Criticism: Essays on the Present and Future in Literary Theory*, West Lafayette: Perdue University Press, 1987, pp. 139–58.

'Cognitive Mapping', in Cary Nelson and Lawrence Grossberg (eds), *Marxism and the Interpretation of Culture*, Chicago: University of Illinois Press, 1988.

'*History and Class Consciousness* as an "Unfinished Project"', *Rethinking MARX-ISM*, vol. 1, no. 1 (1988), pp. 49–72.

The Ideologies of Theory, Essays 1971–1986, vol. 1: *Situations of Theory*, London: Routledge, 1988.

The Ideologies of Theory, Essays 1971–1986, vol. 2: *The Syntax of History*, London: Routledge, 1988.

'Afterword – Marxism and Postmodernism', in Douglas Kellner (ed.), *Postmodernism, Jameson, Critique*, Washington: Maisonneuve Press, 1989.
'Interview' with Stuart Hall, *Marxism Today* (Sept. 1990), pp. 28–31.
Late Marxism: Adorno, or, The Persistence of the Dialectic, London: Verso, 1990.
Signatures of the Visible, London: Routledge, 1990.
Postmodernism, or, The Cultural Logic of Late Capitalism, London: Verso, 1991.
The Geopolitical Aesthetic: Cinema and Space in the World System, London: British Film Institute, 1992.
'Actually Existing Marxism', *Polygraph: An International Journal of Culture and Politics*, vols 6–7 (1993), pp. 170–95.
'On "Cultural Studies" ', *Social Text*, vol. 34 (1993), pp. 17–52.
The Seeds of Time, New York: Columbia University Press, 1994.

Other Works

Adorno, Theodor W., 'Commitment', in Ronald Taylor (ed.), *Aesthetics and Politics*, London: Verso, 1977.
—— 'The Essay as Form', trans. B. Hullot-Kentor and F. Will, *New German Critique*, no. 32 (1984), pp. 151–71.
Ahmad, Aijaz, 'Jameson's Rhetoric of Otherness and the "National Allegory" ', *Social Text*, vol. 17 (1987), pp. 3–25.
Althusser, Louis, *For Marx*, trans. Ben Brewster, Harmondsworth: Penguin, 1969.
—— *Essays on Ideology*, London: Verso, 1984.
—— 'Marxism Today', trans. James H. Kavanagh, in Althusser, *Philosophy and the Spontaneous Philosophy of the Scientists and Other Essays*, ed. Gregory Elliott, London: Verso, 1990.
Althusser, Louis and Balibar, Étienne, *Reading Capital*, trans. Ben Brewster, London: Verso, 1970.
Anderson, Perry, *Considerations on Western Marxism*, London: Verso, 1979.
—— *Arguments within English Marxism*, London: Verso, 1980.
—— *In the Tracks of Historical Materialism*, London: Verso, 1983.
—— 'Modernity and Revolution', *New Left Review*, no. 144 (1984), pp. 96–113.
Arac, Jonathan, *Critical Genealogies: Historical Situations for Postmodern Literary Studies*, New York: Columbia University Press, 1987.
Arato, Andrew, 'Lukács' Theory of Reification', *Telos*, no. 11 (1972), pp. 25–66.
Balibar, Étienne, 'The Non-Contemporaneity of Althusser', in E. Ann Kaplan and Michael Sprinkler (eds), *The Althusserian Legacy*, London: Verso, 1993.
Barrett, Michèle, *The Politics of Truth: From Marx to Foucault*, Cambridge: Polity Press, 1991.
—— 'Althusser's Marx, Althusser's Lacan', in E. Ann Kaplan and Michael Sprinker (eds), *The Althusserian Legacy*, London: Verso, 1993.
Barthes, Roland, *The Pleasure of the Text*, trans. Richard Miller, Oxford: Blackwell, 1990.
Baudrillard, Jean, 'The Ecstasy of Communication', in Hal Foster (ed.), *Postmodern Culture*, London: Pluto Press, 1985.
—— 'For a Critique of the Political Economy of the Sign', in *Jean Baudrillard: Selected Writings*, ed. Mark Poster, Cambridge: Polity Press, 1988.
—— 'The Mirror of Production', in *Jean Baudrillard: Selected Writings*, ed. Mark Poster, Cambridge: Polity Press, 1988.

—— 'Symbolic Exchange and Death', in *Jean Baudrillard: Selected Writings*, ed. Mark Poster, Cambridge: Polity Press, 1988.

—— 'The System of Objects', in *Jean Baudrillard: Selected Writings*, ed. Mark Poster, Cambridge: Polity Press, 1988.

Benjamin, Walter, *Illuminations*, trans. Harry Zohn, London: Fontana, 1992.

Bennington, Geoff, *Lyotard: Writing the Event*, Manchester: Manchester University Press, 1988.

Benton, Ted, *The Rise and Fall of Structural Marxism: Althusser and his Influence*, London: Macmillan, 1984.

Benvenuto, Bice and Kennedy, Roger, *The Works of Jacques Lacan: An Introduction*, New York: St Martins Press, 1986.

Best, Steven, 'Jameson, Totality, and the Poststructuralist Critique', in Douglas Kellner (ed.), *Postmodernism, Jameson, Critique*, Washington: Maisonneuve Press, 1989.

Best, Steven and Kellner, Douglas, *Postmodern Theory: Critical Interrogations*, New York: Guildford Press, 1991.

Bhasker, Roy, *Reclaiming Reality: A Critical Introduction to Contemporary Philosophy*, London: Verso, 1989.

Bottomore, Tom et al. (eds), *A Dictionary of Marxist Thought*, 2nd edn, Oxford: Blackwell, 1991.

Brennan, Teresa, *History after Lacan*, London: Routledge, 1993.

Burke, Kenneth, 'Methodological Repression and/or Strategies of Containment', *Critical Inquiry*, vol. 5, no. 2 (1978), pp. 401–16.

Burnham, Clint, *The Jamesonian Unconscious: The Aesthetics of Marxist Theory*, Durham: Duke University Press, 1995.

Clark, Michael, 'Putting Humpty Together Again: Essays toward Integrative Analysis', *Poetics Today*, vol. 3, no. 1 (1982), pp. 159–70.

—— 'Imagining the Real: Jameson's Use of Lacan', *New Orleans Review*, vol. 11, no. 1 (1984), pp. 67–72.

Clarke, Simon et al., *One-Dimensional Marxism: Althusser and the Politics of Culture*, London: Allison and Busby, 1980.

Cohen, G. A., *Karl Marx's Theory of History: A Defence*, Oxford: Clarendon Press, 1978.

Colás, Santiago, 'The Third World in Jameson's *Postmodernism or the Cultural Logic of Late Capitalism*', *Social Text*, vol. 10, nos 2–3 (1988), pp. 258–70.

Davis, Mike, 'Urban Renaissance and the Spirit of Postmodernism', *New Left Review*, no. 151 (1985), pp. 106–13.

—— *City of Quartz: Excavating the Future in Los Angeles*, London: Verso, 1990.

Deleuze, Gilles and Guattari, Félix, *Anti-Oedipus: Capitalism and Schizophrenia*, vol. 1, trans. Robert Hurley, Mark Seem and Helen R. Lane, London: Athlone Press, 1984.

Dews, Peter, 'The "New Philosophers" and the End of Leftism', *Radical Philosophy*, no. 24 (1980), pp. 2–11.

—— *Logics of Disintegration: Post-Structuralist Thought and the Claims of Critical Theory*, London: Verso, 1987.

Dowling, William C., *Jameson, Althusser, Marx: An Introduction to 'The Political Unconscious'*, London: Methuen, 1984.

Eagleton, Terry, *Criticism and Ideology*, London: Verso, 1976.

—— *Literary Theory: An Introduction*, Oxford: Blackwell, 1983.

—— *Against the Grain: Selected Essays, 1975–1985*, London: Verso, 1986.

—— 'Fredric Jameson: The Politics of Style', in *Against the Grain: Selected Essays*,

1975-1985, London: Verso, 1986, pp. 65–78; repr. from *Diacritics*, vol. 12, no. 3 (1982), pp. 14–22.

—— 'The Idealism of American Criticism', in *Against the Grain: Selected Essays, 1975-1985*, London: Verso, 1986.

—— *The Ideology of the Aesthetic*, Oxford: Blackwell, 1990.

Elliott, Gregory, *Althusser: The Detour of Theory*, London: Verso, 1987.

Featherstone, Mike, 'Postmodernism, Cultural Change, and Social Practice', in Douglas Kellner (ed.), *Postmodernism, Jameson, Critique*, Washington: Maisonneuve Press, 1989.

Fisher-Solomon, J., *Discourse and Reference in the Nuclear Age*, London: University of Oklahoma Press, 1988.

Foucault, Michel, *The Order of Things: An Archaeology of the Human Sciences*, London: Tavistock/Routledge, 1970.

—— 'On the Genealogy of Ethics: An Overview of Work in Progess', in Paul Rabinow (ed.), *The Foucault Reader*, Harmondsworth: Peregrine, 1986.

Frank, Manfred, ' The World as Will and Representation: Deleuze and Guattari's Critique of Capitalism as Schizo-Analysis and Schizo-Discourse', trans. David Berger, *Telos*, no. 64 (1983), pp. 166–76.

Fraser, Nancy, 'From Redistribution to Recognition? Dilemmas of Justice in a "Post-Socialist" Age', *New Left Review*, no. 212 (1995), pp. 68–93.

Frow, John, 'Marxism after Structuralism', *Southern Review Adelaide*, vol. 17, no. 1 (1984), pp. 33-50.

Green, L., Culler, Jonathan and Klein, Richard (eds), Special Issue on Jameson, *Diacritics*, vol. 12, no. 3 (1982).

Habermas, Jürgen, *The Philosophical Discourse of Modernity*, Cambridge: Polity Press, 1990.

Harvey, David, *The Condition of Postmodernity*, Oxford: Blackwell, 1989.

Hegel, G. W. F., *Hegel: The Essential Writings*, ed. Frederick G. Weiss, New York: Harper Torchbooks, 1974.

Homer, Sean, 'A Short History of the Marxist Literary Group', *Mediations*, vol. 19, no. 2 (1995), pp. 68–75.

Hutcheon, Linda, *The Politics of Postmodernism*, London: Routledge, 1989.

Iffland, James, 'The Political Unconscious of Jameson's *The Political Unconscious*', *New Orleans Review*, vol. 11, no. 1 (1984), pp. 36–45.

James, Carol P., 'Does Jameson Have Any Use for Allegory', *New Orleans Review*, vol. 11, no. 1 (1984), pp. 59–66.

Jay, Martin, *Marxism and Totality: The Adventures of a Concept from Lukács to Habermas*, Cambridge: Polity Press, 1984.

Kaplan, E. Ann and Sprinker, Michael (eds), *The Althusserian Legacy*, London: Verso, 1993.

Kavanagh, James H., 'The Jameson-Effect', *New Orleans Review*, vol. 11, no. 1 (1984), pp. 20–8.

—— (ed.), Special Issue on Jameson, *New Orleans Review*, vol. 11, no. 1 (1984).

Kavanagh, James H., and Jameson, Fredric, 'The Weakest Link: Marxism in Literary Studies', in B. Ollman and E. Vernoff (eds), *The Left Academy: Marxist Scholarship on American Campuses*, vol. 11, New York: Pantheon, 1984.

Kellner, Douglas (ed.), *Postmodernism, Jameson, Critique*, Washington: Maisonneuve Press, 1989.

LaCapra, Dominick, 'Review of *The Political Unconscious*', *History and Theory*, vol. 21, no. 1 (1982), pp. 83–106.

Laclau, Ernesto and Mouffe, Chantal, *Hegemony and Socialist Strategy: Toward a*

Radical Democratic Politics, London: Verso, 1985.
—— 'Post-Marxism without Apologies', *New Left Review*, no. 166 (1987), pp. 79–106.
Larsen, Neil, 'Fredric Jameson and the Fate of Dialectical Criticism', Foreword to Fredric Jameson, *The Ideologies of Theory, Essays 1971–1986*, vol. 1: *Situations of Theory*, London: Routledge, 1988.
Latimer, Dan, 'Jameson and Postmodernism', *New Left Review*, no. 148 (1981), pp. 116–28.
Lefebvre, Henri, *The Production of Space*, trans. Donald Nicholson-Smith, Oxford: Blackwell, 1991.
Lentricchia, Frank, *After the New Criticism*, London: Methuen, 1983.
Lévi-Strauss, Claude, *Structural Anthropology*, trans. Claire Jacobson and Brooke Grundfest Schoepf, Harmondsworth: Penguin, 1972.
Levitas, Ruth, *The Concept of Utopia*, Hertfordshire: Philip Allen, 1990.
Lukács, Georg, *History and Class Consciousness*, trans. Rodney Livingston, London: Merlin Press, 1971.
Lyotard, Jean-François, *The Condition of Postmodernity: A Report on Knowledge*, trans. Geoff Bennington and Brian Massumi, Manchester: Manchester University Press, 1984.
Macherey, Pierre, *A Theory Of Literary Production*, trans. Geoffrey Wall, London: Routledge and Kegan Paul, 1978.
Mandel, Ernest, *Late Capitalism*, trans. Joris De Bres, London: Verso, 1975.
Massey, Doreen, 'Politics and Space/Time', *New Left Review*, no. 196 (1992), pp. 65–84.
—— 'Making Spaces, or, Geography is Political Too', *Soundings*, no. 1 (1995), pp. 193–208.
Massumi, Brian, *A User's Guide to Capitalism and Schizophrenia: Deviations from Deleuze and Guattari*, Cambridge: MIT Press, 1993.
Mink, Louis O., 'Narrative Form as a Cognitive Instrument', in R. H. Canary and H. Kozicki (eds), *The Writing of History: Literary Form and Historical Understanding*, Wisconsin: University of Wisconsin Press, 1978.
Nicholls, Peter, 'Divergences: Modernism, Postmodernism, Jameson and Lyotard', *Critical Quarterly*, vol. 33, no. 3 (1991), pp. 1–18.
Nimis, Steven (ed.), 'The Work of Fredric Jameson', Special Issue, *Critical Exchange*, no. 14 (1983).
Ohmann, Richard, *English in America: A Radical View of the Profession*, New York: Oxford University Press, 1976.
Osborne, Peter, 'A Marxism for the Postmodern? Jameson's Adorno', *New German Critique*, no. 56 (1992), pp. 171–92.
—— 'Modernity is a Qualitative, not a Chronological Category', *New Left Review*, no. 192 (1992), pp. 65–84.
Pfeil, Frank, *Another Tale to Tell: Politics and Narrative in Postmodern Culture*, London: Verso, 1990.
Poster, Mark, *Sartre's Marxism*, Cambridge: Cambridge University Press, 1982.
Preziosi, Donald, 'La Vi(ll)e en Rose: Reading Jameson Mapping Space', *Strategies*, vol. 1 (1988), pp. 82–99.
Ricoeur, Paul, 'On Interpretation', in Alan Montefiore (ed.), *Philosophy in France Today*, Cambridge: Cambridge University Press, 1983.
—— *Time and Narrative*, vol. 1, trans. Kathleen McLaughlin and David Pelleur, Chicago: University of Chicago Press, 1984.
Robertson, Roland, 'Glocalization: Time-Space and Homogeneity-Heterogene-

ity', in Mike Featherstone, Scott Lash and Roland Robertson (eds), *Global Modernities*, London: Sage, 1995.

Roustang, François, *The Lacanian Delusion*, trans. Greg Sims, Oxford: Oxford University Press, 1990.

Sohnya Sayers et al. (eds), *The Sixties without Apology*, Minneapolis: University of Minnesota Press, 1984.

Schiller, Herbert I., *Information Inequality: The Deepening Social Crisis in America*, London: Routledge, 1996.

Scholes, Robert, 'Interpretation and Narrative: Kermode and Jameson', *Novel*, vol. 17, no. 3 (1984), pp. 266–78.

—— *Textual Power: Literary Theory and the Teaching of English*, New Haven: Yale University Press, 1985.

Shumway, David, 'Jameson/Hermeneutics/Postmodernism', in Douglas Kellner (ed.), *Postmodernism, Jameson, Critique*, Washington: Maisonneuve Press, 1989.

Smith, Neil, *Uneven Development: Nature, Capital and the Production of Space*, Oxford: Blackwell, 1984.

Soja, Edward W., *Postmodern Geographies: The Reassertion of Space in Critical Theory*, London: Verso, 1989.

Sontag, Susan, *Against Interpretation*, New York: Farrar Straus and Giroux, 1966.

Soper, Kate, 'Postmodernism, Subjectivity and the Question of Value', *New Left Review*, no. 186 (1991), pp. 120–8.

Sprinker, Michael, 'Reinventing Historicism: An Introduction to the Work of Fredric Jameson', in Victor A. Kramer (ed.), *American Critics at Work: Examinations of Contemporary Literary Theory*, New York: Whitson, 1984.

—— 'Politics and Theory: Althusser and Sartre', *Modern Language Notes*, vol. 100, no. 5 (1985), pp. 989–1011.

—— *Imaginary Relations: Aesthetics and Ideology in the Theory of Historical Materialism*, London: Verso, 1987.

Stevenson, Nick, *Understanding Media Cultures: Social Theory and Mass Communication*, London: Sage, 1995.

Taylor, Ronald (ed.), *Aesthetics and Politics*, London: Verso, 1977.

Thompson, Edward P., *The Making of the English Working Class*, Harmondsworth: Pelican, 1968.

—— *The Poverty of Theory and Other Essays*, London: Merlin Press, 1978.

Turkle, Sherry, *Psychoanalytic Politics: Jacques Lacan and Freud's French Revolution*, 2nd edn, London: Free Association Books, 1992.

Williams, Raymond, *Marxism and Literature*, Oxford: Oxford University Press, 1977.

Wood, Philip, 'Sartre, Anglo-American Marxism and the Place of the Subject in History', *Yale French Studies*, vol. 65 (1985), pp. 15–54.

Young, Robert, *White Mythologies: Writing History and the West*, London: Routledge, 1990.

Žižek, Slavoj, *The Sublime Object of Ideology*, London: Verso, 1989.

—— 'Eastern Europe's Republics of Gilead', *New Left Review*, no. 183 (1990), pp. 50–62.

—— 'Eastern European Liberalism and its Discontents', *New German Critique*, no. 57 (1992), pp. 25–49.

—— *Looking Awry: An Introduction to Jacques Lacan through Popular Culture*, Cambridge: MIT Press, 1992.

—— *The Metastases of Enjoyment: Six Essays on Women and Causality*, London: Verso, 1994.

—— 'Between Symbolic Fiction and Fantasmatic Spectre: Toward a Lacanian Theory of Ideology', *Analysis*, no. 5 (1994), pp. 49–62.

Zurbrugg, Nicholas, 'Jameson's Complaint: Video-Art and the Intertextual "Time-Wall"', *Screen*, vol. 32, no. 1 (1991), pp. 16–34.

Index